AF538445

Add your opinion to our next book

Fill out a survey

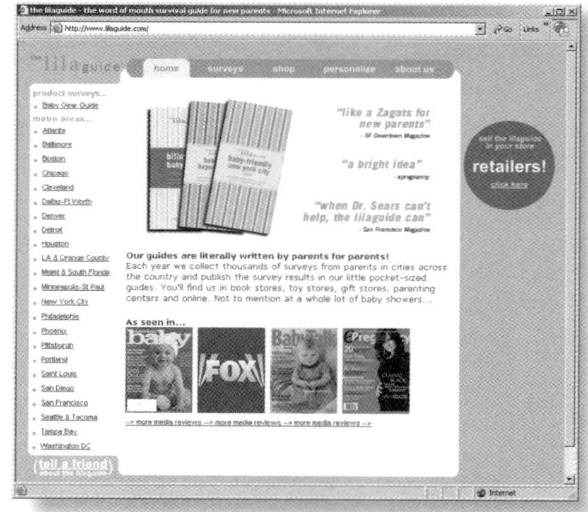

visit www.lilaguide.com

the lila guide

by PARENTS *for* PARENTS

baby-friendly phoenix area

NEW PARENT SURVIVAL GUIDE TO SHOPPING, ACTIVITIES, RESTAURANTS AND MORE...

1ST EDITION

LOCAL EDITOR: MELANIE CARTER-CARVALHO

PUBLISHED BY THE LILAGUIDE/OAM SOLUTIONS, INC.
SAN FRANCISCO, CA WWW.LILAGUIDE.COM

Published by:
OAM Solutions, Inc.
139 Saturn Street
San Francisco, CA 94114, USA
415.252.1300
orders@lilaguide.com
www.lilaguide.com

ISBN. 1-932847-25-1
First Printing: 2005
Printed in the USA

table of contents

No, for the last time, the baby does not come with a handbook. And even if there were a handbook, you wouldn't read it. You'd fill out the warranty card, throw out the box, and start playing right away. Until a few hours passed and you were hit with the epiphany of, "Gee whiz honey, what in the wide, wide world of childcare are we doing here?"

Relax. We had that panicked thought when we had our daughter Delilah. And so did **all the parents** we talked to when they had their children. And while we all knew there was no handbook, there was, we found, a whole lot of **word-of-mouth information**. Everyone we talked to had some bit of child rearing advice about what baby gear store is the most helpful. Some **nugget of parenting wisdom** about which restaurant tolerates strained carrots on the floor. It all really seemed to help. Someone, we thought, should write this down.

And that's when, please pardon the pun, the lilaguide was born. The book you're now holding is a guide **written by local parents for local parents**. It's what happens when someone actually does write it down (and organizes it, calculates it, and presents it in an easy-to-use format).

Nearly 3,400 surveys have produced this first edition of **the lilaguide: Baby-Friendly Phoenix Area**. It provides a truly unique insider's view of over 750 "parent-friendly" stores, activities, restaurants, and service providers that are about to become a very big part of your life. And while this guide won't tell you how to change a diaper or how to get by on little or no sleep (that's what grandparents are for), it will tell you what other **local parents have learned** about the amazing things your city and neighborhood have to offer.

As you peruse these reviews, please remember that this guide is **not intended to be a comprehensive directory** since it does not contain every baby store or activity in the area. Rather, it is intended to provide a short-list of places that your neighbors and friends **deemed exciting and noteworthy**. If a place or business is not listed, it simply means that nobody (or not enough people) rated or submitted information about it to us. **Please let us know** about your favorite parent and baby-friendly businesses and service providers by participating in our online survey at **www.lilaguide.com**. We always want your opinions!

So there you have it. Now go make some phone calls, clean up the house, take a nap, or do something on your list before the baby arrives.

Enjoy!

Oli & Elysa

Oli Mittermaier & Elysa Marco, MD

PS

We love getting feedback (good and bad) so don't be bashful. Email us at **lila@lilaguide.com** with your thoughts, comments and suggestions. We'll be sure to try to include them in next year's edition!

We'd like to take a moment to offer a heart-felt thank you to all the **parents who participated in our survey** and took the time to share their thoughts and opinions. Without your participation, we would never have been able to create this unique guide.

Thanks to our extra helpful Phoenix area contributors **Vivian J Carter**, **Susan Laitin**, **Melanie Romero**, and **Arlene Smyrk** for going above and beyond in the quest for hip tot spots.

Thanks also to **Lisa Barnes**, **Nora Borowsky**, **Todd Cooper**, **Amy Iannone**, **Katy Jacobson**, **Felicity John Odell**, **Shira Johnson**, **Kasia Kappes**, **Jen Krug**, **Dana Kulvin**, **Deborah Schneider**, **Kevin Schwall**, **April Stewart**, and **Nina Thompson** for their tireless editorial eyes, **Satoko Furuta** and **Paul D. Smith** for their beautiful sense of design, and **Lane Foard** for making the words yell.

Special thanks to **Paul D. Smith**, **Ken Miles**, and **Ali Wing** for their consistent support and overall encouragement in all things lilaguide, and of course **our parents** for their unconditional support in this and all our other endeavors.

And last, but certainly not least, thanks to **little Delilah** for inspiring us to embark on this challenging, yet incredibly fulfilling project.

disclaimer

This book is designed to share parents' opinions regarding baby-related products, services and activities. It is sold with the understanding that the information contained in the book **does not represent the publisher's opinion** or recommendations.

The reviews contained in this guide are based on **public opinion surveys** and are therefore subjective in nature. The publisher shall have neither liability nor responsibility to any person or entity with respect to any loss or damage caused, or alleged to have been caused, directly or indirectly, by the information contained in this book.

ratings

Most listings have stars and numbers as part of their write-up. These symbols mean the following:

❺ / ★★★★★	extraordinary
❹ / ★★★★☆	very good
❸ / ★★★☆☆	good
❷ / ★★☆☆☆	fair
❶ / ★☆☆☆☆	poor
✓	available
✗	not available/relevant

If a ★ is listed instead of ★, it means that the rating is less reliable because a small number of parents surveyed the listing. Furthermore, if a listing has **no stars** or **criteria ratings**, it means that although the listing was rated, the number of surveys submitted was so low that we did not feel it justified an actual rating.

quotes & reviews

The quotes/reviews are taken directly from surveys submitted to us via our web site (**www.lilaguide.com**). Other than spelling and minor grammatical changes, they come to you as they came to us. Quotes were selected based on how well they appeared to represent the collective opinions of the surveys submitted.

fact checking

We have contacted all of the businesses listed to verify their address and phone number, as well as to inquire about their hours, class schedules and web site information. Since some of this information may change after this guide has been printed, we appreciate you letting us know of any errors by notifying us via email at **lila@lilaguide.com**.

baby basics & accessories

Central Phoenix

"lila picks"

★Petite Chateau

★This Little Piggy Wears Cotton

★USA Baby

Babies R Us

"...everything baby under one roof... they have a wide selection and carry most 'mainstream' items such as Graco, Fisher-Price, Avent and Britax... great customer service—given how big the stores are, I was pleasantly surprised at how attentive the staff was... easy return policy... super busy on weekends so try to visit on a weekday for the best service... keep an eye out for great coupons, deals and frequent sales... easy and comprehensive registry... shopping here is so easy—you've got to check it out..."

Furniture, Bedding & Decor	✓	$$$	Prices
Gear & Equipment	✓	❹	Product availability
Nursing & Feeding	✓	❹	Staff knowledge
Safety & Babycare	✓	❹	Customer service
Clothing, Shoes & Accessories	✓	❹	Decor
Books, Toys & Entertainment	✓		

WWW.BABIESRUS.COM

PHOENIX—4835 E RAY RD (AT 14TH ST); 480.705.0400; M-SA 9:30-9:30, SU 11-7; PARKING LOT

Baby Bloomers

"...centrally located resale store with clothes in great condition... owner will help compare prices so you get the best deal... staff are helpful and will call you if something you are looking for comes in... organized very nicely... often has good sales..."

Furniture, Bedding & Decor	✗	$$	Prices
Gear & Equipment	✗	❹	Product availability
Nursing & Feeding	✗	❹	Staff knowledge
Safety & Babycare	✗	❹	Customer service
Clothing, Shoes & Accessories	✗	❹	Decor
Books, Toys & Entertainment	✗		

PHOENIX—6505 N 7TH ST (AT E MARYLAND AVE); 602.266.5646; M-SA 10-5, SU 12-5

Baby Boom Rentals

"...a good place to get a temporary breast pump... good people... good place if you are visiting Phoenix and do not want to bring everything with you or find you forgot something...has strollers, highchairs, potty seats, baby monitors and even safety gates..."

Furniture, Bedding & Decor	✗	$$$	Prices
Gear & Equipment	✓	❸	Product availability

Nursing & Feeding ✓ | ❸ Staff knowledge
Safety & Babycare ✓ | ❸ Customer service
Clothing, Shoes & Accessories ✗ | ❸ Decor
Books, Toys & Entertainment ✗

PHOENIX—135 E CLAREMONT ST (AT N 3RD ST); 602.331.8881; M-SA 8-4; PARKING LOT

Baby Depot At Burlington Coat Factory

"...a large, 'super store' layout with a ton of baby gear... wide aisles, packed shelves, barely existent customer service and awesome prices... everything from bottles, car seats and strollers to gliders, cribs and clothes... I always find something worth getting... a little disorganized and hard to locate items you're looking for... the staff is not always knowledgeable about their merchandise... return policy is store credit only..."

Furniture, Bedding & Decor ✓ | $$ Prices
Gear & Equipment ✓ | ❸ Product availability
Nursing & Feeding ✓ | ❸ Staff knowledge
Safety & Babycare ✓ | ❸ Customer service
Clothing, Shoes & Accessories ✓ | ❸ Decor
Books, Toys & Entertainment ✓

WWW.BABYDEPOT.COM

PHOENIX—2728 W PEORIA AVE (AT METRO CENTER); 602.866.2628; M-SA 10-9, SU 11-6; MALL PARKING

PHOENIX—4747 E CACTUS RD (AT TATUM); 602.923.7060; M-SA 10-9, SU 11-6; MALL PARKING

PHOENIX—7611 W THOMAS RD (AT 75TH ST); 623.845.7277; M-SA 10-9, SU 11-6; MALL PARKING

BabyGap/GapKids

"...colorful baby and toddler clothing in clean, well-lit stores... great return policy... it's the Gap, so you know what you're getting—colorful, cute and well-made clothing... best place for baby hats... prices are reasonable especially since there's always a sale of some sort going on... sales, sales, sales—frequent and fantastic... everything I'm looking for in infant clothing—snap crotches, snaps up the front, all natural fabrics and great styling... fun seasonal selections—a great place to shop for gifts as well as for your own kids... although it can get busy, staff generally seem accommodating and helpful..."

Furniture, Bedding & Decor ✗ | $$$ Prices
Gear & Equipment ✗ | ❹ Product availability
Nursing & Feeding ✗ | ❹ Staff knowledge
Safety & Babycare ✗ | ❹ Customer service
Clothing, Shoes & Accessories ✓ | ❹ Decor
Books, Toys & Entertainment ✗

WWW.GAP.COM

PHOENIX—4568 E CACTUS RD (AT PARADISE VALLEY MALL); 602.996.7490; M-SA 10-9, SU 11-7; MALL PARKING

BestFed

"...this store specializes in nursing supplies and clothing... knowledgeable staff who are easy to approach... lactation consultants are very helpful... offers breastfeeding classes... hospital-grade breast pumps available... they do their best to remember your name... web site and newsletters are loaded with information on breastfeeding..."

Furniture, Bedding & Decor ✗ | $$$ Prices
Gear & Equipment ✗ | ❹ Product availability
Nursing & Feeding ✗ | ❺ Staff knowledge
Safety & Babycare ✗ | ❺ Customer service

Clothing, Shoes & Accessories .... ✕ ❸ .... Decor
Books, Toys & Entertainment .... ✕

WWW.EBESTFED.COM

PHOENIX—4920 W THUNDERBIRD RD (AT N 49TH AVE); 602.843.4111; M-SA 9-7, SU 12-5; PARKING LOT

Bookman's

Furniture, Bedding & Decor .... ✕ ✕ .... Gear & Equipment
Nursing & Feeding .... ✕ ✕ .... Safety & Babycare
Clothing, Shoes & Accessories .... ✕ ✓ .... Books, Toys & Entertainment

WWW.BOOKMANS.COM

PHOENIX—8034 N 19TH AVE (AT W NORTHERN AVE); 602.433.0255; DAILY 9-10

Children's Place, The ★★★½☆

"...great bargains on cute clothing... shoes, socks, swimsuits, sunglasses and everything in between... lots of '3 for $20' type deals on sleepers, pants and mix-and-match separates... so much more affordable than the other 'big chains'... don't expect the most unique stuff here, but it wears and washes well... cheap clothing for cheap prices... you can leave the store with bags full of clothes without putting a huge dent in your wallet..."

Furniture, Bedding & Decor .... ✕ $$ .... Prices
Gear & Equipment .... ✕ ❹ .... Product availability
Nursing & Feeding .... ✕ ❹ .... Staff knowledge
Safety & Babycare .... ✕ ❹ .... Customer service
Clothing, Shoes & Accessories ...... ✓ ❹ .... Decor
Books, Toys & Entertainment .... ✓

WWW.CHILDRENSPLACE.COM

PHOENIX—4550 E CACTUS RD (AT PARADISE VALLEY); 602.485.4229; M-SA 10-9, SU 11-6; PARKING LOT

Consign-It ★★★☆☆

"...a furniture consignment shop that carries maternity and kids wear... if you want designer clothes for reasonable prices I recommend going secondhand... when you are finished you can sell them back... quite a variety of stuff if you are willing to do a little exploring..."

Furniture, Bedding & Decor .... ✕ $$ .... Prices
Gear & Equipment .... ✕ ❸ .... Product availability
Nursing & Feeding .... ✕ ❸ .... Staff knowledge
Safety & Babycare .... ✕ ❸ .... Customer service
Clothing, Shoes & Accessories .... ✕ ❸ .... Decor
Books, Toys & Entertainment .... ✕

PHOENIX—724 W INDIAN SCHOOL RD (AT 7TH AVE); 602.277.0048; M-SA 9:30-6 ; PARKING LOT

Costco ★★★½☆

"...dependable place for bulk diapers, wipes and formula at discount prices... clothing selection is very hit-or-miss... avoid shopping there during nights and weekends if possible, because parking and checkout lines are brutal... they don't have a huge selection of brands, but the brands they do have are almost always in stock and at a great price... lowest prices around for diapers and formula... kid's clothing tends to be picked through, but it's worth looking for great deals on name-brand items like Carter's..."

Furniture, Bedding & Decor .... ✓ $$ .... Prices
Gear & Equipment .... ✓ ❸ .... Product availability
Nursing & Feeding .... ✓ ❸ .... Staff knowledge
Safety & Babycare .... ✓ ❸ .... Customer service
Clothing, Shoes & Accessories ...... ✓ ❷ .... Decor
Books, Toys & Entertainment .... ✓

WWW.COSTCO.COM

PHOENIX—1646 W MONTEBELLO AVE (AT CHRIS-TOWN MALL); 623.293.4524; M-F 11-8:30, SA 9:30-6, SU 10-6

PHOENIX—19001 N 27TH AVE (AT W WESTCOTT DR); 623.293.4403; M-F 11-8:30, SA 9:30-6, SU 10-6

PHOENIX—3801 N 33RD AVE (AT W GRAND AVE); 480.293.2123; M-F 8-6, SA 9:30-6

PHOENIX—4502 E OAK ST (AT ARCADIA CROSSING SHOPPING CTR); 602.808.0101; M-F 10-8:30, SA 9:30-6, SU 10-6

Dillard's

"...this store has beautiful clothes, and if you catch a sale, you can get great quality clothes at super bargain prices... good customer service and helpful staff... a huge selection of merchandise for boys and girls... nice layette department... some furnishings like little tables and chairs... beautiful displays... the best part is that in addition to shopping for your kids, you can also shop for yourself..."

Furniture, Bedding & Decor	✓	$$$	Prices
Gear & Equipment	✗	❹	Product availability
Nursing & Feeding	✗	❸	Staff knowledge
Safety & Babycare	✗	❹	Customer service
Clothing, Shoes & Accessories	✓	❹	Decor
Books, Toys & Entertainment	✓		

WWW.DILLARDS.COM

PHOENIX—10002 N METRO PKWY (AT METRO CENTER); 602.953.9600; M-SA 10-9, SU 12-6

PHOENIX—4610 E CACTUS RD (OFF TATUM BLVD); 602.953.9600; M-SA 10-9, SU 12-6

PHOENIX—7621 W THOMAS RD (AT 75TH AVE); 623.849.0100; M-SA 10-9, SU 12-6

Good Samaritan Hospital Gift Shop

"...great selection of baby gifts for the new arrivals... prices are reasonable and quality is first class... has a mobile gift cart on the maternity floor that has more baby products than the store... rents breast pumps... be patient with the limited staff..."

Furniture, Bedding & Decor	✗	$$$	Prices
Gear & Equipment	✗	❸	Product availability
Nursing & Feeding	✓	❹	Staff knowledge
Safety & Babycare	✗	❹	Customer service
Clothing, Shoes & Accessories	✗	❹	Decor
Books, Toys & Entertainment	✗		

WWW.BANNERHEALTH.COM

PHOENIX—1111 E MCDOWELL RD (AT 12TH ST); 602.239.6818; M-SA 9-5, SU 11-5; PARKING LOT

Gymboree

"...beautiful clothing and great quality... colorful and stylish baby and kids wear... lots of fun birthday gift ideas... easy exchange and return policy... items usually go on sale pretty quickly... save money with Gymbucks... many stores have a play area which makes shopping with my kids fun (let alone feasible)..."

Furniture, Bedding & Decor	✗	$$$	Prices
Gear & Equipment	✗	❹	Product availability
Nursing & Feeding	✗	❹	Staff knowledge
Safety & Babycare	✗	❹	Customer service
Clothing, Shoes & Accessories	✓	❹	Decor
Books, Toys & Entertainment	✓		

WWW.GYMBOREE.COM

PHOENIX—4500 E CACTUS RD (AT TATUM); 602.996.7940; M-SA 10-9, SU 11-6; PARKING LOT

It's My Turn

"...a good selection of used toys, cribs, maternity, baby and kids clothes... great quality of merchandise and priced considerably well... really cute little store... worth digging around for the right item... very organized..."

Furniture, Bedding & Decor	✓	$$	Prices
Gear & Equipment	✗	❸	Product availability
Nursing & Feeding	✗	❹	Staff knowledge
Safety & Babycare	✗	❹	Customer service
Clothing, Shoes & Accessories	✓	❸	Decor
Books, Toys & Entertainment	✓		

WWW.ITSMYTURNRESALE.COM

PHOENIX—19401 N CAVE CREEK RD (AT E UTOPIA RD); 602.765.0530; 10-5 M-SU; STREET PARKING

JCPenney

"...always a good place to find clothes and other baby basics... the registry process was seamless... staff is generally friendly but the lines always seem long and slow... they don't have the greatest selection of toddler clothes, but their baby section is great... we had some damaged furniture delivered but customer service was easy and accommodating... a pretty limited selection of gear, but what they have is priced right..."

Furniture, Bedding & Decor	✓	$$	Prices
Gear & Equipment	✓	❸	Product availability
Nursing & Feeding	✓	❸	Staff knowledge
Safety & Babycare	✓	❸	Customer service
Clothing, Shoes & Accessories	✓	❸	Decor
Books, Toys & Entertainment	✓		

WWW.JCPENNEY.COM

PHOENIX—4510 E CACTUS RD (AT PARADISE VALLEY MALL); 602.996.2550; M-SA 10-9, SU 11-6; PARKING LOT

PHOENIX—9809 N METRO PKWY W (AT METRO CENTER); 602.371.8545; M-SA 10-9, SU 11-6; PARKING LOT

Kid's Foot Locker

"...Nike, Reebok and Adidas for your little ones... hip, trendy and quite pricey... perfect for the sports addict dad who wants his kid sporting the latest NFL duds... shoes cost close to what the adult variety costs... generally good quality... they carry infant and toddler sizes..."

Furniture, Bedding & Decor	✗	$$$	Prices
Gear & Equipment	✗	❸	Product availability
Nursing & Feeding	✗	❸	Staff knowledge
Safety & Babycare	✗	❸	Customer service
Clothing, Shoes & Accessories	✓	❸	Decor
Books, Toys & Entertainment	✗		

WWW.KIDSFOOTLOCKER.COM

PHOENIX—9648 N METRO PKWY E (AT METRO CENTER); 602.861.1837; M-SA 10-9, SU 11-6

Kohl's

"...nice one-stop shopping for the whole family—everything from clothing to baby gear... great sales on clothing and a good selection of higher-end brands... stylish, inexpensive clothes for babies through 24 months... very easy shopping experience... dirt-cheap sales and

clearance prices... nothing super fancy, but just right for those everyday romper outfits... Graco, Eddie Bauer and other well-known brands... ”

Furniture, Bedding & Decor .... ✓
Gear & Equipment .... ✓
Nursing & Feeding .... ✓
Safety & Babycare .... ✓
Clothing, Shoes & Accessories .... ✓
Books, Toys & Entertainment .... ✓

$$ .... Prices
4 .... Product availability
3 .... Staff knowledge
3 .... Customer service
3 .... Decor

WWW.KOHLS.COM

PHOENIX—17323 N 19TH AVE (AT W BELL RD); 602.298.1893; M-SA 8-10, SU 10-8; FREE PARKING

PHOENIX—21001 N TATUM BLVD (AT E DEER VALLEY DR); 480.538.1750; M-SA 8-10, SU 10-8; FREE PARKING

PHOENIX—4637 E CHANDLER BLVD (AT S 46TH ST); 480.785.7561; M-SA 8-10, SU 9-9; PARKING LOT

Lakeshore Learning Store

“*...this is a teachers supply store that also sells to individuals... a wonderful place to find age appropriate crafts and learning tools for children... good variety of books, puzzles, blocks, music, instruments, etc....*”

Furniture, Bedding & Decor .... ×
Gear & Equipment .... ✓
Nursing & Feeding .... ✓
Safety & Babycare .... ×
Clothing, Shoes & Accessories .... ×
Books, Toys & Entertainment .... ✓

$$$ .... Prices
4 .... Product availability
4 .... Staff knowledge
4 .... Customer service
4 .... Decor

WWW.LAKESHORELEARNING.COM

PHOENIX—4819 E RAY RD (AT FOOTHILLS PARK PL); 480.940.7700; M-SA 9-9, SU 11-6

Macy's

“*...Macy's has it all and I never leave empty-handed... if you time your visit right you can find some great deals... go during the week so you don't get overwhelmed with the weekend crowd... good for staples as well as beautiful party dresses for girls... lots of brand-names like Carter's, Guess, and Ralph Lauren... not much in terms of assistance... newspaper coupons and sales help keep the cost down... some stores are better organized and maintained than others... if you're going to shop at a department store for your baby, then Macy's is a safe bet...*”

Furniture, Bedding & Decor .... ✓
Gear & Equipment .... ×
Nursing & Feeding .... ×
Safety & Babycare .... ×
Clothing, Shoes & Accessories .... ✓
Books, Toys & Entertainment .... ✓

$$$ .... Prices
3 .... Product availability
3 .... Staff knowledge
3 .... Customer service
3 .... Decor

WWW.MACYS.COM

PHOENIX—2410 E CAMELBACK RD (AT BALTIMORE FASHION PARK); 602.468.2100; M-SA 10-9, SU 11-8

PHOENIX—4520 E CACTUS RD (AT PARADISE VALLEY MALL); 602.494.2100; M-SA 10-9, SU 11-8

Mervyn's

“*...wide selection of baby and kids' clothing, including OshKosh and Carter's... limited shoe selection without any real sizing assistance... lots of good sales... you might not always be able to find the size and color you want, but there's enough selection here that you're sure to find something else that will work just as well... cheap, cheap, cheap... okay for cheap basics, but don't expect anything super special...*”

Furniture, Bedding & Decor .... ×

$$ .... Prices

Gear & Equipment ✗ | 4 Product availability
Nursing & Feeding ✗ | 3 Staff knowledge
Safety & Babycare ✗ | 3 Customer service
Clothing, Shoes & Accessories ✓ | 3 Decor
Books, Toys & Entertainment ✓

WWW.MERVYNS.COM

PHOENIX—1869 E CAMELBACK RD (AT SQUAW PEAK PKWY); 602.266.2500; DAILY 10-9; FREE PARKING

PHOENIX—4255 W THUNDERBIRD RD (AT N 43RD AVE); 602.978.4330; DAILY 10-9; FREE PARKING

PHOENIX—4643 E CACTUS RD (AT N TATUM BLVD); 602.996.7780; DAILY 10-9; FREE PARKING

PHOENIX—4710 E RAY RD (AT S 48TH ST); 480.893.8880; DAILY 10-9; FREE PARKING

PHOENIX—7537 W THOMAS RD (AT N 75TH AVE); 623.849.8880; DAILY 10-9; FREE PARKING

Naartjie

"...moderately priced, high-quality clothes... lots of choices for boys... festive fabrics... deep discounts during their regular sales events... durable onesies and pajamas that have stood up to hundreds of washings... comfortable clothing with an emphasis on earth tones and patterns..."

Furniture, Bedding & Decor ✗ | $$$ Prices
Gear & Equipment ✗ | 4 Product availability
Nursing & Feeding ✗ | 4 Staff knowledge
Safety & Babycare ✗ | 4 Customer service
Clothing, Shoes & Accessories ✓ | 4 Decor
Books, Toys & Entertainment ✗

WWW.NAARTJIE.COM

PHOENIX—4250 W ANTHEM WAY (AT N 43RD AVE); 623.465.9949; M-SA 9-8, SU 11-6

Old Navy

"...hip and 'in' clothes for infants and tots... plenty of steals on clearance items... T-shirts and pants for $10 or less... busy, busy, busy—long lines, especially on weekends... nothing fancy and you won't mind when your kids get down and dirty in these clothes... easy to wash, decent quality... you can shop for your baby, your toddler, your teen and yourself all at the same time... clothes are especially affordable when you hit their sales (post-holiday sales are amazing!)..."

Furniture, Bedding & Decor ✗ | $$ Prices
Gear & Equipment ✗ | 4 Product availability
Nursing & Feeding ✗ | 3 Staff knowledge
Safety & Babycare ✗ | 3 Customer service
Clothing, Shoes & Accessories ✗ | 3 Decor
Books, Toys & Entertainment ✗

WWW.OLDNAVY.COM

PHOENIX—1949 E CAMELBACK RD (AT CAMELBACK COLONNADE); 602.240.5405; M-F 9-9, SU 10-6

PHOENIX—21001 N TATUM BLVD (AT HWY 101); 480.502.1672; M-TH 9-9, F-SA 9-9:30, SU 9-6; PARKING LOT

PHOENIX—4550 E CACTUS RD (AT PARADISE VALLEY MALL); 602.404.3005; M-SA 9-10, SU 10-9; PARKING LOT

PHOENIX—9617 N METRO PKWY (AT METRO CENTER); 602.216.0016; M-SA 9-9, SU 10-6

Other Mothers

"...a chain resale shop that carries maternity and kids clothes, furniture and toys... everything you may want or need without the department store prices... take the things your child outgrows in exchange for new 'used' items... great for breastfeeding mothers... my favorite place to look for gently used baby products... a hit or miss, but there are a lot more hits..."

Furniture, Bedding & Decor	✓	$$	Prices
Gear & Equipment	✓	❹	Product availability
Nursing & Feeding	✓	❹	Staff knowledge
Safety & Babycare	✗	❹	Customer service
Clothing, Shoes & Accessories	✓	❸	Decor
Books, Toys & Entertainment	✗		

PHOENIX—2734 W BELL RD (AT I-17); 602.548.2343; M-F10-8, SA 12-5, SU 9-6; PARKING LOT

PHOENIX—3133 E GREENWAY RD (AT 32ND ST); 602.482.6978; M-SA 9-6, SU 12-5; PARKING LOT

Payless Shoe Source

"...a good place for deals on children's shoes... staff is helpful with sizing... the selection and prices for kids' shoes can't be beat, but the quality isn't always spectacular... good leather shoes for cheap... great variety of all sizes and widths... I get my son's shoes here and don't feel like I'm wasting my money since he'll outgrow them in 3 months anyway..."

Furniture, Bedding & Decor	✗	$$	Prices
Gear & Equipment	✗	❸	Product availability
Nursing & Feeding	✗	❸	Staff knowledge
Safety & Babycare	✗	❸	Customer service
Clothing, Shoes & Accessories	✓	❸	Decor
Books, Toys & Entertainment	✗		

WWW.PAYLESS.COM

PHOENIX—1615 E INDIAN SCHOOL RD (N 16TH ST); 602.265.0633; M-SA 10-8

PHOENIX—1623 W BETHANY HOME RD (AT N 19TH AVE); 602.246.0028; M-SA 10-9

PHOENIX—DESERT PALMS POWER CTR (AT E CAMELBACK RD & N 24TH ST); 602.231.0062; M-SA 9-9

PHOENIX—K MART PLAZA SHOPPING CTR (AT N 19TH AVE); 602.276.9717; M-SA 9-9, SU 10-6

PHOENIX—LEGACY VILLAGE (AT S GILBERT RD & E WARNER RD); 602.276.0574; M-SA 9-9

PHOENIX—PARK LEE CTR (AT W CAMELBACK RD); 602.266.1320; M-SA 10-7, SU 10-6

PHOENIX—SOUTH PLAZA SHOPPING CTR (AT S PLAZA SHOPPING CTR); 602.243.7077; M-SA 9-8, SU 10-6

Petite Chateau

"...the best boutique for high-end baby decor and furniture in Phoenix... don't miss the darling slogan onesies and the softest blankets in town... very hip store for mommy and baby... their prices are high, but their selection is unmatched in the area... cool diaper bags, dressers... beautiful items... great ideas for decorating your nursery..."

Furniture, Bedding & Decor	✓	$$$$	Prices
Gear & Equipment	✓	❹	Product availability
Nursing & Feeding	✗	❹	Staff knowledge
Safety & Babycare	✗	❹	Customer service
Clothing, Shoes & Accessories	✓	❺	Decor
Books, Toys & Entertainment	✗		

WWW.PETITE-CHATEAU.COM

PHOENIX—3939 E CAMPBELL AVE (AT 40TH ST); 602.667.3551; M-F 10-6, SA 10-5; PARKING IN FRONT OF BLDG

Phoenix Childrens Hospital Gift Shop

"...a hospital gift store convenient for last minute baby gifts... wide variety of products to choose from... many items benefit the hospital... nice staff and decor..."

Furniture, Bedding & Decor	✗	$$$	Prices
Gear & Equipment	✗	❹	Product availability
Nursing & Feeding	✗	❹	Staff knowledge
Safety & Babycare	✗	❹	Customer service
Clothing, Shoes & Accessories	✗	❹	Decor
Books, Toys & Entertainment	✗		

WWW.PHOENIXCHILDRENSHOSPITAL.COM

PHOENIX—1919 E THOMAS RD (AT 18TH ST); 602.546.0900; M-F 9-8, SA-SU 11-4; PARKING LOT

Rainbow Kids

"...fun clothing styles for infants and tots at low prices... the quality isn't the same as the more expensive brands, but the sleepers and play outfits always hold up well... great place for basics... cute trendy shoe selection for your little walker... we love the prices... up-to-date selection..."

Furniture, Bedding & Decor	✗	$$	Prices
Gear & Equipment	✓	❸	Product availability
Nursing & Feeding	✗	❸	Staff knowledge
Safety & Babycare	✗	❸	Customer service
Clothing, Shoes & Accessories	✓	❸	Decor
Books, Toys & Entertainment	✓		

WWW.RAINBOWSHOPS.COM

PHOENIX—1625B W BETHANY HOME (AT CHRIS-TOWN MALL); 602.589.5133; M-F 10-9, SA 10-7, SU 11-6

Ross Dress For Less

"...if you're in the mood for bargain hunting and are okay with potentially coming up empty-handed, then Ross is for you... don't expect to get educated about baby products here... go early on a week day and you'll find an organized store and staff that is helpful and available—forget weekends... their selection is pretty inconsistent, but I have found some incredible bargains... a great place to stock up on birthday presents or stocking stuffers..."

Furniture, Bedding & Decor	✗	$$	Prices
Gear & Equipment	✗	❸	Product availability
Nursing & Feeding	✗	❸	Staff knowledge
Safety & Babycare	✗	❸	Customer service
Clothing, Shoes & Accessories	✓	❸	Decor
Books, Toys & Entertainment	✓		

WWW.ROSSSTORES.COM

PHOENIX—10625 N 43RD AVE (AT PEORIA); 602.843.1668; M-SA 9:30-9, SU 11-7; PARKING LOT

PHOENIX—10835 N TATUM BLVD (AT E SHEA BLVD); 480.922.7785; M-SA 9:30-9:30, SU 11-7; PARKING LOT

PHOENIX—1751 W BETHANY HOME RD (AT 19TH AVE); 602.544.0338; M-SA 9:30-9:30, SU 11-7; PARKING LOT

PHOENIX—220 E BELL ST (AT 3RD ST); 602.504.1125; M-SA 9:30-9:30, SU 11-7; PARKING LOT

PHOENIX—2821 W PEORIA AVE (AT 28TH AVE); 602.944.7800; M-SA 9:30-9:30, SU 11-7; PARKING LOT

PHOENIX—2929 W AGUA FRIA FWY (AT 27TH AVE); 623.780.3277; M-SA 9:30-9:30, SU 11-7; PARKING LOT

PHOENIX—4509 E THOMAS RD (AT 44TH ST); 602.840.0330; M-SA 9:30-9:30, SU 11-7; PARKING LOT

PHOENIX—7333 W THOMAS RD (AT N 75TH AVE); 623.247.6030; M-SA 9:30-9:30, SU 11-7; PARKING LOT

Sears

“...a decent selection of clothes and basic baby equipment... check out the Kids Club program—it's a great way to save money... you go to Sears to save money, not to be pampered... the quality of their merchandise is better than Wal-Mart, but don't expect anything too special or different... not much in terms of gear, but tons of well-priced baby and toddler clothing...”

Furniture, Bedding & Decor	✓	$$	Prices
Gear & Equipment	✓	❸	Product availability
Nursing & Feeding	✓	❸	Staff knowledge
Safety & Babycare	✓	❸	Customer service
Clothing, Shoes & Accessories	✓	❸	Decor
Books, Toys & Entertainment	✓		

WWW.SEARS.COM

PHOENIX—10001 N METRO PKWY W (AT METRO CENTER); 602.395.2995; M-SA 10-9, SU 10-6; PARKING LOT

PHOENIX—4531 E THOMAS RD (AT ARCADIA CROSSING SHOPPING CTR); 602.474.8451; M-F 10-9, SA 10-6, SU 11-5

PHOENIX—4604 E CACTUS RD (AT PARADISE VALLEY MALL); 602.953.7116; M-F 10-9, SA 8-9, SU 10-6

PHOENIX—7611 W THOMAS RD (AT 75TH AVE); 623.849.7960; M-F 10-9, SA 8-9, SU 10-7

Stride Rite Shoes

“...wonderful selection of baby and toddler shoes... sandals, sneakers, and even special-occasion shoes... decent quality shoes that last... they know a lot about kids' shoes and take the time to get it right—they always measure my son's feet before fittings... store sizes vary, but they always have something in stock that works... they've even special ordered shoes for my daughter... a fun 'first shoe' buying experience...”

Furniture, Bedding & Decor	✗	$$$	Prices
Gear & Equipment	✗	❹	Product availability
Nursing & Feeding	✗	❹	Staff knowledge
Safety & Babycare	✗	❹	Customer service
Clothing, Shoes & Accessories	✓	❹	Decor
Books, Toys & Entertainment	✗		

WWW.STRIDERITE.COM

PHOENIX—4568 E CACTUS RD (AT PARADISE VILLAGE); 602.787.1909; M-SA 10-9, SU11-6

Target

“...our favorite place to shop for kids' stuff—good selection and very affordable... guilt-free shopping—kids grow so fast so I don't want to pay high department-store prices... everything from diapers and sippy cups to car seats and strollers... easy return policy... generally helpful staff, but you don't go for the service—you go for the prices... decent registry that won't freak your friends out with outrageous prices... easy, convenient shopping for well-priced items... all the big-box brands available—Graco, Evenflo, Eddie Bauer, etc....”

Furniture, Bedding & Decor	✓	$$	Prices

Gear & Equipment ✓
Nursing & Feeding ✓
Safety & Babycare ✓
Clothing, Shoes & Accessories ✓
Books, Toys & Entertainment ✓

❹ Product availability
❸ Staff knowledge
❸ Customer service
❸ Decor

WWW.TARGET.COM

PHOENIX—12602 N PARADISE VILLAGE PKY W (AT CACTUS RD); 602.953.2151; M-SA 8-10, SU 8-9; PARKING LOT

PHOENIX—16806 N 7TH ST (AT BELL RD); 602.375.1500; M-SA 8-10, SU 8-9; PARKING LOT

PHOENIX—1818 E BASELINE RD (AT 24TH ST); 602.281.1119; M-SA 8-10, SU 8-9; PARKING LOT

PHOENIX—21001 N TATUM BLVD (AT E DEER VALLEY DR); 480.419.9380; M-SA 8-10, SU 8-9; PARKING LOT

PHOENIX—2727 W AGUA FRIA FWY (AT 27TH AVE); 623.869.8070; M-SA 8-10, SU 8-9; PARKING LOT

PHOENIX—4515 E THOMAS RD (AT ARCADIA CROSSING SHOPPING CTR); 602.952.1797; M-SA 8-10, SU 8-9; PARKING LOT

PHOENIX—4734 E RAY RD (AT 48TH ST); 480.893.0588; M-SA 8-10, SU 8-9; PARKING LOT

PHOENIX—740 W CAMELBACK RD (AT 7TH AVE); 602.263.6035; M-SA 8-10, SU 8-9; PARKING LOT

PHOENIX—7409 W VIRGINIA AVE (AT 48TH ST); 480.893.9333; M-SA 8-10, SU 8-9; PARKING LOT

This Little Piggy Wears Cotton ★★★★☆

"...a fun store full of adorable baby clothes, toys and gear... not cheap, but they really have a knack for finding cute things... high-quality kid's clothing, including layette and baby items... fashionable clothes include plenty of European brands... makes shopping a fun experience... great cotton PJs for kids..."

Furniture, Bedding & Decor ✗
Gear & Equipment ✓
Nursing & Feeding ✗
Safety & Babycare ✗
Clothing, Shoes & Accessories ✓
Books, Toys & Entertainment ✓

$$$$ Prices
❹ Product availability
❹ Staff knowledge
❹ Customer service
❹ Decor

WWW.LITTLEPIGGY.COM

PHOENIX—2468 E CAMELBACK RD (AT BILTMORE FASHION PARK); 602.224.0801; M-W 10-7, TH-F 10-8, SA 10-6, SU 12-6

Twice Is Nice

"...lots of used items in very good condition at reasonable prices... trade in your gently used baby clothes and use the store credit to get more... they donate what they don't want to charity... you can find some great deals if you shop there frequently and plan on really digging around... aisles can be a bit crowded... definitely worth a trip..."

Furniture, Bedding & Decor ✗
Gear & Equipment ✗
Nursing & Feeding ✗
Safety & Babycare ✗
Clothing, Shoes & Accessories ✓
Books, Toys & Entertainment ✗

$$ Prices
❸ Product availability
❸ Staff knowledge
❹ Customer service
❸ Decor

WWW.TWICEISNICE.COM

PHOENIX—10653 N 43RD AVE (AT W PEORIA AVE); 602.564.1022; M-F 9-8, SA 9-7, SU 11-6

USA Baby

"...they carry an extensive selection of high-end nursery products such as furniture, bedding, accessories and highchairs... popular place to do all the shopping for your nursery... the staff knows their products well and can help you sort through their vast selection... allow plenty of time for your products to arrive, especially the big-ticket items (they offer loaners while you wait for your order to arrive)... they have great sales a few times a year and will match competitor prices... good selection, especially if you're getting ready to set up your nursery..."

Furniture, Bedding & Decor	✓	$$$$	Prices
Gear & Equipment	✓	4	Product availability
Nursing & Feeding	✓	4	Staff knowledge
Safety & Babycare	✓	4	Customer service
Clothing, Shoes & Accessories	×	4	Decor
Books, Toys & Entertainment	✓		

WWW.USABABY.COM

PHOENIX—10630 N 32ND ST (AT E SHEA BLVD); 602.788.8200; M F 10-8, T-TH SA 10-6, SU 12-5; MALL PARKING

Northwest Valley

Babies R Us

“...everything baby under one roof... they have a wide selection and carry most 'mainstream' items such as Graco, Fisher-Price, Avent and Britax... great customer service—given how big the stores are, I was pleasantly surprised at how attentive the staff was... easy return policy... super busy on weekends so try to visit on a weekday for the best service... keep an eye out for great coupons, deals and frequent sales... easy and comprehensive registry... shopping here is so easy—you've got to check it out...”

Furniture, Bedding & Decor	✓	$$$	Prices
Gear & Equipment	✓	❹	Product availability
Nursing & Feeding	✓	❹	Staff knowledge
Safety & Babycare	✓	❹	Customer service
Clothing, Shoes & Accessories	✓	❹	Decor
Books, Toys & Entertainment	✓		

WWW.BABIESRUS.COM

GLENDALE—7540 W BELL RD (AT ARROWHEAD TOWNE CTR); 623.878.3810; M-SA 9:30-9:30, SU 11-7; PARKING IN FRONT OF BLDG

Bombay Kids

“...the kids section of this furniture store carries out-of-the-ordinary items... whimsical, pastel grandfather clocks... zebra bean bags... perfect for my eclectic taste... I now prefer my daughter's room to my own... clean bathroom with changing area and wipes... they have a little table with crayons and coloring books for the kids... easy and relaxed shopping destination...”

Furniture, Bedding & Decor	✓	$$$	Prices
Gear & Equipment	✗	❹	Product availability
Nursing & Feeding	✗	❹	Staff knowledge
Safety & Babycare	✗	❹	Customer service
Clothing, Shoes & Accessories	✗	❹	Decor
Books, Toys & Entertainment	✗		

WWW.BOMBAYKIDS.COM

GLENDALE—20028 N 67TH AVE (OFF AQUA FRIA FWY); 623.561.8580; M-SA 9-8, SU 11-6

Children's Place, The

“...great bargains on cute clothing... shoes, socks, swimsuits, sunglasses and everything in between... lots of '3 for $20' type deals on sleepers, pants and mix-and-match separates... so much more affordable than the other 'big chains'... don't expect the most unique stuff here, but it wears and washes well... cheap clothing for cheap prices... you can leave the store with bags full of clothes without putting a huge dent in your wallet...”

Furniture, Bedding & Decor	✗	$$	Prices
Gear & Equipment	✗	❹	Product availability
Nursing & Feeding	✗	❹	Staff knowledge
Safety & Babycare	✗	❹	Customer service
Clothing, Shoes & Accessories	✓	❹	Decor
Books, Toys & Entertainment	✓		

WWW.CHILDRENSPLACE.COM

GLENDALE—7700 W ARROWHEAD TOWNE CTR (AT ARROWHEAD MALL); 623.334.3186; M-SA 10-9, SU 11-6; PARKING LOT

Costco

"...dependable place for bulk diapers, wipes and formula at discount prices... clothing selection is very hit-or-miss... avoid shopping there during nights and weekends if possible, because parking and checkout lines are brutal... they don't have a huge selection of brands, but the brands they do have are almost always in stock and at a great price... lowest prices around for diapers and formula... kid's clothing tends to be picked through, but it's worth looking for great deals on name-brand items like Carter's..."

Furniture, Bedding & Decor	✓	$$	Prices
Gear & Equipment	✓	❸	Product availability
Nursing & Feeding	✓	❸	Staff knowledge
Safety & Babycare	✓	❸	Customer service
Clothing, Shoes & Accessories	✓	❷	Decor
Books, Toys & Entertainment	✓		

WWW.COSTCO.COM

GLENDALE—17550 N 79TH AVE (AT ARROWHEAD TOWNE CTR); 623.776.4003; M-F 10-8:30, SA 9:30-6, SU 10-6

Dillard's

"...this store has beautiful clothes, and if you catch a sale, you can get great quality clothes at super bargain prices... good customer service and helpful staff... a huge selection of merchandise for boys and girls... nice layette department... some furnishings like little tables and chairs... beautiful displays... the best part is that in addition to shopping for your kids, you can also shop for yourself..."

Furniture, Bedding & Decor	✓	$$$	Prices
Gear & Equipment	✗	❹	Product availability
Nursing & Feeding	✗	❸	Staff knowledge
Safety & Babycare	✗	❹	Customer service
Clothing, Shoes & Accessories	✓	❹	Decor
Books, Toys & Entertainment	✓		

WWW.DILLARDS.COM

GLENDALE—7800 W ARROWHEAD TWN CTR (AT W CAMPO BELLO DR); 623.979.1128; M-SA 10-9, SU 12-6

Gymboree

"...beautiful clothing and great quality... colorful and stylish baby and kids wear... lots of fun birthday gift ideas... easy exchange and return policy... items usually go on sale pretty quickly... save money with Gymbucks... many stores have a play area which makes shopping with my kids fun (let alone feasible)..."

Furniture, Bedding & Decor	✗	$$$	Prices
Gear & Equipment	✗	❹	Product availability
Nursing & Feeding	✗	❹	Staff knowledge
Safety & Babycare	✗	❹	Customer service
Clothing, Shoes & Accessories	✓	❹	Decor
Books, Toys & Entertainment	✓		

WWW.GYMBOREE.COM

GLENDALE—7700 W ARROWHEAD TOWNE CTR (AT N 77TH AVE); 623.878.2405; M-SA 10-9, SU 11-6

JCPenney

"...always a good place to find clothes and other baby basics... the registry process was seamless... staff is generally friendly but the lines always seem long and slow... they don't have the greatest selection of toddler clothes, but their baby section is great... we had some damaged furniture delivered but customer service was easy and accommodating... a pretty limited selection of gear, but what they have is priced right..."

Furniture, Bedding & Decor	✓	$$	Prices
Gear & Equipment	✓	❸	Product availability
Nursing & Feeding	✓	❸	Staff knowledge
Safety & Babycare	✓	❸	Customer service
Clothing, Shoes & Accessories	✓	❸	Decor
Books, Toys & Entertainment	✓		

WWW.JCPENNEY.COM

GLENDALE—7750 W ARROWHEAD TOWNE CTR (AT N 77TH AVE); 623.412.1121; M-F 10-9, SA 10-7, SU 11-6; PARKING LOT

PEORIA—8235 W BELL RD (AT N VALLEY POWER CTR); 623.487.9775; M-F 10-9, SA 10-7, SU 11-6; PARKING LOT

Kohl's

★★★★☆

"...nice one-stop shopping for the whole family—everything from clothing to baby gear... great sales on clothing and a good selection of higher-end brands... stylish, inexpensive clothes for babies through 24 months... very easy shopping experience... dirt-cheap sales and clearance prices... nothing super fancy, but just right for those everyday romper outfits... Graco, Eddie Bauer and other well-known brands..."

Furniture, Bedding & Decor	✓	$$	Prices
Gear & Equipment	✓	❹	Product availability
Nursing & Feeding	✓	❸	Staff knowledge
Safety & Babycare	✓	❸	Customer service
Clothing, Shoes & Accessories	✓	❸	Decor
Books, Toys & Entertainment	✓		

WWW.KOHLS.COM

GLENDALE—5408 W BELL RD (AT N 55TH AVE); 602.298.5456; M-SA 8-10, SU 10-8; FREE PARKING

PEORIA—9220 W NORTHERN AVE (AT N 91ST AVE); 623.877.0177; M-SA 8-10, SU 10-8; FREE PARKING

SURPRISE—14020 W BELL RD (AT N LITCHFIELD RD); 623.544.6330; M-SA 8-10, SU 10-8; FREE PARKING

Liz's Too Resale Furniture

Furniture, Bedding & Decor	✓	✗	Gear & Equipment
Nursing & Feeding	✗	✗	Safety & Babycare
Clothing, Shoes & Accessories	✗	✗	Books, Toys & Entertainment

SUN CITY—10050 W BELL RD (AT 99TH AVE); 623.977.1655; M-SA 8-3:30; PARKING LOT

Mervyn's

★★★☆☆

"...wide selection of baby and kids' clothing, including OshKosh and Carter's... limited shoe selection without any real sizing assistance... lots of good sales... you might not always be able to find the size and color you want, but there's enough selection here that you're sure to find something else that will work just as well... cheap, cheap, cheap... okay for cheap basics, but don't expect anything super special..."

Furniture, Bedding & Decor	✗	$$	Prices
Gear & Equipment	✗	❹	Product availability
Nursing & Feeding	✗	❸	Staff knowledge
Safety & Babycare	✗	❸	Customer service
Clothing, Shoes & Accessories	✓	❸	Decor
Books, Toys & Entertainment	✓		

WWW.MERVYNS.COM

GLENDALE—7650 W ARROWHEAD TOWNE CTR (AT N 75TH AVE); 623.486.8800; M-SA 9-10, SU 9-9; FREE PARKING

Old Navy

"...hip and 'in' clothes for infants and tots... plenty of steals on clearance items... T-shirts and pants for $10 or less... busy, busy,

busy—long lines, especially on weekends... nothing fancy and you won't mind when your kids gets down and dirty in these clothes... easy to wash, decent quality... you can shop for your baby, your toddler, your teen and yourself all at the same time... clothes are especially affordable when you hit their sales (post-holiday sales are amazing!)... ❞

Furniture, Bedding & Decor	✗	$$	Prices
Gear & Equipment	✗	❹	Product availability
Nursing & Feeding	✗	❸	Staff knowledge
Safety & Babycare	✗	❸	Customer service
Clothing, Shoes & Accessories	✓	❸	Decor
Books, Toys & Entertainment	✗		

WWW.OLDNAVY.COM

PEORIA—7375 W BELL RD (AT 75TH AVE); 623.776.8274; M-SA 9-9, SU 10-6; PARKING LOT

Ross Dress For Less

❝*...if you're in the mood for bargain hunting and are okay with potentially coming up empty-handed, then Ross is for you... don't expect to get educated about baby products here... go early on a week day and you'll find an organized store and staff that is helpful and available—forget weekends... their selection is pretty inconsistent, but I have found some incredible bargains... a great place to stock up on birthday presents or stocking stuffers...* ❞

Furniture, Bedding & Decor	✗	$$	Prices
Gear & Equipment	✗	❸	Product availability
Nursing & Feeding	✗	❸	Staff knowledge
Safety & Babycare	✗	❸	Customer service
Clothing, Shoes & Accessories	✓	❸	Decor
Books, Toys & Entertainment	✓		

WWW.ROSSSTORES.COM

PEORIA—8115 W BELL RD (AT 83RD AVE); 623.486.9311; M-SA 9:30-9:30, SU 11-7; PARKING LOT

PEORIA—9460 W NORTHERN AVE (AT 91ST AVE); 623.772.1228; M-SA 9:30-9:30, SU 11-7; PARKING LOT

SURPRISE—13715 W BELL RD (AT N W POINT PKWY); 623.537.9278; M-SA 9:30-9:30, SU 11-7

Sears

❝*...a decent selection of clothes and basic baby equipment... check out the Kids Club program—it's a great way to save money... you go to Sears to save money, not to be pampered... the quality of their merchandise is better than Wal-Mart, but don't expect anything too special or different... not much in terms of gear, but tons of well-priced baby and toddler clothing...* ❞

Furniture, Bedding & Decor	✓	$$	Prices
Gear & Equipment	✓	❸	Product availability
Nursing & Feeding	✓	❸	Staff knowledge
Safety & Babycare	✓	❸	Customer service
Clothing, Shoes & Accessories	✓	❸	Decor
Books, Toys & Entertainment	✓		

WWW.SEARS.COM

GLENDALE—7780 W ARROWHEAD TOWNE CTR (AT N 77TH AVE); 623.776.4500; M-F 10-9, SA 8-9, SU 10-6

PEORIA—10140 N 91ST AVE (AT W PEORIA AVE); 623.687.2400; M-SA 8-10, SU 8-8

Stride Rite Shoes

❝*...wonderful selection of baby and toddler shoes... sandals, sneakers, and even special-occasion shoes... decent quality shoes that last... they*

know a lot about kids' shoes and take the time to get it right—they always measure my son's feet before fittings... store sizes vary, but they always have something in stock that works... they've even special ordered shoes for my daughter... a fun 'first shoe' buying experience... ”

Furniture, Bedding & Decor .... ✗
Gear & Equipment .... ✗
Nursing & Feeding .... ✗
Safety & Babycare .... ✗
Clothing, Shoes & Accessories ...... ✓
Books, Toys & Entertainment .... ✗

$$$ .... Prices
❹ .... Product availability
❹ .... Staff knowledge
❹ .... Customer service
❹ .... Decor

WWW.STRIDERITE.COM

GLENDALE—7700 W ARROWHEAD TOWNE CTR (AT 75TH AVE); 623.773.3286; M-SA 10-9, SU 11-6; PARKING LOT

Target

“*...our favorite place to shop for kids' stuff—good selection and very affordable... guilt-free shopping—kids grow so fast so I don't want to pay high department-store prices... everything from diapers and sippy cups to car seats and strollers... easy return policy... generally helpful staff, but you don't go for the service—you go for the prices... decent registry that won't freak your friends out with outrageous prices... easy, convenient shopping for well-priced items... all the big-box brands available—Graco, Evenflo, Eddie Bauer, etc....* ”

Furniture, Bedding & Decor .... ✓
Gear & Equipment .... ✓
Nursing & Feeding .... ✓
Safety & Babycare .... ✓
Clothing, Shoes & Accessories ...... ✓
Books, Toys & Entertainment .... ✓

$$ .... Prices
❹ .... Product availability
❸ .... Staff knowledge
❸ .... Customer service
❸ .... Decor

WWW.TARGET.COM

GLENDALE—10230 N 43RD AVE (AT FRY RD); 480.281.0008; M-SA 8-10, SU 8-9; PARKING LOT

GLENDALE—9350 W NORTHERN AVE (AT LOOP 101); 623.877.8440; M-SA 8-10, SU 8-9; PARKING LOT

PEORIA—8055 W BELL RD (AT 79TH AVE); 623.773.2172; M-SA 8-10, SU 8-9; PARKING LOT

SURPRISE—13731 W BELL RD (AT GRAND AVE); 623.975.4122; M-SA 8-10, SU 8-9; PARKING LOT

Wal-Mart

“*...inexpensive source for all your children's needs... the quality is sometimes lacking so shop carefully... you can shop anytime day or night... low prices on diapers, wipes, formula and other basics... you will always walk out of here with bargains, just be prepared to work for them... some stores are more disorganized than others and staff may not be as knowledgeable as smaller shops... you go for the deals, not the service... well known brands for very little money... the crowds can be intimidating, especially if you're shopping with your kids...* ”

Furniture, Bedding & Decor .... ✓
Gear & Equipment .... ✓
Nursing & Feeding .... ✓
Safety & Babycare .... ✓
Clothing, Shoes & Accessories ...... ✓
Books, Toys & Entertainment .... ✓

$$ .... Prices
❹ .... Product availability
❸ .... Staff knowledge
❸ .... Customer service
❸ .... Decor

WWW.WALMART.COM

GLENDALE—5845 W BELL RD (AT 59TH AVE); 602.978.8205; M-SA 6-12; PARKING LOT

Northeast Valley

"lila picks"

★Babystyle

★Bellini

★Jacadi

April Cornell

"...beautiful, classic dresses and accessories for special occasions... I love the matching 'mommy and me' outfits... lots of fun knickknacks for sale... great selection of baby wear on their web site... rest assured your baby won't look like every other child in these adorable outfits... very frilly and girlie—beautiful..."

Furniture, Bedding & Decor .... ✗
Gear & Equipment .... ✗
Nursing & Feeding .... ✗
Safety & Babycare .... ✗
Clothing, Shoes & Accessories....... ✓
Books, Toys & Entertainment .... ✗

$$$ .... Prices
❸ .... Product availability
❹ .... Staff knowledge
❹ .... Customer service
❹ .... Decor

WWW.APRILCORNELL.COM

SCOTTSDALE—15054 N SCOTTSDALE RD (AT KIERLAND COMMONS); 480.607.7790; M-TH 10-8, F-SA 10-9, SU 12-6

Babies R Us

"...everything baby under one roof... they have a wide selection and carry most 'mainstream' items such as Graco, Fisher-Price, Avent and Britax... great customer service—given how big the stores are, I was pleasantly surprised at how attentive the staff was... easy return policy... super busy on weekends so try to visit on a weekday for the best service... keep an eye out for great coupons, deals and frequent sales... easy and comprehensive registry... shopping here is so easy—you've got to check it out..."

Furniture, Bedding & Decor .... ✓
Gear & Equipment .... ✓
Nursing & Feeding .... ✓
Safety & Babycare .... ✓
Clothing, Shoes & Accessories....... ✓
Books, Toys & Entertainment .... ✓

$$$ .... Prices
❹ .... Product availability
❹ .... Staff knowledge
❹ .... Customer service
❹ .... Decor

WWW.BABIESRUS.COM

SCOTTSDALE—7000 E MAYO BLVD (AT SCOTTSDALE RD); 480.585.7362; M-SA 9:30-9:30, SU 11-7; PARKING LOT

Baby Couture & Caviar Kids

"...unique nursery decorations... baby toys are fun and safe... adorable clothing for boys and girls... a place for aunts and grandmothers who like to spoil kids... pricey, but worth it for the little treasures you may find..."

Furniture, Bedding & Decor .... ✓
Gear & Equipment .... ✗

$$$$$ .... Prices
❹ .... Product availability

Nursing & Feeding .... ✗
Safety & Babycare .... ✗
Clothing, Shoes & Accessories ...... ✓
Books, Toys & Entertainment .... ✗

❹ .... Staff knowledge
❹ ....Customer service
❺ .... Decor

PARADISE VALLEY—8787 N SCOTTSDALE RD (AT E SUNNYVALE RD); 480.951.9696; M-SA 10-5:30; PARKING LOT

BabyGap/GapKids ★★★★☆

"...colorful baby and toddler clothing in clean, well-lit stores... great return policy... it's the Gap, so you know what you're getting—colorful, cute and well-made clothing... best place for baby hats... prices are reasonable especially since there's always a sale of some sort going on... sales, sales, sales—frequent and fantastic... everything I'm looking for in infant clothing—snap crotches, snaps up the front, all natural fabrics and great styling... fun seasonal selections—a great place to shop for gifts as well as for your own kids... although it can get busy, staff generally seem accommodating and helpful..."

Furniture, Bedding & Decor .... ✗
Gear & Equipment .... ✗
Nursing & Feeding .... ✗
Safety & Babycare .... ✗
Clothing, Shoes & Accessories ...... ✓
Books, Toys & Entertainment .... ✗

$$$ .... Prices
❹ .... Product availability
❹ .... Staff knowledge
❹ ....Customer service
❹ .... Decor

WWW.GAP.COM

SCOTTSDALE—7014 E CAMELBACK RD (AT FASHION SQUARE MALL); 480.949.8767; M-SA 10-9, SU 11-7; MALL PARKING

Babystyle ★★★★★

"...they offer a wonderful range of children's clothing, educational toys, gear and even maternity items... the atmosphere is great for babies—you really feel the staff there want you to be comfortable... great, friendly service... unfortunately what is on their web site is not always in the store... if you are looking for a special occasion gift or a really chic diaper bag then you should come here... their line of baby and toddler clothing is really cute and wears well..."

Furniture, Bedding & Decor .... ✓
Gear & Equipment .... ✓
Nursing & Feeding .... ✓
Safety & Babycare .... ✓
Clothing, Shoes & Accessories ...... ✓
Books, Toys & Entertainment .... ✓

$$$$ .... Prices
❹ .... Product availability
❹ .... Staff knowledge
❹ ....Customer service
❹ .... Decor

WWW.BABYSTYLE.COM

SCOTTSDALE—15215 N KIERLAND BLVD (AT N 71ST ST); 480.596.9201; M-F 10-9, SA 10-7, SU 11-6; PARKING LOT

SCOTTSDALE—7014 E CAMELBACK RD (AT SCOTTSDALE RD); 480.994.5800; M-F 10-9, SA 10-7, SU 11-6; PARKING LOT

Bearly Kidding ★★★★☆

"...carries Giggle Moon, Baby Lulu, Robeez and other high-quality brands... size selection is limited... staff is knowledgeable...they carry a nice selection of European designer clothes from newborn to preteen..."

Furniture, Bedding & Decor .... ✓
Gear & Equipment .... ✓
Nursing & Feeding .... ✗
Safety & Babycare .... ✗
Clothing, Shoes & Accessories ...... ✓
Books, Toys & Entertainment .... ✓

$$$ .... Prices
❸ .... Product availability
❹ .... Staff knowledge
❸ ....Customer service
❹ .... Decor

SCOTTSDALE—6107 N SCOTTSDALE RD (AT E MCDONALD DR); 480.483.7522; DAILY 10-5:30; STREET PARKING

Bellini

"...high-end furniture for a gorgeous nursery... if you're looking for the kind of furniture you see in magazines then this is the place to go... excellent quality... yes, it's pricey, but the quality is impeccable... free delivery and setup... their furniture is built to withstand the abuse my tots dish out... they sell very unique merchandise, ranging from cribs to bedding and even some clothes... our nursery design was inspired by their store decor... I wish they had more frequent sales..."

Furniture, Bedding & Decor	✓	$$$$	Prices
Gear & Equipment	✗	4	Product availability
Nursing & Feeding	✗	4	Staff knowledge
Safety & Babycare	✗	4	Customer service
Clothing, Shoes & Accessories	✗	4	Decor
Books, Toys & Entertainment	✓		

WWW.BELLINI.COM

SCOTTSDALE—15227 N NORTHSIGHT BLVD (AT RAINTREE); 480.368.0086; M-W F-SA 10-6, TH 10-7, SU 11-5

SCOTTSDALE—7366 E SHEA BLVD (AT N SCOTTSDALE RD); M-SA 10-5; FREE PARKING

Bombay Kids

"...the kids section of this furniture store carries out-of-the-ordinary items... whimsical, pastel grandfather clocks... zebra bean bags... perfect for my eclectic taste... I now prefer my daughter's room to my own... clean bathroom with changing area and wipes... they have a little table with crayons and coloring books for the kids... easy and relaxed shopping destination..."

Furniture, Bedding & Decor	✓	$$$	Prices
Gear & Equipment	✗	4	Product availability
Nursing & Feeding	✗	4	Staff knowledge
Safety & Babycare	✗	4	Customer service
Clothing, Shoes & Accessories	✗	4	Decor
Books, Toys & Entertainment	✗		

WWW.BOMBAYKIDS.COM

SCOTTSDALE—4513 N SCOTTSDALE RD (AT CAMELBACK RD); 480.994.8859; M-SA 10-8, SU 11-6

Children's Place, The

"...great bargains on cute clothing... shoes, socks, swimsuits, sunglasses and everything in between... lots of '3 for $20' type deals on sleepers, pants and mix-and-match separates... so much more affordable than the other 'big chains'... don't expect the most unique stuff here, but it wears and washes well... cheap clothing for cheap prices... you can leave the store with bags full of clothes without putting a huge dent in your wallet..."

Furniture, Bedding & Decor	✗	$$	Prices
Gear & Equipment	✗	4	Product availability
Nursing & Feeding	✗	4	Staff knowledge
Safety & Babycare	✗	4	Customer service
Clothing, Shoes & Accessories	✓	4	Decor
Books, Toys & Entertainment	✓		

WWW.CHILDRENSPLACE.COM

SCOTTSDALE—7014 E CAMELBACK RD (AT SCOTTSDALE RD); 480.946.9015; M-SA 10-9, SU 11-6; PARKING LOT

Costco

"...dependable place for bulk diapers, wipes and formula at discount prices... clothing selection is very hit-or-miss... avoid shopping there during nights and weekends if possible, because parking and checkout lines are brutal... they don't have a huge selection of brands, but the

brands they do have are almost always in stock and at a great price... lowest prices around for diapers and formula... kid's clothing tends to be picked through, but it's worth looking for great deals on name-brand items like Carter's... ❞

Furniture, Bedding & Decor .... ✓
Gear & Equipment .... ✓
Nursing & Feeding .... ✓
Safety & Babycare .... ✓
Clothing, Shoes & Accessories ...... ✓
Books, Toys & Entertainment .... ✓

$$ .... Prices
❸ .... Product availability
❸ .... Staff knowledge
❸ .... Customer service
❷ .... Decor

WWW.COSTCO.COM

SCOTTSDALE—15255 N HAYDEN RD (AT N 83RD PL); 408.948.5040; M-F 10-8:30, SA 9:30-6, SU 10-6

Dillard's

❝*...this store has beautiful clothes, and if you catch a sale, you can get great quality clothes at super bargain prices... good customer service and helpful staff... a huge selection of merchandise for boys and girls... nice layette department... some furnishings like little tables and chairs... beautiful displays... the best part is that in addition to shopping for your kids, you can also shop for yourself...* ❞

Furniture, Bedding & Decor .... ✓
Gear & Equipment .... ×
Nursing & Feeding .... ×
Safety & Babycare .... ×
Clothing, Shoes & Accessories ...... ✓
Books, Toys & Entertainment .... ✓

$$$ .... Prices
❹ .... Product availability
❸ .... Staff knowledge
❹ .... Customer service
❹ .... Decor

WWW.DILLARDS.COM

SCOTTSDALE—6900 E CAMELBACK RD (AT GOLDWATER BLVD); 480.949.5869; M-SA 10-9, SU 12-6

Ecco Shoes

Furniture, Bedding & Decor .... ×
Nursing & Feeding .... ×
Clothing, Shoes & Accessories ...... ✓

× .... Gear & Equipment
× .... Safety & Babycare
× .... Books, Toys & Entertainment

WWW.ECCO.COM

SCOTTSDALE—7030 E GREENWAY PKWY (AT SCOTTSDALE RD); 480.443.0558; M-TH 10-8, F-SA 10-9, SU 12-6; PARKING LOT

Frou Frou

Furniture, Bedding & Decor .... ✓
Nursing & Feeding .... ×
Clothing, Shoes & Accessories ...... ✓

× .... Gear & Equipment
× .... Safety & Babycare
✓ .... Books, Toys & Entertainment

WWW.FROUFROULIFE.COM

CAREFREE—7212 HO HUM RD (AT SPANISH VILLAGE); 480.437.9998; DAILY 11-5; PARKING LOT

Gigi's Second Time Around

Furniture, Bedding & Decor .... ×
Nursing & Feeding .... ×
Clothing, Shoes & Accessories .... ×

× .... Gear & Equipment
× .... Safety & Babycare
× .... Books, Toys & Entertainment

SCOTTSDALE—7126 E BECKER LN (AT SHAY); 480.998.5978; M-F 10-6, SA 9-4:30 ; PARKING LOT

Gymboree

❝*...beautiful clothing and great quality... colorful and stylish baby and kids wear... lots of fun birthday gift ideas... easy exchange and return policy... items usually go on sale pretty quickly... save money with Gymbucks... many stores have a play area which makes shopping with my kids fun (let alone feasible)...* ❞

Furniture, Bedding & Decor	✗	$$$	Prices
Gear & Equipment	✗	❹	Product availability
Nursing & Feeding	✗	❹	Staff knowledge
Safety & Babycare	✗	❹	Customer service
Clothing, Shoes & Accessories	✓	❹	Decor
Books, Toys & Entertainment	✓		

WWW.GYMBOREE.COM

SCOTTSDALE—7014 E CAMELBACK RD (AT SCOTTSDALE MALL); 480.970.8262; M-SA 10-9, SU 11-6; PARKING LOT

Jacadi ★★★★★

"...beautiful French clothes, baby bumpers and quilts... elegant and perfect for special occasions... quite expensive, but the clothing is hip and the quality really good... many handmade clothing and bedding items... take advantage of their sales... more of a store to buy gifts than practical, everyday clothes... beautiful, special clothing—especially for newborns and toddlers... velvet pajamas, coordinated nursery items... stores are as pretty as the clothes... they have a huge (half-off everything) sale twice a year that makes it very affordable..."

Furniture, Bedding & Decor	✓	$$$$	Prices
Gear & Equipment	✗	❹	Product availability
Nursing & Feeding	✗	❹	Staff knowledge
Safety & Babycare	✗	❹	Customer service
Clothing, Shoes & Accessories	✓	❹	Decor
Books, Toys & Entertainment	✓		

WWW.JACADIUSA.COM

SCOTTSDALE—15044 N SCOTTSDALE RD (AT KIERLAND COMMONS); 480.443.3921; M-SA 10-7, SU 12-6; MALL PARKING

Janie And Jack ★★★★☆

"...gorgeous clothing and some accessories (shoes, socks, etc.)... fun to look at, somewhat pricey, but absolutely adorable clothes for little ones... boutique-like clothes at non-boutique prices—especially on sale... high-quality infant and toddler clothes anyone would love—always good for a baby gift... I always check the clearance racks in the back of the store... their decor is darling—a really fun shopping experience..."

Furniture, Bedding & Decor	✗	$$$$	Prices
Gear & Equipment	✓	❹	Product availability
Nursing & Feeding	✗	❹	Staff knowledge
Safety & Babycare	✗	❹	Customer service
Clothing, Shoes & Accessories	✓	❹	Decor
Books, Toys & Entertainment	✗		

WWW.JANIEANDJACK.COM

SCOTTSDALE—7014 E CAMELBACK RD (AT SCOTTSDALE FASHION SQUARE); 480.941.3072; 24 HRS; FREE PARKING

Kid to Kid

"...best selection and best finds of all the secondhand children's stores that I have been to... wonderful resale outlet for high-end children's clothing, furniture, and toys... I make out really well there with books... beautifully arranged, the stock and the prices are great... the place to go for used equipment... they only accept items in excellent condition, many of them look brand new... finally I can actually fit my double stroller in the aisle of a children's clothing store..."

Furniture, Bedding & Decor	✗	$$	Prices
Gear & Equipment	✗	❹	Product availability
Nursing & Feeding	✗	❹	Staff knowledge
Safety & Babycare	✗	❹	Customer service
Clothing, Shoes & Accessories	✓	❸	Decor
Books, Toys & Entertainment	✓		

WWW.KIDTOKID.COM

SCOTTSDALE—8664 E SHEA BLVD (AT PIEDMONT CROSSING); 480.556.9781; M-F 10-6, SA 10-5, SU 12-4; PARKING LOT

Kids Room By Breuners

Furniture, Bedding & Decor	✓	✗	Gear & Equipment
Nursing & Feeding	✗	✗	Safety & Babycare
Clothing, Shoes & Accessories	✗	✗	Books, Toys & Entertainment

WWW.BREUNERSAZ.COM

SCOTTSDALE—1800 N SCOTTSDALE RD (AT MCDOWELL RD); 480.941.2600; M 10-8, T-SA 10-6, SU 12-6

Kidstop Learning Fun

Furniture, Bedding & Decor	✗	✗	Gear & Equipment
Nursing & Feeding	✗	✗	Safety & Babycare
Clothing, Shoes & Accessories	✗	✓	Books, Toys & Entertainment

SCOTTSDALE—6990 E SHEA BLVD (AT N SCOTTSDALE RD); 480.609.9012; M-SA 10-6

Kohl's

"...nice one-stop shopping for the whole family—everything from clothing to baby gear... great sales on clothing and a good selection of higher-end brands... stylish, inexpensive clothes for babies through 24 months... very easy shopping experience... dirt-cheap sales and clearance prices... nothing super fancy, but just right for those everyday romper outfits... Graco, Eddie Bauer and other well-known brands..."

Furniture, Bedding & Decor	✓	$$	Prices
Gear & Equipment	✓	❹	Product availability
Nursing & Feeding	✓	❸	Staff knowledge
Safety & Babycare	✓	❸	Customer service
Clothing, Shoes & Accessories	✓	❸	Decor
Books, Toys & Entertainment	✓		

WWW.KOHLS.COM

SCOTTSDALE—8680 E RAINTREE DR (AT PIMA FWY); 480.609.9830; M-SA 8-10, SU 10-8; FREE PARKING

Macy's

"...Macy's has it all and I never leave empty-handed... if you time your visit right you can find some great deals... go during the week so you don't get overwhelmed with the weekend crowd... good for staples as well as beautiful party dresses for girls... lots of brand-names like Carter's, Guess, and Ralph Lauren... not much in terms of assistance... newspaper coupons and sales help keep the cost down... some stores are better organized and maintained than others... if you're going to shop at a department store for your baby, then Macy's is a safe bet..."

Furniture, Bedding & Decor	✓	$$$	Prices
Gear & Equipment	✗	❸	Product availability
Nursing & Feeding	✗	❸	Staff knowledge
Safety & Babycare	✗	❸	Customer service
Clothing, Shoes & Accessories	✓	❸	Decor
Books, Toys & Entertainment	✓		

WWW.MACYS.COM

SCOTTSDALE—7014 E CAMELBACK RD (AT SCOTTSDALE FASHION SQ); 480.840.0333; M-SA 10-9, SU 11-8

Mervyn's

"...wide selection of baby and kids' clothing, including OshKosh and Carter's... limited shoe selection without any real sizing assistance... lots of good sales... you might not always be able to find the size and color you want, but there's enough selection here that you're sure to

find something else that will work just as well... cheap, cheap, cheap... okay for cheap basics, but don't expect anything super special... ”

Furniture, Bedding & Decor	✗	$$	Prices
Gear & Equipment	✗	4	Product availability
Nursing & Feeding	✗	3	Staff knowledge
Safety & Babycare	✗	3	Customer service
Clothing, Shoes & Accessories	✓	3	Decor
Books, Toys & Entertainment	✓		

WWW.MERVYNS.COM

SCOTTSDALE—9109 E INDIAN BEND RD (AT PIMA FWY); 480.443.8885; DAILY 10-9; FREE PARKING

Mothers' Milk Boutique

“*...locally-owned and operated store carrying unique maternity and nursing products... amazing lactation counseling... great place for alternatives... interesting selection of diaper bags... authorized Medela retailer... staff are helpful, kind and not pushy...*”

Furniture, Bedding & Decor	✓	$$$	Prices
Gear & Equipment	✓	4	Product availability
Nursing & Feeding	✓	4	Staff knowledge
Safety & Babycare	✗	4	Customer service
Clothing, Shoes & Accessories	✓	4	Decor
Books, Toys & Entertainment	✓		

WWW.MOTHERSMILKBOUTIQUE.COM

SCOTTSDALE—10816 N SCOTTSDALE RD (AT E SHEA BLVD); 480.922.4615; M-F 10-6, SA 10-5 ; PARKING LOT

Nordstrom

“*...quality service and quality clothes... awesome kids shoe department—almost as good as the one for adults... free balloons in the children's shoe area as well as drawing tables... in addition to their own brand, they carry a very nice selection of other high-end baby clothing including Ralph Lauren, Robeez, etc... adorable baby clothes—they make great shower gifts... such a wonderful shopping experience—their lounge is perfect for breastfeeding and for changing diapers... well-rounded selection of baby basics as well as fancy clothes for special events...*”

Furniture, Bedding & Decor	✓	$$$$	Prices
Gear & Equipment	✓	4	Product availability
Nursing & Feeding	✗	4	Staff knowledge
Safety & Babycare	✗	4	Customer service
Clothing, Shoes & Accessories	✓	4	Decor
Books, Toys & Entertainment	✓		

WWW.NORDSTROM.COM

SCOTTSDALE—7055 E CAMELBACK RD (AT SCOTTSDALE FASHION SQ); 480.946.4111; M-SA 10, SU11-7; MALL PARKING

Old Navy

“*...hip and 'in' clothes for infants and tots... plenty of steals on clearance items... T-shirts and pants for $10 or less... busy, busy, busy—long lines, especially on weekends... nothing fancy and you won't mind when your kids gets down and dirty in these clothes... easy to wash, decent quality... you can shop for your baby, your toddler, your teen and yourself all at the same time... clothes are especially affordable when you hit their sales (post-holiday sales are amazing!)...*”

Furniture, Bedding & Decor	✗	$$	Prices
Gear & Equipment	✗	4	Product availability
Nursing & Feeding	✗	3	Staff knowledge
Safety & Babycare	✗	3	Customer service
Clothing, Shoes & Accessories	✗	3	Decor

Books, Toys & Entertainment .... ×

WWW.OLDNAVY.COM

SCOTTSDALE—16215 N SCOTTSDALE RD (AT E PARADISE LN); 480.998.0234; M-SA 9-9, SU 10-6

Payless Shoe Source

"...a good place for deals on children's shoes... staff is helpful with sizing... the selection and prices for kids' shoes can't be beat, but the quality isn't always spectacular... good leather shoes for cheap... great variety of all sizes and widths... I get my son's shoes here and don't feel like I'm wasting my money since he'll outgrow them in 3 months anyway..."

Furniture, Bedding & Decor	×	$$	Prices
Gear & Equipment	×	❸	Product availability
Nursing & Feeding	×	❸	Staff knowledge
Safety & Babycare	×	❸	Customer service
Clothing, Shoes & Accessories	✓	❸	Decor
Books, Toys & Entertainment	×		

WWW.PAYLESS.COM

SCOTTSDALE—SCOTTSDALE PAVILIONS (AT N PIMA RD & E INDIAN BEND RD); 480.948.3263; M-F 10-9, SA-SU 10-7

Rascal's Ranch

"...very cute clothes and accessories... upscale and hard-to-find brands..."

Furniture, Bedding & Decor	×	$$$$	Prices
Gear & Equipment	×	❹	Product availability
Nursing & Feeding	×	❹	Staff knowledge
Safety & Babycare	×	❸	Customer service
Clothing, Shoes & Accessories	✓	❹	Decor
Books, Toys & Entertainment	×		

SCOTTSDALE—8912 E PINNACLE PEAK RD (AT PIMA); 480.473.7272; M-SA 10-5 ; PARKING LOT

Ross Dress For Less

"...if you're in the mood for bargain hunting and are okay with potentially coming up empty-handed, then Ross is for you... don't expect to get educated about baby products here... go early on a week day and you'll find an organized store and staff that is helpful and available—forget weekends... their selection is pretty inconsistent, but I have found some incredible bargains... a great place to stock up on birthday presents or stocking stuffers..."

Furniture, Bedding & Decor	×	$$	Prices
Gear & Equipment	×	❸	Product availability
Nursing & Feeding	×	❸	Staff knowledge
Safety & Babycare	×	❸	Customer service
Clothing, Shoes & Accessories	✓	❸	Decor
Books, Toys & Entertainment	✓		

WWW.ROSSSTORES.COM

SCOTTSDALE—15694 N FRANK LLOYD WRIGHT BLVD (AT 101); 480.391.2617; M-SA 9:30-9:30, SU 11-7; PARKING LOT

SCOTTSDALE—8970 INDIAN BEND RD (AT 101); 480.951.1338; M-SA 9:30-9:30, SU 11-7; PARKING LOT

T J Maxx

"...a hit or miss kind of place for kids' stuff, but the prices can't be beat... their book selections are great... lots of new stuff all reasonably priced..."

Furniture, Bedding & Decor	×	$$	Prices
Gear & Equipment	×	❸	Product availability

Nursing & Feeding .... ✗	❸ .... Staff knowledge
Safety & Babycare .... ✗	❸ .... Customer service
Clothing, Shoes & Accessories .... ✓	❸ .... Decor
Books, Toys & Entertainment .... ✗	

WWW.TJMAXX.COM

SCOTTSDALE—15464 N FRANK LLOYD WRIGHT BLVD (AT RT 101); 480.661.7720; M-SA 9:30-9:30, SU 11-6; PARKING LOT

Target ★★★★☆

"...our favorite place to shop for kids' stuff—good selection and very affordable... guilt-free shopping—kids grow so fast so I don't want to pay high department-store prices... everything from diapers and sippy cups to car seats and strollers... easy return policy... generally helpful staff, but you don't go for the service—you go for the prices... decent registry that won't freak your friends out with outrageous prices... easy, convenient shopping for well-priced items... all the big-box brands available—Graco, Evenflo, Eddie Bauer, etc...."

Furniture, Bedding & Decor .... ✓	$$ .... Prices
Gear & Equipment .... ✓	❹ .... Product availability
Nursing & Feeding .... ✓	❸ .... Staff knowledge
Safety & Babycare .... ✓	❸ .... Customer service
Clothing, Shoes & Accessories .... ✓	❸ .... Decor
Books, Toys & Entertainment .... ✓	

WWW.TARGET.COM

FOUNTAIN HILLS—16825 E SHEA BLVD (AT N TECHNOLOGY DR); 480.837.8557; M-SA 8-10, SU 8-9; PARKING LOT

SCOTTSDALE—15444 N FRANK LLOYD WRIGHT BLVD (AT 101); 480.661.7720; M-SA 9:30-9:30, SU 11-6 ; PARKING LOT

SCOTTSDALE—32351 N SCOTTSDALE RD (AT ASHLER HILLS); 480.575.7043; M-SA 8-10, SU 8-9; PARKING LOT

SCOTTSDALE—9000 E INDIAN BEND RD (AT SCOTTSDALE PAVILIONS); 480.951.4403; M-SA 8-10, SU 8-9; PARKING LOT

Two Little Monkeys

Furniture, Bedding & Decor .... ✓	✓ .... Gear & Equipment
Nursing & Feeding .... ✗	✗ .... Safety & Babycare
Clothing, Shoes & Accessories .... ✓	✗ .... Books, Toys & Entertainment

WWW.2LITTLEMONKEYS.COM

SCOTTSDALE—480.361.2656; CALL FOR APPT

Southeast Valley

"lila picks"

★Changing Hands Bookstore

★Crimsons Baby Boutique

★IKEA

★USA Baby

Baby Bargains

"...the staff here were very knowledgeable and helpful... I'd highly recommend this store... great staff and easy to work with... love shopping at Baby Bargains in Mesa... small used store with excellent customer service, employees always willing to help..."

Furniture, Bedding & Decor	✗	$	Prices
Gear & Equipment	✗	❹	Product availability
Nursing & Feeding	✗	❺	Staff knowledge
Safety & Babycare	✗	❺	Customer service
Clothing, Shoes & Accessories	✓	❹	Decor
Books, Toys & Entertainment	✗		

MESA—2111 S ALMA SCHOOL RD (AT W BASELINE RD); 480.820.6406; CALL FOR HRS

Baby Depot At Burlington Coat Factory

"...a large, 'super store' layout with a ton of baby gear... wide aisles, packed shelves, barely existent customer service and awesome prices... everything from bottles, car seats and strollers to gliders, cribs and clothes... I always find something worth getting... a little disorganized and hard to locate items you're looking for... the staff is not always knowledgeable about their merchandise... return policy is store credit only..."

Furniture, Bedding & Decor	✓	$$	Prices
Gear & Equipment	✓	❸	Product availability
Nursing & Feeding	✓	❸	Staff knowledge
Safety & Babycare	✓	❸	Customer service
Clothing, Shoes & Accessories	✓	❸	Decor
Books, Toys & Entertainment	✓		

WWW.BABYDEPOT.COM

MESA—6225 E SOUTHERN AVE (AT SUPERSTITION SPRINGS BLVD); 480.325.4796; M-SA 10-9, SU 11-6; MALL PARKING

TEMPE—5000 S ARIZONA MILLS CIR (AT ARIZONA MILLS); 480.897.4700; M-SA 10-9:30, SU 11-7; MALL PARKING

Baby Mother & More

"...nursing bras and assorted items... fantastic service and a lactation specialist to assist when needed... a nursing resource Mecca... baby gifts too... everything to make nursing your new baby easy..."

Furniture, Bedding & Decor	✗	$$$	Prices
Gear & Equipment	✓	5	Product availability
Nursing & Feeding	✓	5	Staff knowledge
Safety & Babycare	✗	5	Customer service
Clothing, Shoes & Accessories	✗	4	Decor
Books, Toys & Entertainment	✗		

WWW.MILKSMILE.COM

MESA—1235 S GILBERT RD (AT SOUTHERN); 480.890.1870; M-SA 10-6, SU 12-4; PARKING LOT

BabyGap/GapKids

"...colorful baby and toddler clothing in clean, well-lit stores... great return policy... it's the Gap, so you know what you're getting—colorful, cute and well-made clothing... best place for baby hats... prices are reasonable especially since there's always a sale of some sort going on... sales, sales, sales—frequent and fantastic... everything I'm looking for in infant clothing—snap crotches, snaps up the front, all natural fabrics and great styling... fun seasonal selections—a great place to shop for gifts as well as for your own kids... although it can get busy, staff generally seem accommodating and helpful..."

Furniture, Bedding & Decor	✗	$$$	Prices
Gear & Equipment	✗	4	Product availability
Nursing & Feeding	✗	4	Staff knowledge
Safety & Babycare	✗	4	Customer service
Clothing, Shoes & Accessories	✓	4	Decor
Books, Toys & Entertainment	✗		

WWW.GAP.COM

CHANDLER—3111 W CHANDLER BLVD (AT N FEDERAL); 480.726.0426; M-SA 10-9, SU 11-7; MALL PARKING

Bearly Worn Kids Wear

"...a resale shop for kids wear with more items for the younger child... a great place to get seat covers for those supermarket shopping carts... the prices have me returning all the time... I love this store... you can rent strollers, carseats and other baby gear..."

Furniture, Bedding & Decor	✓	$$	Prices
Gear & Equipment	✓	3	Product availability
Nursing & Feeding	✓	4	Staff knowledge
Safety & Babycare	✗	4	Customer service
Clothing, Shoes & Accessories	✗	3	Decor
Books, Toys & Entertainment	✓		

WWW.BEARLYWORN.COM

GILBERT—1430 W WARNER RD (AT MCQUEEN); 480.756.2543; M-SA 10-6, SU 10-3; PARKING LOT

Bookman's

Furniture, Bedding & Decor	✗	✗	Gear & Equipment
Nursing & Feeding	✗	✗	Safety & Babycare
Clothing, Shoes & Accessories	✗	✓	Books, Toys & Entertainment

WWW.BOOKMANS.COM

MESA—1056 S COUNTRY CLUB DR (AT W 10TH AVE); 480.835.0505; DAILY 9-10

Buffalo Kids

"...part of the chain of used clothing consignment stores... great little store with good prices... they only accept decent clothes so I was not wary to shop here... a small space with a limited selection..."

Furniture, Bedding & Decor .... ✗
Gear & Equipment .... ✗
Nursing & Feeding .... ✗
Safety & Babycare .... ✗
Clothing, Shoes & Accessories .... ✗
Books, Toys & Entertainment .... ✗

$$ .... Prices
3 .... Product availability
4 .... Staff knowledge
4 .... Customer service
4 .... Decor

WWW.BUFFALOEXCHANGE.COM

TEMPE—1720 E WARNER RD (AT S MCCLINTOCK DR); 480.545.2868; M-SA 10-6, SU 12-5; PARKING LOT

Changing Hands Bookstore

"...amazing bookstore...nice little items for babies and young children and of course they have an amazing selection of books for adults (lots about pregnancy, parental advice, baby names etc)... the staff is very knowledgeable and will order any book you do not find in the store... nice place to find a gift for a new mother or birthday gift..."

Furniture, Bedding & Decor .... ✗
Gear & Equipment .... ✗
Nursing & Feeding .... ✗
Safety & Babycare .... ✗
Clothing, Shoes & Accessories .... ✗
Books, Toys & Entertainment .... ✓

$$ .... Prices
4 .... Product availability
4 .... Staff knowledge
5 .... Customer service
4 .... Decor

WWW.CHANGINGHANDS.COM

TEMPE—6428 S MCCLINTOCK DR (AT E GUADALUPE RD); 480.730.0205; M-F 10-9, SA 9-9, SU 10-7; FREE PARKING

Children's Orchard

"...a friendly resale boutique... the clothes and gear are super clean and sold at amazing prices... amazing prices on clothing that is hardly used and practically brand new... shoes, toys, furniture, hair pretties, crib sets, etc... fantastic deals on well-selected used items... prices are great and you can pretty much always find something useful... a great place to buy those everyday play outfits... a lot of name brands at steeply discounted prices..."

Furniture, Bedding & Decor .... ✓
Gear & Equipment .... ✓
Nursing & Feeding .... ✓
Safety & Babycare .... ✓
Clothing, Shoes & Accessories .... ✓
Books, Toys & Entertainment .... ✓

$$ .... Prices
3 .... Product availability
4 .... Staff knowledge
4 .... Customer service
3 .... Decor

WWW.CHILDRENSORCHARD.COM

GILBERT—1395 E WARNER RD (AT S CACTUS WREN); 480.503.2720; M-SA 10-6; MALL PARKING

Children's Place, The

"...great bargains on cute clothing... shoes, socks, swimsuits, sunglasses and everything in between... lots of '3 for $20' type deals on sleepers, pants and mix-and-match separates... so much more affordable than the other 'big chains'... don't expect the most unique stuff here, but it wears and washes well... cheap clothing for cheap prices... you can leave the store with bags full of clothes without putting a huge dent in your wallet..."

Furniture, Bedding & Decor .... ✗
Gear & Equipment .... ✗
Nursing & Feeding .... ✗
Safety & Babycare .... ✗

$$ .... Prices
4 .... Product availability
4 .... Staff knowledge
4 .... Customer service

Clothing, Shoes & Accessories....... ✓
Books, Toys & Entertainment .... ✓

❹ .... Decor

WWW.CHILDRENSPLACE.COM

CHANDLER—3111 W CHANDLER BLVD (AT CHANDLER MALL); 480.855.0632; M-SA 10-9, SU 11-6; MALL PARKING

Costco ★★★½☆

"...dependable place for bulk diapers, wipes and formula at discount prices... clothing selection is very hit-or-miss... avoid shopping there during nights and weekends if possible, because parking and checkout lines are brutal... they don't have a huge selection of brands, but the brands they do have are almost always in stock and at a great price... lowest prices around for diapers and formula... kid's clothing tends to be picked through, but it's worth looking for great deals on name-brand items like Carter's..."

Furniture, Bedding & Decor .... ✓
Gear & Equipment .... ✓
Nursing & Feeding .... ✓
Safety & Babycare .... ✓
Clothing, Shoes & Accessories....... ✓
Books, Toys & Entertainment .... ✓

$$ .... Prices
❸ .... Product availability
❸ .... Staff knowledge
❸ .... Customer service
❷ .... Decor

WWW.COSTCO.COM

GILBERT—1415 N ARIZONA AVE (AT W BASELINE RD); 480.293.0053; M-F 11-8:30, SA 9:30-6, SU 10-6

MESA—1235 S POWER RD (AT E SOUTHERN AVE); 480.641.4216; M-F 10-8:30, SA 9:30-6, SU 10-6

TEMPE—1445 W ELLIOT RD (AT S PRIEST DR); 480.496.6651; M-F 11-8:30, SA 9:30-6, SU 10-6

Crismons Baby Boutique ★★★★★

"...top quality baby and children's boutique... they carry many original items that you can't find anywhere else... store had the most cribs of any store that I have seen in Mesa... most were very affordable and well made... very impressed with the store and the stores ability to work with you on shopping for anything baby..."

Furniture, Bedding & Decor .... ✓
Gear & Equipment .... ✓
Nursing & Feeding .... ✗
Safety & Babycare .... ✗
Clothing, Shoes & Accessories....... ✓
Books, Toys & Entertainment .... ✗

$$$ .... Prices
❹ .... Product availability
❹ .... Staff knowledge
❹ .... Customer service
❸ .... Decor

WWW.CRISMONSBABY.COM

MESA—1455 E UNIVERSITY DR (AT GILBERT); 480.969.0462; W-F 9-6, SA 9-4; PARKING LOT

Dillard's ★★★★☆

"...this store has beautiful clothes, and if you catch a sale, you can get great quality clothes at super bargain prices... good customer service and helpful staff... a huge selection of merchandise for boys and girls... nice layette department... some furnishings like little tables and chairs... beautiful displays... the best part is that in addition to shopping for your kids, you can also shop for yourself..."

Furniture, Bedding & Decor .... ✓
Gear & Equipment .... ✗
Nursing & Feeding .... ✗
Safety & Babycare .... ✗
Clothing, Shoes & Accessories....... ✓
Books, Toys & Entertainment .... ✓

$$$ .... Prices
❹ .... Product availability
❸ .... Staff knowledge
❹ .... Customer service
❹ .... Decor

WWW.DILLARDS.COM

CHANDLER—3101 W CHANDLER BLVD (OFF PRICE FWY); 480.735.2060; M-SA 10-9, SU 12-6

MESA—1435 E SOUTHERN AVE (OFF STAPLEY DR); 480.833.7777; M-SA 10-9, SU 12-6

MESA—6545 E SOUTHERN AVE (AT POWER RD); 480.832.1247; M-SA 10-9, SU 12-6

Domestic Bliss

"...a great and fun store, although the prices are very high..."

Furniture, Bedding & Decor	✓	$$$$$	Prices
Gear & Equipment	✗	❹	Product availability
Nursing & Feeding	✗	❹	Staff knowledge
Safety & Babycare	✗	❹	Customer service
Clothing, Shoes & Accessories	✓	❺	Decor
Books, Toys & Entertainment	✗		

WWW.DOMESTICBLISSDESIGN.COM

MESA—140 W MAIN ST (AT COUNTRY CLUB); 480.733.0552; M-SA 10-5 ; PARKING LOT

Gymboree

"...beautiful clothing and great quality... colorful and stylish baby and kids wear... lots of fun birthday gift ideas... easy exchange and return policy... items usually go on sale pretty quickly... save money with Gymbucks... many stores have a play area which makes shopping with my kids fun (let alone feasible)..."

Furniture, Bedding & Decor	✗	$$$	Prices
Gear & Equipment	✗	❹	Product availability
Nursing & Feeding	✗	❹	Staff knowledge
Safety & Babycare	✗	❹	Customer service
Clothing, Shoes & Accessories	✓	❹	Decor
Books, Toys & Entertainment	✓		

WWW.GYMBOREE.COM

CHANDLER—3111 W CHANDLER BLVD (AT CHANDLER FASHION CTR); 480.917.3769; M-SA 10-9, SU 11-6; PARKING LOT

MESA—1445 W SOUTHERN AVE (AT ALMA SCHOOL); 480.827.1206; M-SA 10-9, SU 11-6; PARKING LOT

IKEA

"...the coolest-looking and best-priced bedding, bibs and eating utensils in town... fun, practical style and the prices are definitely right... one of the few stores around that lets kids climb and crawl on furniture... the kids' area has a slide, tunnels, tents... is it an indoor playground or a store?.. unending decorating ideas for families on a budget (lamps, rugs, beds, bedding)... it's all about organization—cubbies, drawers, shelves, seats that double as a trunk and step stool... arts and crafts galore... free childcare while you shop... cheap eats if you get hungry..."

Furniture, Bedding & Decor	✓	$$	Prices
Gear & Equipment	✗	❹	Product availability
Nursing & Feeding	✓	❹	Staff knowledge
Safety & Babycare	✓	❹	Customer service
Clothing, Shoes & Accessories	✗	❹	Decor
Books, Toys & Entertainment	✓		

WWW.IKEA.COM

TEMPE—2110 W IKEA WY (AT WARNER AND PRIEST); 480.496.5658; M-SA 10-9, SU 10-7; PARKING LOT

JCPenney

"...always a good place to find clothes and other baby basics... the registry process was seamless... staff is generally friendly but the lines

always seem long and slow... they don't have the greatest selection of toddler clothes, but their baby section is great... we had some damaged furniture delivered but customer service was easy and accommodating... a pretty limited selection of gear, but what they have is priced right... ❞

Furniture, Bedding & Decor .... ✓ $$ .... Prices
Gear & Equipment .... ✓ ❸ .... Product availability
Nursing & Feeding .... ✓ ❸ .... Staff knowledge
Safety & Babycare .... ✓ ❸ .... Customer service
Clothing, Shoes & Accessories....... ✓ ❸ .... Decor
Books, Toys & Entertainment .... ✓

WWW.JCPENNEY.COM

MESA—6525 E SOUTHERN AVE (AT SUPERSTITION SPRINGS CTR); 480.832.0400; M-SA 10-9, SU 11-6; PARKING LOT

TEMPE—1140 W ELLIOT RD (AT SPORTS AUTHORITY PLAZA); 480.456.8828; M-SA 10-8, SU 10-6; PARKING LOT

Kid City

Furniture, Bedding & Decor .... ✓ ✓ .... Gear & Equipment
Nursing & Feeding .... ✓ ✗ .... Safety & Babycare
Clothing, Shoes & Accessories....... ✗ ✗ .... Books, Toys & Entertainment

WWW.AKIDCITY.COM

MESA—1455 S STAPLEY DR (AT US 60); 480.813.5813; M-SA 10-5:30; PARKING LOT

Kid's Foot Locker

❝*...Nike, Reebok and Adidas for your little ones... hip, trendy and quite pricey... perfect for the sports addict dad who wants his kid sporting the latest NFL duds... shoes cost close to what the adult variety costs... generally good quality... they carry infant and toddler sizes...* ❞

Furniture, Bedding & Decor .... ✗ $$$ .... Prices
Gear & Equipment .... ✗ ❸ .... Product availability
Nursing & Feeding .... ✗ ❸ .... Staff knowledge
Safety & Babycare .... ✗ ❸ .... Customer service
Clothing, Shoes & Accessories....... ✓ ❸ .... Decor
Books, Toys & Entertainment .... ✗

WWW.KIDSFOOTLOCKER.COM

MESA—1114 W SOUTHERN AVE (AT POCA FIESTA SHOPPING CTR); 480.833.3141; M-SA 10-9, SU 11-6

Kohl's

❝*...nice one-stop shopping for the whole family—everything from clothing to baby gear... great sales on clothing and a good selection of higher-end brands... stylish, inexpensive clothes for babies through 24 months... very easy shopping experience... dirt-cheap sales and clearance prices... nothing super fancy, but just right for those everyday romper outfits... Graco, Eddie Bauer and other well-known brands...* ❞

Furniture, Bedding & Decor .... ✓ $$ .... Prices
Gear & Equipment .... ✓ ❹ .... Product availability
Nursing & Feeding .... ✓ ❸ .... Staff knowledge
Safety & Babycare .... ✓ ❸ .... Customer service
Clothing, Shoes & Accessories....... ✓ ❸ .... Decor
Books, Toys & Entertainment .... ✓

WWW.KOHLS.COM

GILBERT—1121 E BASELINE RD (AT N COOPER RD); 480.926.0290; M-SA 8-10, SU 10-8; FREE PARKING

MESA—5833 E MCKELLIPS RD (AT N RECKER RD); 480.924.8527; M-SA 8-10, SU 10-8; FREE PARKING

Macy's

"...Macy's has it all and I never leave empty-handed... if you time your visit right you can find some great deals... go during the week so you don't get overwhelmed with the weekend crowd... good for staples as well as beautiful party dresses for girls... lots of brand-names like Carter's, Guess, and Ralph Lauren... not much in terms of assistance... newspaper coupons and sales help keep the cost down... some stores are better organized and maintained than others... if you're going to shop at a department store for your baby, then Macy's is a safe bet..."

Furniture, Bedding & Decor	✓	$$$	Prices
Gear & Equipment	✗	❸	Product availability
Nursing & Feeding	✗	❸	Staff knowledge
Safety & Babycare	✗	❸	Customer service
Clothing, Shoes & Accessories	✓	❸	Decor
Books, Toys & Entertainment	✓		

WWW.MACYS.COM

MESA—4000 FIESTA MALL (OFF SOUTHERN AVE); 480.835.4500; M-SA 10-9, SU 11-8

Mervyn's

"...wide selection of baby and kids' clothing, including OshKosh and Carter's... limited shoe selection without any real sizing assistance... lots of good sales... you might not always be able to find the size and color you want, but there's enough selection here that you're sure to find something else that will work just as well... cheap, cheap, cheap... okay for cheap basics, but don't expect anything super special..."

Furniture, Bedding & Decor	✗	$$	Prices
Gear & Equipment	✗	❹	Product availability
Nursing & Feeding	✗	❸	Staff knowledge
Safety & Babycare	✗	❸	Customer service
Clothing, Shoes & Accessories	✓	❸	Decor
Books, Toys & Entertainment	✓		

WWW.MERVYNS.COM

CHANDLER—2992 N ALMA SCHOOL RD (AT W ELLIOT RD); 480.821.1891; M-SA 9-10, SU 9-9; FREE PARKING

MESA—1240 E MAIN ST (AT N STAPLEY DR); 480.835.8800; DAILY 10-9; FREE PARKING

TEMPE—800 E SOUTHERN AVE (AT S RURAL RD); 480.894.9281; DAILY 10-9; FREE PARKING

Nordstrom

"...quality service and quality clothes... awesome kids shoe department—almost as good as the one for adults... free balloons in the children's shoe area as well as drawing tables... in addition to their own brand, they carry a very nice selection of other high-end baby clothing including Ralph Lauren, Robeez, etc... adorable baby clothes—they make great shower gifts... such a wonderful shopping experience—their lounge is perfect for breastfeeding and for changing diapers... well-rounded selection of baby basics as well as fancy clothes for special events..."

Furniture, Bedding & Decor	✓	$$$$	Prices
Gear & Equipment	✓	❹	Product availability
Nursing & Feeding	✗	❹	Staff knowledge
Safety & Babycare	✗	❹	Customer service
Clothing, Shoes & Accessories	✓	❹	Decor
Books, Toys & Entertainment	✓		

WWW.NORDSTROM.COM

CHANDLER—3199 W CHANDLER BLVD (AT CHANDLER FASHION CTR); 480.855.2500; M-SA 10-9, SU 11-6; PARKING LOT

Old Navy

"...hip and 'in' clothes for infants and tots... plenty of steals on clearance items... T-shirts and pants for $10 or less... busy, busy, busy—long lines, especially on weekends... nothing fancy and you won't mind when your kids gets down and dirty in these clothes... easy to wash, decent quality... you can shop for your baby, your toddler, your teen and yourself all at the same time... clothes are especially affordable when you hit their sales (post-holiday sales are amazing!)..."

Furniture, Bedding & Decor	✗	$$	Prices
Gear & Equipment	✗	❹	Product availability
Nursing & Feeding	✗	❸	Staff knowledge
Safety & Babycare	✗	❸	Customer service
Clothing, Shoes & Accessories	✓	❸	Decor
Books, Toys & Entertainment	✗		

WWW.OLDNAVY.COM

GILBERT—1055 E BASELINE RD (AT STAPLEY); 480.503.0395; M-SA 9-9, SU 10-6; PARKING LOT

TEMPE—5000 S ARIZONA MILLS CR (AT BASELINE); 480.752.9230; M-SA 10-9, SU 10-7; PARKING LOT

Once Upon A Child

"...new and used items... the place for bargain baby items in like-new condition... a great bargain spot with a wide variety of clothes for baby... some inexpensive furniture... good selection, staff and prices... cluttered and hard to get through the store with kids... good toys and gear... some items are definitely more than 'gently used'... a kid's play area... good end-of-season sales... expect to sort through items... cash for your old items..."

Furniture, Bedding & Decor	✓	$$	Prices
Gear & Equipment	✓	❸	Product availability
Nursing & Feeding	✗	❹	Staff knowledge
Safety & Babycare	✗	❹	Customer service
Clothing, Shoes & Accessories	✓	❸	Decor
Books, Toys & Entertainment	✓		

WWW.OUAC.COM

CHANDLER—1994 N ALMA SCHOOL RD (AT W WARNER RD); 480.963.9092; M-F 10-8, SA 10-6, SU 12-5; PARKING LOT

GILBERT—3701 E BASELINE RD (AT S VAL VISTA DR); 480.539.1338; M-SA 9-7 ; PARKING LOT

Payless Shoe Source

"...a good place for deals on children's shoes... staff is helpful with sizing... the selection and prices for kids' shoes can't be beat, but the quality isn't always spectacular... good leather shoes for cheap... great variety of all sizes and widths... I get my son's shoes here and don't feel like I'm wasting my money since he'll outgrow them in 3 months anyway..."

Furniture, Bedding & Decor	✗	$$	Prices
Gear & Equipment	✗	❸	Product availability
Nursing & Feeding	✗	❸	Staff knowledge
Safety & Babycare	✗	❸	Customer service
Clothing, Shoes & Accessories	✓	❸	Decor
Books, Toys & Entertainment	✗		

WWW.PAYLESS.COM

MESA—1265 W MAIN ST (AT N ALMA SCHOOL RD); 480.969.1461; M-SA 9-9

MESA—FIESTA MALL (AT W SOUTHERN AVE & S ALMA SCHOOL RD); 480.649.1989; M-SA 10-9, SU 10-6

MESA—SHERWOOD SHOPPING CTR (AT S POWER RD & E BROADWAY RD); 480.962.6594; M-SA 9-9

TEMPE—ARIZONA MILLS (OFF MARICOPA FWY); 480.755.4197; M-SA 10-9:30, SU 11-7

Polka Dot Dreams

Furniture, Bedding & Decor	✓	✓	Gear & Equipment
Nursing & Feeding	✗	✗	Safety & Babycare
Clothing, Shoes & Accessories	✓	✗	Books, Toys & Entertainment

WWW.POLKADOTDREAMS.COM

CHANDLER—7131 W RAY RD (AT I-10 HWY); 480.496.9494; M-SA 10-6, SU 12-5; PARKING LOT

Pottery Barn Kids

"...stylish furniture, rugs, rockers and much more... they've found the right mix between quality and price... finally a company that stands behind what they sell—their customer service is great... gorgeous baby decor and furniture that will make your nursery to-die-for... the play area is so much fun—my daughter never wants to leave... a beautiful store with tons of ideas for setting up your nursery or kid's room... bright colors and cute patterns with basics to mix and match... if you see something in the catalog, but not in the store, just ask because they often have it in the back..."

Furniture, Bedding & Decor	✓	$$$$	Prices
Gear & Equipment	✗	4	Product availability
Nursing & Feeding	✗	4	Staff knowledge
Safety & Babycare	✗	4	Customer service
Clothing, Shoes & Accessories	✗	5	Decor
Books, Toys & Entertainment	✓		

WWW.POTTERYBARNKIDS.COM

CHANDLER—3111 W CHANDLER BLVD (AT CHANDLER FASHION CTR); 480.899.7155; M-SA 10-9, SU 10-6; PARKING LOT

Sears

"...a decent selection of clothes and basic baby equipment... check out the Kids Club program—it's a great way to save money... you go to Sears to save money, not to be pampered... the quality of their merchandise is better than Wal-Mart, but don't expect anything too special or different... not much in terms of gear, but tons of well-priced baby and toddler clothing..."

Furniture, Bedding & Decor	✓	$$	Prices
Gear & Equipment	✓	3	Product availability
Nursing & Feeding	✓	3	Staff knowledge
Safety & Babycare	✓	3	Customer service
Clothing, Shoes & Accessories	✓	3	Decor
Books, Toys & Entertainment	✓		

WWW.SEARS.COM

CHANDLER—3177 CHANDLER VILLAGE DR (AT CHANDLER FASHION CTR); 480.855.2800; M-F 10-9, SA 8-9, SU 10-6

MESA—1425 W SOUTHERN AVE (AT ALMA SCHOOL RD); 480.833.6767; M-F 10-9, SA 8-9, SU 10-6

Seeds for Learning

Furniture, Bedding & Decor	✗	✗	Gear & Equipment
Nursing & Feeding	✗	✗	Safety & Babycare
Clothing, Shoes & Accessories	✗	✓	Books, Toys & Entertainment

WWW.TEACHINGSUPPLIES.COM

GILBERT—645 N GILBERT RD (AT GUADALUPE); 480.497.4274; CALL FOR HRS; FREE PARKING

Spoiled Silly Kids Resale

"...the best kids resale store I have been to... good quality of clothing and accessories... I always leave with a bag full of name brand stuff... can be pricey for a consignment shop and stocks more stuff for girls than boys..."

Furniture, Bedding & Decor .... ✗
Gear & Equipment .... ✗
Nursing & Feeding .... ✗
Safety & Babycare .... ✗
Clothing, Shoes & Accessories .... ✓
Books, Toys & Entertainment .... ✗

$$ .... Prices
❸ .... Product availability
❹ .... Staff knowledge
❹ .... Customer service
❹ .... Decor

MESA—1829 N POWER RD (AT MCKELLIPS RD); 480.807.0110; M-F10-7, SA 10-6, SU 12-4; PARKING LOT

Stride Rite Shoes

"...wonderful selection of baby and toddler shoes... sandals, sneakers, and even special-occasion shoes... decent quality shoes that last... they know a lot about kids' shoes and take the time to get it right—they always measure my son's feet before fittings... store sizes vary, but they always have something in stock that works... they've even special ordered shoes for my daughter... a fun 'first shoe' buying experience..."

Furniture, Bedding & Decor .... ✗
Gear & Equipment .... ✗
Nursing & Feeding .... ✗
Safety & Babycare .... ✗
Clothing, Shoes & Accessories .... ✓
Books, Toys & Entertainment .... ✗

$$$ .... Prices
❹ .... Product availability
❹ .... Staff knowledge
❹ .... Customer service
❹ .... Decor

WWW.STRIDERITE.COM

CHANDLER—2432-3111 W CHANDLER BLVD (AT CHANDLER BLVD); 480.814.1590; M-SA 10-9, SU 11-6; PARKING LOT

Target

"...our favorite place to shop for kids' stuff—good selection and very affordable... guilt-free shopping—kids grow so fast so I don't want to pay high department-store prices... everything from diapers and sippy cups to car seats and strollers... easy return policy... generally helpful staff, but you don't go for the service—you go for the prices... decent registry that won't freak your friends out with outrageous prices... easy, convenient shopping for well-priced items... all the big-box brands available—Graco, Evenflo, Eddie Bauer, etc...."

Furniture, Bedding & Decor .... ✓
Gear & Equipment .... ✓
Nursing & Feeding .... ✓
Safety & Babycare .... ✓
Clothing, Shoes & Accessories .... ✓
Books, Toys & Entertainment .... ✓

$$ .... Prices
❹ .... Product availability
❸ .... Staff knowledge
❸ .... Customer service
❸ .... Decor

WWW.TARGET.COM

CHANDLER—2020 N ARIZONA AVE (AT WARNER RD); 480.899.7986; M-SA 8-10, SU 8-9; PARKING LOT

CHANDLER—2880 S ALMA SCHOOL RD (AT QUEEN CREEK); 480.782.1881; M-SA 8-10, SU 8-9; PARKING LOT

CHANDLER—3425 W FRYE RD (AT S PRICE RD); 480.281.0007; M-SA 8-10, SU 8-9; PARKING LOT

GILBERT—1515 E WARNER RD (AT S VAL VISTA DR); 480.892.2282; M-SA 8-10, SU 8-9

MESA—1135 S GILBERT RD (AT E SOUTHERN AVE); 480.926.3443; M-SA 8-10, SU 8-9

MESA—1525 S POWER RD (AT SUPERSTITIONS FWY); 480.396.0403; M-SA 8-10, SU 8-9; PARKING LOT

MESA—2151 N POWER RD (AT E MCKELLIPS RD); 480.830.2035; M-SA 8-10, SU 8-9; PARKING LOT

MESA—66 S DOBSON RD (AT W MAIN ST); 480.892.2283; F-SA 10-1, SU-TH 10-12; PARKING LOT

Twinkle Toes

"...so many great ideas on the walls for nurseries... a lot of one of a kind items... lots of cute girl clothes and accessories, blankets and decor... I fell in love with so many things... if you want something very special then this is the place to go..."

Furniture, Bedding & Decor	✓	$$$$	Prices
Gear & Equipment	×	❸	Product availability
Nursing & Feeding	×	❹	Staff knowledge
Safety & Babycare	×	❹	Customer service
Clothing, Shoes & Accessories	✓	❹	Decor
Books, Toys & Entertainment	×		

CHANDLER—3355 W CHANDLER BLVD (AT 101); 480.722.7672; M-SA 10-6 ; PARKING LOT

USA Baby

"...they carry an extensive selection of high-end nursery products such as furniture, bedding, accessories and highchairs... popular place to do all the shopping for your nursery... the staff knows their products well and can help you sort through their vast selection... allow plenty of time for your products to arrive, especially the big-ticket items (they offer loaners while you wait for your order to arrive)... they have great sales a few times a year and will match competitor prices... good selection, especially if you're getting ready to set up your nursery..."

Furniture, Bedding & Decor	✓	$$$$	Prices
Gear & Equipment	✓	❹	Product availability
Nursing & Feeding	✓	❹	Staff knowledge
Safety & Babycare	✓	❹	Customer service
Clothing, Shoes & Accessories	×	❹	Decor
Books, Toys & Entertainment	✓		

WWW.USABABY.COM

TEMPE—3143 S MCCLINTOCK DR (AT E SOUTHERN AVE); 480.897.2229; T TH SA 10-6, M W F 10-8, SU 12-5; MALL PARKING

West Valley

Costco

"...dependable place for bulk diapers, wipes and formula at discount prices... clothing selection is very hit-or-miss... avoid shopping there during nights and weekends if possible, because parking and checkout lines are brutal... they don't have a huge selection of brands, but the brands they do have are almost always in stock and at a great price... lowest prices around for diapers and formula... kid's clothing tends to be picked through, but it's worth looking for great deals on name-brand items like Carter's..."

Furniture, Bedding & Decor ✓
Gear & Equipment ✓
Nursing & Feeding ✓
Safety & Babycare ✓
Clothing, Shoes & Accessories ✓
Books, Toys & Entertainment ✓

$$ Prices
❸ Product availability
❸ Staff knowledge
❸ Customer service
❷ Decor

WWW.COSTCO.COM

AVONDALE—10000 W MCDOWELL RD (AT N 99TH AVE); 623.907.5663; M-F 10-8:30, SA 9:30-6, SU 10-6

Kohl's

"...nice one-stop shopping for the whole family—everything from clothing to baby gear... great sales on clothing and a good selection of higher-end brands... stylish, inexpensive clothes for babies through 24 months... very easy shopping experience... dirt-cheap sales and clearance prices... nothing super fancy, but just right for those everyday romper outfits... Graco, Eddie Bauer and other well-known brands..."

Furniture, Bedding & Decor ✓
Gear & Equipment ✓
Nursing & Feeding ✓
Safety & Babycare ✓
Clothing, Shoes & Accessories ✓
Books, Toys & Entertainment ✓

$$ Prices
❹ Product availability
❸ Staff knowledge
❸ Customer service
❸ Decor

WWW.KOHLS.COM

AVONDALE—1611 N DYSART RD (AT W MCDOWELL RD); 623.536.2700; M-SA 8-10, SU 10-8; FREE PARKING

Ross Dress For Less

"...if you're in the mood for bargain hunting and are okay with potentially coming up empty-handed, then Ross is for you... don't expect to get educated about baby products here... go early on a week day and you'll find an organized store and staff that is helpful and available—forget weekends... their selection is pretty inconsistent, but I have found some incredible bargains... a great place to stock up on birthday presents or stocking stuffers..."

Furniture, Bedding & Decor ✗
Gear & Equipment ✗
Nursing & Feeding ✗
Safety & Babycare ✗
Clothing, Shoes & Accessories ✓
Books, Toys & Entertainment ✓

$$ Prices
❸ Product availability
❸ Staff knowledge
❸ Customer service
❸ Decor

WWW.ROSSSTORES.COM

GOODYEAR—1408 N LITCHFIELD RD (AT MCDOWELL RD); 623.535.7242; M-SA 9:30-9:30, SU 11-7; PARKING LOT

Target

"...our favorite place to shop for kids' stuff—good selection and very affordable... guilt-free shopping—kids grow so fast so I don't want to pay high department-store prices... everything from diapers and sippy cups to car seats and strollers... easy return policy... generally helpful staff, but you don't go for the service—you go for the prices... decent registry that won't freak your friends out with outrageous prices... easy, convenient shopping for well-priced items... all the big-box brands available—Graco, Evenflo, Eddie Bauer, etc...."

Furniture, Bedding & Decor	✓	$$	Prices
Gear & Equipment	✓	❹	Product availability
Nursing & Feeding	✓	❸	Staff knowledge
Safety & Babycare	✓	❸	Customer service
Clothing, Shoes & Accessories	✓	❸	Decor
Books, Toys & Entertainment	✓		

WWW.TARGET.COM

GOODYEAR—1515 N LITCHFIELD RD (AT MCDOWELL RD); 623.935.3510; M-SA 8-10, SU 8-9; PARKING LOT

Online

"lila picks"

★ babycenter.com ★ babystyle.com

★ babyuniverse.com ★ joggingstroller.com

ababy.com

Furniture, Bedding & Decor	✓	✓	Gear & Equipment
Nursing & Feeding	×	✓	Safety & Babycare
Clothing, Shoes & Accessories	✓	×	Books, Toys & Entertainment

aikobaby.com ★★★☆☆

"...high end clothes that are so cute... everything from Catamini to Jack and Lily... you can find super expensive infant and baby clothes at discounted prices... amazing selection of diaper bags so you don't have to look like a frumpy mom (or dad)..."

Furniture, Bedding & Decor	×	✓	Gear & Equipment
Nursing & Feeding	×	×	Safety & Babycare
Clothing, Shoes & Accessories	✓	×	Books, Toys & Entertainment

albeebaby.com ★★★★☆

"...they offer a really comprehensive selection of baby gear... their prices are some of the best online... great discounts on Maclarens before the new models come out... good product availability—fast shipping and easy transactions... the site is pretty easy to use... the prices are surprisingly great..."

Furniture, Bedding & Decor	✓	✓	Gear & Equipment
Nursing & Feeding	✓	✓	Safety & Babycare
Clothing, Shoes & Accessories	✓	✓	Books, Toys & Entertainment

amazon.com ★★★★½

"...unless you've been living under a rock, you know that in addition to books, Amazon carries an amazing amount of baby stuff too... they have the best prices and offer free shipping on bigger purchases... you can even buy used items for dirt cheap... I always read the comments written by others—they're very useful in helping make my decisions... I love Amazon for just about everything, but their baby selection only carries the big box standards..."

Furniture, Bedding & Decor	×	✓	Gear & Equipment
Nursing & Feeding	✓	✓	Safety & Babycare
Clothing, Shoes & Accessories	✓	✓	Books, Toys & Entertainment

arunningstroller.com ★★★★½

"...the prices are very competitive and the customer service is great... I talked to them on the phone for a while and they totally hooked me up with the right model... if you're looking for a new stroller, look no further... talk to Marilyn—she's the best... shipping costs are reasonable and their prices overall are good..."

Furniture, Bedding & Decor	✓	✓	Gear & Equipment
Nursing & Feeding	✗	✗	Safety & Babycare
Clothing, Shoes & Accessories	✗	✗	Books, Toys & Entertainment

babiesinthesun.com ★★★★☆

"...one-stop shopping for cloth diapers... run by a fantastic woman who had 3 cloth diapered babies herself and is a wealth of knowledge... if you live in South Florida, the owner will let you into her home to see the merchandise and ask questions... great selection and the customer service is the best..."

Furniture, Bedding & Decor	✗	✓	Gear & Equipment
Nursing & Feeding	✗	✓	Safety & Babycare
Clothing, Shoes & Accessories	✗	✗	Books, Toys & Entertainment

babiesrus.com ★★★★☆

"...terrific web site with all the baby gear you'll need... registering online made it easy for my family and friends... getting the registry activated was a bit tricky... super convenient and ideal for the moms-to-be who are on bedrest... web site prices are comparable to in-store prices... shipping is usually free... a very efficient way to buy and send baby gifts... our local Babies R Us said they will accept returns if they carry the same item... not all online items are available in your local store..."

Furniture, Bedding & Decor	✓	✓	Gear & Equipment
Nursing & Feeding	✓	✓	Safety & Babycare
Clothing, Shoes & Accessories	✓	✓	Books, Toys & Entertainment

babiestravellite.com ★★★★½

"...caters to traveling families... they deliver baby items to your hotel room anywhere in the country... all of the different baby supplies you will need when you travel with a baby or a toddler... they sell almost every major brand for each product and their prices are sometimes cheaper than you would find at your local store..."

Furniture, Bedding & Decor	✗	✗	Gear & Equipment
Nursing & Feeding	✓	✓	Safety & Babycare
Clothing, Shoes & Accessories	✗	✓	Books, Toys & Entertainment

babyage.com ★★★★☆

"...fast shipping and the best prices around... flat rate shipping is great after the baby has arrived and you don't have time to go to the store... very attentive customer service... clearance items are a great deal (regular items are very competitive too)... ordering and delivery were super smooth... I usually check this web site before I purchase any baby gear... sign up for their newsletter and they'll notify you when they are having a sale..."

Furniture, Bedding & Decor	✓	✓	Gear & Equipment
Nursing & Feeding	✓	✓	Safety & Babycare
Clothing, Shoes & Accessories	✓	✓	Books, Toys & Entertainment

babyant.com ★★★★☆

"...wide variety of brands and products available through their site... super easy to navigate... fun, whimsical ideas... nice people and helpful... easy to return items and you can call them with questions... often has the best prices and low shipping costs..."

Furniture, Bedding & Decor	✓	✓	Gear & Equipment
Nursing & Feeding	✓	✓	Safety & Babycare
Clothing, Shoes & Accessories	✓	✓	Books, Toys & Entertainment

babybazaar.com

"...high-end baby stuff available on an easy-to-use web site... lots of European styles... quick processing and shipping... mom's tips, educational toys, exclusive favorites Bugaboo and Stokke..."

Furniture, Bedding & Decor .... ✓ | ✓ .... Gear & Equipment
Nursing & Feeding .... ✓ | ✓ .... Safety & Babycare
Clothing, Shoes & Accessories....... ✓ | ✓ .... Books, Toys & Entertainment

babybestbuy.com

Furniture, Bedding & Decor .... ✓ | ✓ .... Gear & Equipment
Nursing & Feeding .... ✓ | ✓ .... Safety & Babycare
Clothing, Shoes & Accessories....... ✓ | ✓ .... Books, Toys & Entertainment

babycatalog.com ★★★★☆

"...great deals on many essentials... wide selection of rockers but fewer options in other categories... the web site could be more user-friendly... customer service and delivery was fast and efficient... check out their seasonal specials... the baby club is a great way to save additional money... sign up for their wonderful pregnancy/new baby email newsletter... check this web site before you buy anywhere else..."

Furniture, Bedding & Decor .... ✓ | ✓ .... Gear & Equipment
Nursing & Feeding .... ✓ | ✓ .... Safety & Babycare
Clothing, Shoes & Accessories....... ✓ | ✓ .... Books, Toys & Entertainment

babycenter.com ★★★★★

"...a terrific selection of all things baby, plus quick shipping... free shipping on big orders... makes shopping convenient for new parents... web site is very user friendly... they always email you about sale items and special offers... lots of useful information for parents... carries everything you may need... online registry is simple, easy and a great way to get what you need... includes helpful products ratings by parents... they've created a nice online community in addition to their online store..."

Furniture, Bedding & Decor .... ✓ | ✓ .... Gear & Equipment
Nursing & Feeding .... ✓ | ✓ .... Safety & Babycare
Clothing, Shoes & Accessories....... ✓ | ✓ .... Books, Toys & Entertainment

babydepot.com ★★★☆☆

"...carries everything you'll find in a big department store but at cheaper prices and with everything all in one place... be certain you know what you want because returns can be difficult... site could be more user-friendly... online selection can differ from instore selection... love the online registry..."

Furniture, Bedding & Decor .... ✓ | ✓ .... Gear & Equipment
Nursing & Feeding .... ✓ | ✓ .... Safety & Babycare
Clothing, Shoes & Accessories....... ✓ | ✓ .... Books, Toys & Entertainment

babygeared.com

Furniture, Bedding & Decor .... ✓ | ✓ .... Gear & Equipment
Nursing & Feeding .... ✓ | ✓ .... Safety & Babycare
Clothing, Shoes & Accessories....... ✓ | ✓ .... Books, Toys & Entertainment

babyphd.com

Furniture, Bedding & Decor .... ✓ | ✗ .... Gear & Equipment
Nursing & Feeding .... ✗ | ✗ .... Safety & Babycare
Clothing, Shoes & Accessories....... ✓ | ✓ .... Books, Toys & Entertainment

babystyle.com ★★★★★

"...their web site is just like their stores—terrific... an excellent source for everything a parent needs... fantastic maternity and baby clothes...

they always respond quickly by email... their site seems to have even more merchandise than their stores... I started shopping on their site after receiving a gift card—very easy and convenient... wonderful selection... ❞

Furniture, Bedding & Decor ✓	✓ Gear & Equipment
Nursing & Feeding ✓	✓ Safety & Babycare
Clothing, Shoes & Accessories ✓	✓ Books, Toys & Entertainment

babysupermall.com

Furniture, Bedding & Decor ✓	✓ Gear & Equipment
Nursing & Feeding ✓	✓ Safety & Babycare
Clothing, Shoes & Accessories ✓	✓ Books, Toys & Entertainment

babyuniverse.com ★★★★★

❝*...nice large selection of specialty and basic items... easy-to-use web site with decent prices... carries Carter's clothes and many other popular brands... great bedding selection - they're one of the few places with the Kidsline bedding I wanted... adorable backpacks for toddlers and preschoolers... check out the site for strollers and car seats... this was my first online shopping experience and they made it so easy, convenient and fast, I was hooked... fine customer service... flat rate (if not free) shipping takes the 'ouch' factor out of those big ticket purchases...* ❞

Furniture, Bedding & Decor ✓	✓ Gear & Equipment
Nursing & Feeding ✓	✓ Safety & Babycare
Clothing, Shoes & Accessories ✓	✓ Books, Toys & Entertainment

barebabies.com

Furniture, Bedding & Decor ✓	✓ Gear & Equipment
Nursing & Feeding ✓	✓ Safety & Babycare
Clothing, Shoes & Accessories ✓	✓ Books, Toys & Entertainment

birthandbaby.com ★★★★☆

❝*...incredible site for buying a nursing bra... there is more information about different manufacturers than you can imagine... I've even received a phone call from the owner after placing an order to clarify something... free shipping, so it's easy to buy multiple sizes and send back the ones that don't fit... their selection of nursing bras is better than any other place I've found... if you are a hard to fit size, this is the place to go...* ❞

Furniture, Bedding & Decor ✗	✓ Gear & Equipment
Nursing & Feeding ✓	✓ Safety & Babycare
Clothing, Shoes & Accessories ✗	✓ Books, Toys & Entertainment

blueberrybabies.com

Furniture, Bedding & Decor ✓	✓ Gear & Equipment
Nursing & Feeding ✓	✓ Safety & Babycare
Clothing, Shoes & Accessories ✓	✓ Books, Toys & Entertainment

buybuybaby.com ★★★★½

❝*...this is the web site for the popular New York-based baby retailer... you name it, they've got it... all the items in their store can also be found on their web site... prices are fair - especially since things get shipped right to your door... we had some items that were damaged and their online customer service took care of it without any problems...* ❞

Furniture, Bedding & Decor ✓	✓ Gear & Equipment
Nursing & Feeding ✓	✓ Safety & Babycare
Clothing, Shoes & Accessories ✓	✓ Books, Toys & Entertainment

childcarriers.com

Furniture, Bedding & Decor ✗	✓ Gear & Equipment

Nursing & Feeding ✗ | ✗ Safety & Babycare
Clothing, Shoes & Accessories ✗ | ✗ Books, Toys & Entertainment

clothdiaper.com

Furniture, Bedding & Decor ✗ | ✓ Gear & Equipment
Nursing & Feeding ✓ | ✓ Safety & Babycare
Clothing, Shoes & Accessories ✗ | ✗ Books, Toys & Entertainment

cocoacrayon.com

Furniture, Bedding & Decor ✓ | ✓ Gear & Equipment
Nursing & Feeding ✓ | ✓ Safety & Babycare
Clothing, Shoes & Accessories ✓ | ✓ Books, Toys & Entertainment

cvs.com ★★★★☆

"...super convenient web site for any 'drug store' items... items are delivered in a reasonable amount of time... decent selection of baby products... prices are competitive and ordering online definitely beats making the trip out to the drugstore... order a bunch of stuff at a time so shipping is free... I used them for my baby announcements and everyone loved them... super easy to refill prescriptions... it was a real relief to order all my formula, baby wipes and diapers online..."

Furniture, Bedding & Decor ✗ | ✗ Gear & Equipment
Nursing & Feeding ✓ | ✓ Safety & Babycare
Clothing, Shoes & Accessories ✗ | ✗ Books, Toys & Entertainment

dreamtimebaby.com

Furniture, Bedding & Decor ✓ | ✓ Gear & Equipment
Nursing & Feeding ✓ | ✓ Safety & Babycare
Clothing, Shoes & Accessories ✓ | ✓ Books, Toys & Entertainment

drugstore.com ★★★★☆

Furniture, Bedding & Decor ✗ | ✗ Gear & Equipment
Nursing & Feeding ✓ | ✓ Safety & Babycare
Clothing, Shoes & Accessories ✗ | ✗ Books, Toys & Entertainment

ebay.com ★★★★☆

"...great way to save money on everything from maternity clothes to breast pumps... be careful with whom you do business... it's always worth checking out what's available... I picked up a brand new jogger for dirt cheap... great deals to be had if you have patience to browse and be willing to resell or exchange what you don't like... baby stuff is easily found and often reasonably priced... keep an eye on shipping costs when you're bidding..."

Furniture, Bedding & Decor ✓ | ✓ Gear & Equipment
Nursing & Feeding ✓ | ✓ Safety & Babycare
Clothing, Shoes & Accessories ✓ | ✓ Books, Toys & Entertainment

egiggle.com ★★★★☆

"...nice selection—not overwhelming... don't expect the big box store brands here—they carry higher-end, specialty items that you won't find elsewhere... smooth shopping experience... nice site—convenient and easy to use..."

Furniture, Bedding & Decor ✓ | ✓ Gear & Equipment
Nursing & Feeding ✓ | ✓ Safety & Babycare
Clothing, Shoes & Accessories ✓ | ✓ Books, Toys & Entertainment

gagagifts.com ★★★★☆

"...great online store that carries fun clothes and unique gifts and toys for kids and adults... unique and special gifts like designer diaper bags, Whoozit learning toys and handmade quilts... this site makes gift buying incredibly easy—I'm done in less than 5 minutes... prices are high but products are special..."

Furniture, Bedding & Decor ✓ — ✓ Gear & Equipment
Nursing & Feeding ✓ — ✓ Safety & Babycare
Clothing, Shoes & Accessories ✓ — ✓ Books, Toys & Entertainment

gap.com ★★★★☆

"...I love the Gap's online store—all the cool things in their stores available via my computer... terrific selection of boys and girls clothes plus cute shoes... you can find awesome deals and return online purchases to Gap stores... their clothes are very durable... it's easy to purchase items online and delivery is prompt... a very practical and affordable way to shop... site makes it easy to quickly find what you need... sign up for the weekly newsletter and you'll find out about online sales..."

Furniture, Bedding & Decor ✓ — ✓ Gear & Equipment
Nursing & Feeding ✗ — ✗ Safety & Babycare
Clothing, Shoes & Accessories ✓ — ✓ Books, Toys & Entertainment

geniusbabies.com ★★★½☆

"...the best selection available of developmental toys and gifts... the only place to order real puppets from the Baby Einstein video series... cool place for unique baby shower and birthday gifts... their site navigation could use an upgrade..."

Furniture, Bedding & Decor ✗ — ✗ Gear & Equipment
Nursing & Feeding ✗ — ✗ Safety & Babycare
Clothing, Shoes & Accessories ✗ — ✓ Books, Toys & Entertainment

gymboree.com ★★★★☆

"...beautiful clothing and great quality... colorful and stylish baby and kids wear... lots of fun birthday gift ideas... easy exchange and return policy... items usually go on sale pretty quickly... save money with gymbucks... many stores have a play area which makes shopping with my kids fun (let alone feasible)..."

Furniture, Bedding & Decor ✗ — ✗ Gear & Equipment
Nursing & Feeding ✗ — ✗ Safety & Babycare
Clothing, Shoes & Accessories ✓ — ✓ Books, Toys & Entertainment

hannaandersson.com

Furniture, Bedding & Decor ✓ — ✗ Gear & Equipment
Nursing & Feeding ✓ — ✗ Safety & Babycare
Clothing, Shoes & Accessories ✓ — ✓ Books, Toys & Entertainment

jcpenney.com

Furniture, Bedding & Decor ✓ — ✗ Gear & Equipment
Nursing & Feeding ✗ — ✓ Safety & Babycare
Clothing, Shoes & Accessories ✓ — ✗ Books, Toys & Entertainment

joggingstroller.com ★★★★★

"...an excellent resource when you're choosing a jogging stroller... the entire site is devoted to joggers... very helpful information that's worth checking whether you plan to buy from them or not... the best online guide for researching jogging strollers... includes helpful comparisons and parent reviews on the top strollers..."

Furniture, Bedding & Decor ✗ — ✓ Gear & Equipment
Nursing & Feeding ✗ — ✗ Safety & Babycare
Clothing, Shoes & Accessories ✗ — ✗ Books, Toys & Entertainment

kidsurplus.com

Furniture, Bedding & Decor ✓ — ✗ Gear & Equipment
Nursing & Feeding ✓ — ✗ Safety & Babycare
Clothing, Shoes & Accessories ✓ — ✓ Books, Toys & Entertainment

landofnod.com

★★★★☆

"...cool site with adorable and unique furnishings... hip kid style art work... fabulous furniture and bedding... the catalog is amusing and nicely laid out... lots of sweet selections for both boys and girls... good customer service... fun but small selection of music, books, toys and more... a great way to get ideas for putting rooms together..."

Furniture, Bedding & Decor	✓	✗	Gear & Equipment
Nursing & Feeding	✗	✗	Safety & Babycare
Clothing, Shoes & Accessories	✗	✓	Books, Toys & Entertainment

landsend.com

"...carries the best quality in children's wear—their stuff lasts forever... durable and adorable clothing, shoes and bedding... they offer a huge variety of casual clothing and awesome pajamas... not as inexpensive as other sites, but you can't beat the quality... the very best diaper bags... site is easy to navigate and has great finds for the entire family... love the flannel sheets, maternity clothes and shoes for mom..."

Furniture, Bedding & Decor	✓	✗	Gear & Equipment
Nursing & Feeding	✗	✗	Safety & Babycare
Clothing, Shoes & Accessories	✓	✗	Books, Toys & Entertainment

letsgostrolling.com

Furniture, Bedding & Decor	✓	✓	Gear & Equipment
Nursing & Feeding	✓	✗	Safety & Babycare
Clothing, Shoes & Accessories	✓	✓	Books, Toys & Entertainment

llbean.com

"...high quality clothing for babies, toddlers and kids at reasonable prices... the clothes are extremely durable and stand up to wear and tear very well... a great site for winter clothing and gear shopping... wonderful selection for older kids, too... fewer options for infants... an awesome way to shop for clothing basics... you can't beat the diaper bags..."

Furniture, Bedding & Decor	✗	✗	Gear & Equipment
Nursing & Feeding	✗	✗	Safety & Babycare
Clothing, Shoes & Accessories	✓	✗	Books, Toys & Entertainment

modernseed.com

"...it was fun finding many unique items for my son's nursery... I wanted a contemporary theme and they had lots of wonderful items including crib linens, wall art and lighting... the place to find super cool baby and kid stuff and the best place for modern nursery decor... they also carry children and adult clothing and furniture and toys... not cheap but one of my favorite places..."

Furniture, Bedding & Decor	✓	✓	Gear & Equipment
Nursing & Feeding	✓	✓	Safety & Babycare
Clothing, Shoes & Accessories	✓	✓	Books, Toys & Entertainment

naturalbaby-catalog.com

"...all natural products—clothes, toys, herbal medicines, bathing, etc... fine quality and a great alternative to the usual products... site is fairly easy to navigate and has a good selection... dealing with returns is pretty painless... love the catalogue and the products... excellent customer service... lots of organic clothing made with natural materials... high quality shoes in a range of prices..."

Furniture, Bedding & Decor	✓	✓	Gear & Equipment
Nursing & Feeding	✓	✓	Safety & Babycare
Clothing, Shoes & Accessories	✓	✓	Books, Toys & Entertainment

netkidswear.com

Furniture, Bedding & Decor	✓	✓	Gear & Equipment
Nursing & Feeding	✓	✓	Safety & Babycare
Clothing, Shoes & Accessories	✓	✓	Books, Toys & Entertainment

nordstrom.com ★★★★☆

"...just like their stores, the site carries a great selection of high-quality items... you can't go wrong with Nordstrom—even online... quick shipping and easy site navigation... a little pricey, but great quality items... I've purchased a bunch of baby stuff from their website and have never had a problem... a great shoe selection for all ages..."

Furniture, Bedding & Decor	✓	✓	Gear & Equipment
Nursing & Feeding	✗	✓	Safety & Babycare
Clothing, Shoes & Accessories	✓	✓	Books, Toys & Entertainment

oldnavy.com ★★★★☆

"...shopping online with Old Navy makes it easy to find incredible bargains... site was easy to use and my products arrived quickly... site carries items that aren't necessarily available in their stores... an inexpensive way to get trendy baby clothes... you can return items directly to any store... check out the sale page of this web site for deep discounts on current season clothing... I signed up for the email savings and get free shipping several times a year..."

Furniture, Bedding & Decor	✗	✗	Gear & Equipment
Nursing & Feeding	✗	✗	Safety & Babycare
Clothing, Shoes & Accessories	✓	✗	Books, Toys & Entertainment

oliebollen.com ★★★★½

"...perfect for the busy mom looking for a fun baby shower gift... this online-only store has all the best brands—Catamini and Tea Collection to name a couple... great for gifts and home stuff, too... lots of style... very easy to use... 30 days full refund, 60 days store credit..."

Furniture, Bedding & Decor	✓	✗	Gear & Equipment
Nursing & Feeding	✓	✗	Safety & Babycare
Clothing, Shoes & Accessories	✓	✓	Books, Toys & Entertainment

onestepahead.com ★★★★½

"...one stop shopping site with everything parents are looking for... huge variety of items to choose from... I bought everything from a crib to a nursery bottle... high quality items, many of which are developmental in nature... great line of safety equipment... easy to order and fast delivery but you will pay for shipping... web site has helpful reviews... great site for hard to find items..."

Furniture, Bedding & Decor	✓	✓	Gear & Equipment
Nursing & Feeding	✓	✓	Safety & Babycare
Clothing, Shoes & Accessories	✓	✓	Books, Toys & Entertainment

peapods.com

Furniture, Bedding & Decor	✓	✓	Gear & Equipment
Nursing & Feeding	✗	✓	Safety & Babycare
Clothing, Shoes & Accessories	✓	✓	Books, Toys & Entertainment

pokkadots.com

Furniture, Bedding & Decor	✓	✓	Gear & Equipment
Nursing & Feeding	✓	✗	Safety & Babycare
Clothing, Shoes & Accessories	✓	✓	Books, Toys & Entertainment

poshtots.com ★★★★☆

"...incredible selection of whimsical and out-of-the-ordinary nursery decor... beautiful, unique designer room sets in multiple styles... they do boys and girls bedrooms... great for the baby that has everything—

including parents with an unlimited cash account... you can get great ideas about decor just from browsing the site, even if you don't buy... ”

Furniture, Bedding & Decor .... ✓ ✓ .... Gear & Equipment
Nursing & Feeding .... ✓ ✗ .... Safety & Babycare
Clothing, Shoes & Accessories....... ✓ ✓ .... Books, Toys & Entertainment

potterybarnkids.com ★★★★☆

“*...beautiful high end furniture and bedding... they have a way with matching everything perfectly and I am always a sucker for that look... adorable merchandise of great quality... you will get what you pay for: high quality furniture at high prices... web site is easy to navigate... items like hooded towels and plush blankets make this place special... if I could afford it I would buy everything in the store...* ”

Furniture, Bedding & Decor .... ✓ ✓ .... Gear & Equipment
Nursing & Feeding .... ✗ ✗ .... Safety & Babycare
Clothing, Shoes & Accessories....... ✗ ✓ .... Books, Toys & Entertainment

preemie.com

Furniture, Bedding & Decor .... ✗ ✓ .... Gear & Equipment
Nursing & Feeding .... ✓ ✓ .... Safety & Babycare
Clothing, Shoes & Accessories....... ✓ ✓ .... Books, Toys & Entertainment

rei.com

Furniture, Bedding & Decor .... ✗ ✓ .... Gear & Equipment
Nursing & Feeding .... ✗ ✗ .... Safety & Babycare
Clothing, Shoes & Accessories....... ✓ ✓ .... Books, Toys & Entertainment

royalnursery.com ★★★☆☆

“*...this used to be a store in San Diego and now it is only online... if you need a silver rattle, luxury baby blanket or shower gift—this is the place... a beautiful site with elegant baby clothes, jewelry, and gifts...love the hand print kits—they are my current favorite gift... high end baby wear and gear... be sure to check out the sale items...* ”

Furniture, Bedding & Decor .... ✓ ✗ .... Gear & Equipment
Nursing & Feeding .... ✗ ✓ .... Safety & Babycare
Clothing, Shoes & Accessories....... ✓ ✓ .... Books, Toys & Entertainment

showeryourbaby.com

Furniture, Bedding & Decor .... ✓ ✓ .... Gear & Equipment
Nursing & Feeding .... ✓ ✓ .... Safety & Babycare
Clothing, Shoes & Accessories....... ✓ ✓ .... Books, Toys & Entertainment

snipsnsnails.com ★★★★☆

“*...a great boys clothing store for infants to 14 years old... clothes for every occasion, from casual to special occasion... pajamas and swimsuits, too... pricey, but upscale and fun... items on the web site are not always in stock ...* ”

Furniture, Bedding & Decor .... ✓ ✗ .... Gear & Equipment
Nursing & Feeding .... ✗ ✗ .... Safety & Babycare
Clothing, Shoes & Accessories....... ✓ ✗ .... Books, Toys & Entertainment

strollerdepot.com

Furniture, Bedding & Decor .... ✗ ✓ .... Gear & Equipment
Nursing & Feeding .... ✗ ✗ .... Safety & Babycare
Clothing, Shoes & Accessories....... ✗ ✓ .... Books, Toys & Entertainment

strollers4less.com ★★★☆☆

“*...some of the best prices on strollers... I love this site... we purchased our stroller online for a lot less than it costs locally... online ordering went smoothly—from ordering through receiving... wide* *selection and some incredible deals... shipping is relatively fast... free shipping if you spend $100, which isn't hard to do... "*

Furniture, Bedding & Decor .... ✗ ✓ .... Gear & Equipment
Nursing & Feeding .... ✗ ✗ .... Safety & Babycare
Clothing, Shoes & Accessories ...... ✗ ✓ .... Books, Toys & Entertainment

target.com ★★★★☆

"...our favorite place to shop for kids stuff—good selection and very affordable... guilt free shopping—kids grow so fast so I don't want to pay high department store prices... everything from diapers and sippy cups to car seats and strollers... easy return policy... decent registry that won't freak your friends out with outrageous prices... easy, convenient shopping for well-priced items... all the big box brands available—Graco, Evenflo, Eddie Bauer, etc.... "

Furniture, Bedding & Decor .... ✓ ✓ .... Gear & Equipment
Nursing & Feeding .... ✓ ✓ .... Safety & Babycare
Clothing, Shoes & Accessories ...... ✓ ✓ .... Books, Toys & Entertainment

teddylux.com

Furniture, Bedding & Decor .... ✗ ✗ .... Gear & Equipment
Nursing & Feeding .... ✗ ✗ .... Safety & Babycare
Clothing, Shoes & Accessories ...... ✗ ✓ .... Books, Toys & Entertainment

thebabyhammock.com ★★★★☆

"...a family owned business selling parent-tested products from morning sickness relief products to baby carriers, natural skincare, gift sets and more... fast friendly service... natural products and waldorf influenced toys... "

Furniture, Bedding & Decor .... ✓ ✓ .... Gear & Equipment
Nursing & Feeding .... ✓ ✓ .... Safety & Babycare
Clothing, Shoes & Accessories ...... ✓ ✗ .... Books, Toys & Entertainment

thebabyoutlet.com

Furniture, Bedding & Decor .... ✗ ✓ .... Gear & Equipment
Nursing & Feeding .... ✓ ✓ .... Safety & Babycare
Clothing, Shoes & Accessories ...... ✗ ✓ .... Books, Toys & Entertainment

tinyride.com

Furniture, Bedding & Decor .... ✗ ✓ .... Gear & Equipment
Nursing & Feeding .... ✓ ✗ .... Safety & Babycare
Clothing, Shoes & Accessories ...... ✗ ✗ .... Books, Toys & Entertainment

toadsandtulips.com

Furniture, Bedding & Decor .... ✓ ✗ .... Gear & Equipment
Nursing & Feeding .... ✗ ✗ .... Safety & Babycare
Clothing, Shoes & Accessories ...... ✓ ✓ .... Books, Toys & Entertainment

toysrus.com ★★★★☆

"...makes shopping incredibly easy... well organized site with discount prices... makes registering for gifts super simple... even more products are online than in the actual stores... check out the outlet section and coupon codes for even more discounts... I did most of my Christmas shopping here, paid no shipping and had my gifts delivered in 3 days... web site includes helpful toy reviews... use this to send your wish lists to relatives... "

Furniture, Bedding & Decor .... ✓ ✓ .... Gear & Equipment
Nursing & Feeding .... ✓ ✓ .... Safety & Babycare
Clothing, Shoes & Accessories ...... ✓ ✓ .... Books, Toys & Entertainment

tuttibella.com ★★★★☆

"...well designed web site with beautiful, original clothing, toys, bedding and accessories... cute vintage stuff for babies and kids...

stylish designer goods from here and abroad... your child will stand out among the Baby Gap-clothed masses... gorgeous fabrics... a great place to find that perfect gift for someone special and stylish... ❞

Furniture, Bedding & Decor	✓	✓	Gear & Equipment
Nursing & Feeding	✗	✗	Safety & Babycare
Clothing, Shoes & Accessories	✓	✗	Books, Toys & Entertainment

usillygoose.com

Furniture, Bedding & Decor	✓	✗	Gear & Equipment
Nursing & Feeding	✗	✗	Safety & Babycare
Clothing, Shoes & Accessories	✗	✓	Books, Toys & Entertainment

walmart.com

❝*...the site is packed with information, which can be a little difficult to navigate... anything and everything you need at a huge discount... good idea to browse the site and research prices before you visit a store... my order was delivered well before the estimated delivery date... I've found cheaper deals online than in the store...* ❞

Furniture, Bedding & Decor	✓	✓	Gear & Equipment
Nursing & Feeding	✓	✓	Safety & Babycare
Clothing, Shoes & Accessories	✓	✓	Books, Toys & Entertainment

maternity clothing

Central Phoenix

"lila picks"

★Motherhood Maternity

A Pea In The Pod

"...excellent if you are looking for stylish maternity clothes and don't mind paying for them... start here for special occasions and business wear... the decor is lovely and most of the clothes are beautiful... stylish fashion solutions, but expect to pay more than at department stores... keep your eyes open for the sale rack—the markdowns can be terrific... an upscale shop that carries everything from intimates to fancy dresses... stylish, fun and non-maternity-like..."

Casual wear	✓	$$$$	Prices
Business wear	✓	❹	Product availability
Intimate apparel	✓	❹	Customer service
Nursing wear	✓	❹	Decor

WWW.APEAINTHEPOD.COM

PHOENIX—7014 E CAMELBACK RD (AT N GOLDWATER BLVD); 480.421.9851; M-SA 10-9, SU 11-9

Baby Bloomers

"...handmade baby gifts, clothing and accessories... maternity clothes... for gently used items, this is the place to go—you'll save a ton!..."

Casual wear	✓	$$	Prices
Business wear	✗	❹	Product availability
Intimate apparel	✗	❺	Customer service
Nursing wear	✗	❹	Decor

PHOENIX—6505 N 7TH ST (AT E MARYLAND AVE); 602.266.5646; M-SA 10-5, SU 12-5

Baby Depot At Burlington Coat Factory

"...a surprisingly good selection of maternity clothes at great prices... staff can be hard to find so be prepared to dig... cute pants, skirts and sets... I wouldn't have thought that their selection would be as good as it is... not much other than casual items, but what they have is pretty good..."

Casual wear	✓	$$	Prices
Business wear	✗	❸	Product availability
Intimate apparel	✗	❸	Customer service
Nursing wear	✗	❸	Decor

WWW.BABYDEPOT.COM

PHOENIX—2728 W PEORIA AVE (AT METRO CENTER); 602.866.2628; M-SA 10-9, SU 11-6; MALL PARKING

PHOENIX—4747 E CACTUS RD (AT TATUM); 602.923.7060; M-SA 10-9, SU 11-6; MALL PARKING

PHOENIX—7611 W THOMAS RD (AT 75TH ST); 623.845.7277; M-SA 10-9, SU 11-6; MALL PARKING

Coming Event Maternity Boutique

"...small boutique with trendy, cute, stylish clothes... this store was way out of my price range for maternity clothes... unique clothing that looks and feels good, and makes you feel good too... lots to choose from, and very helpful service..."

Casual wear	✓	$$$$	Prices
Business wear	✓	❹	Product availability
Intimate apparel	✓	❹	Customer service
Nursing wear	✓	❸	Decor

PHOENIX—7000 E MAYO BLVD (AT N 70TH ST); 480.998.8016; M-SA 10-6, SU 12-5

Fashion Bug

"...not the hippest collection around, but the clothes are really cheap and perfectly presentable... basics like cropped pants and babydoll shirts... plus-sizes are a 'plus' in my book... sale prices are great... check the web for coupons..."

Casual wear	✓	$$$	Prices
Business wear	✓	❸	Product availability
Intimate apparel	✓	❸	Customer service
Nursing wear	✓	❹	Decor

WWW.FASHIONBUG.COM

PHOENIX—1626 W MONTEBELLO AVE (NEXT TO CHRIS TOWN MALL); 602.246.2701; M-SA 10-9, SU 12-6; FREE PARKING

PHOENIX—2020 N 75TH AVE (AT W ENCANTO BLVD); 623.873.1022; M-SA 10-9, SU 12-6; FREE PARKING

PHOENIX—4523 E THOMAS RD (AT ARCADIA CROSSING SHOPPING CTR); 602.553.3188; M-SA 10-9, SU 12-6

Good Threads Consignment

"...source for quality consignment clothing, accessories, shoes, and specialty gift items... great selection..."

Casual wear	✓	$$$	Prices
Business wear	✓	❸	Product availability
Intimate apparel	✗	❸	Customer service
Nursing wear	✗	❸	Decor

PHOENIX—3145 E CHANDLER BLVD (AT S 32ND ST); 480.759.9722; DAILY 10-6; FREE PARKING

It's My Turn

"...variety of nice maternity, baby and toddler clothing and they even have other items from cribs to videos and books..."

Casual wear	✓	$	Prices
Business wear	✗	❹	Product availability
Intimate apparel	✓	❸	Customer service
Nursing wear	✓	❸	Decor

PHOENIX—19401 N CAVE CREEK RD (AT E UTOPIA RD); 602.765.0530; M-SA 10-5

JCPenney

"...competitive prices and a surprisingly cute selection... they carry bigger sizes that are very hard to find at other stores... much cheaper than most maternity boutiques and they always seem to have some sort

of sale going on... an especially large selection of maternity jeans for plus sizes... a more conservative collection than the smaller, hipper boutiques... good for casual basics, but not much for special occasions... ”

Casual wear	✓	$$	Prices
Business wear	✓	❸	Product availability
Intimate apparel	✓	❸	Customer service
Nursing wear	✗	❸	Decor

WWW.JCPENNEY.COM

PHOENIX—4510 E CACTUS RD (AT PARADISE VALLEY MALL); 602.996.2550; M-SA 10-9, SU 11-6; PARKING LOT

PHOENIX—9809 N METRO PKWY W (AT METRO CENTER); 602.371.8545; M-SA 10-9, SU 11-6; PARKING LOT

Kohl's

“*...a small maternity selection but I always manage to find several items I like... our favorite shopping destination—clean, wide open aisles... not a huge amount of maternity, but if you find something the price is always right... the selection is very inconsistent but sometimes you can find nice casuals... best for the bare-bone basics like T-shirts, shorts or casual pants...*”

Casual wear	✓	$$	Prices
Business wear	✗	❸	Product availability
Intimate apparel	✗	❸	Customer service
Nursing wear	✗	❸	Decor

WWW.KOHLS.COM

PHOENIX—17323 N 19TH AVE (AT W BELL RD); 602.298.1893; M-SA 8-10, SU 10-8; FREE PARKING

PHOENIX—21001 N TATUM BLVD (AT E DEER VALLEY DR); 480.538.1750; M-SA 8-10, SU 10-8; FREE PARKING

PHOENIX—4637 E CHANDLER BLVD (AT S 46TH ST); 480.785.7561; M-SA 8-10, SU 9-9; PARKING LOT

Macy's

“*...if your local Macy's has a maternity section, you're in luck... I bought my entire pregnancy work wardrobe at Macy's... the styles are all relatively recent and the brands are well known... you can generally find some attractive dresses at very reasonable prices on their sales rack... like other large department stores, you're bound to find something that works if you dig enough... very convenient because you can get your other shopping done at the same time... the selection isn't huge, but what they have is nice...*”

Casual wear	✓	$$$	Prices
Business wear	✓	❸	Product availability
Intimate apparel	✓	❸	Customer service
Nursing wear	✗	❸	Decor

WWW.MACYS.COM

PHOENIX—2410 E CAMELBACK RD (AT BALTIMORE FASHION PARK); 602.468.2100; M-SA 10-9, SU 11-8

PHOENIX—4520 E CACTUS RD (AT PARADISE VALLEY MALL); 602.494.2100; M-SA 10-9, SU 11-8

Motherhood Maternity

“*...a wide variety of styles, from business to weekend wear, all at a good price... affordable and cute... everything from bras and swimsuits to work outfits... highly recommended for those who don't want to spend a fortune on maternity clothes... less fancy and pricey than their sister stores—A Pea in the Pod and Mimi Maternity... they have frequent sales, so you just need to keep dropping in—you're bound to find something good...*”

Casual wear ✓ | $$$ Prices
Business wear ✓ | ❹ Product availability
Intimate apparel ✓ | ❹ Customer service
Nursing wear ✓ | ❸ Decor

WWW.MOTHERHOOD.COM

PHOENIX—21001 N TATUM BLVD (AT E DEER VALLEY DR); 480.419.7562; M-SA 10-9, SU 11-6

PHOENIX—4250 W ANTHEM WY (AT BLACK CANYON ACCESS RD); 623.465.7793; M-SA 9-8, SU 11-6

PHOENIX—4550 E CACTUS RD (AT PARADISE VALLEY MALL); 602.996.8971; M-SA 10-9, SU 11-6; MALL PARKING

PHOENIX—9812 N METRO PKWY E (AT METRO CENTER); 602.371.1468; M-SA 10-9, SU 11-6

Old Navy

“...the best for casual maternity clothing like stretchy T-shirts with Lycra and comfy jeans... prices are so reasonable it's ridiculous... not much for the workplace, but you can't beat the prices on casual clothes... not all Old Navy locations carry their maternity line... don't expect a huge or diverse selection... the staff is not always knowledgeable about maternity clothing and can't really help with questions about sizing... they have the best return policy—order online and return to the nearest store location... perfect for inexpensive maternity duds...”

Casual wear ✓ | $$ Prices
Business wear ✗ | ❹ Product availability
Intimate apparel ✗ | ❸ Customer service
Nursing wear ✗ | ❸ Decor

WWW.OLDNAVY.COM

PHOENIX—1949 E CAMELBACK RD (AT CAMELBACK COLONNADE); 602.240.5405; M-F 9-9, SU 10-6

PHOENIX—9617 N METRO PKWY (AT METRO CENTER); 602.216.0016; M-SA 9-9, SU 10-6

Ross Dress For Less

“...if you don't mind looking through a lot of clothes you can find some good pieces at great prices... they sometimes have larger sizes too... totally hit or miss depending on their most recent shipment... not the most fashionable clothing, but great for that everyday, casual T-shirt or stretchy pair of pants...”

Casual wear ✓ | $$$ Prices
Business wear ✓ | ❸ Product availability
Intimate apparel ✗ | ❷ Customer service
Nursing wear ✗ | ❷ Decor

WWW.ROSSSTORES.COM

PHOENIX—10625 N 43RD AVE (AT PEORIA); 602.843.1668; M-SA 9:30-9, SU 11-7; PARKING LOT

PHOENIX—10835 N TATUM BLVD (AT E SHEA BLVD); 480.922.7785; M-SA 9:30-9:30, SU 11-7; PARKING LOT

PHOENIX—1751 W BETHANY HOME RD (AT 19TH AVE); 602.544.0338; M-SA 9:30-9:30, SU 11-7; PARKING LOT

PHOENIX—220 E BELL ST (AT 3RD ST); 602.504.1125; M-SA 9:30-9:30, SU 11-7; PARKING LOT

PHOENIX—2821 W PEORIA AVE (AT 28TH AVE); 602.944.7800; M-SA 9:30-9:30, SU 11-7; PARKING LOT

PHOENIX—2929 W AGUA FRIA FWY (AT 27TH AVE); 623.780.3277; M-SA 9:30-9:30, SU 11-7; PARKING LOT

PHOENIX—4509 E THOMAS AVE (AT 44TH ST); 602.840.0330; M-SA 9:30-9:30, SU 11-7; PARKING LOT

PHOENIX—7333 W THOMAS RD (AT N 75TH AVE); 623.247.6030; M-SA 9:30-9:30, SU 11-7; PARKING LOT

Sears

"...good place to get maternity clothes for a low price... the clearance rack always has good deals and their sales are quite frequent... not necessarily super high-quality, but if you just need them for nine months, who cares... good selection of nursing bras... I love the fact that they carry maternity wear in larger sizes—I got so tired of looking in those cutesy boutiques and then being disappointed because they didn't have my size... the only place I found maternity for plus-sized women..."

Casual wear	✓	$$	Prices
Business wear	✗	❸	Product availability
Intimate apparel	✓	❸	Customer service
Nursing wear	✓	❸	Decor

WWW.SEARS.COM

PHOENIX—10001 N METRO PKWY W (AT METRO CENTER); 602.395.2995; M-SA 10-9, SU 10-6; PARKING LOT

PHOENIX—4531 E THOMAS RD (AT ARCADIA CROSSING SHOPPING CTR); 602.474.8451; M-F 10-9, SA 10-6, SU 11-5

PHOENIX—4604 E CACTUS RD (AT PARADISE VALLEY MALL); 602.953.7116; M-F 10-9, SA 8-9, SU 10-6

PHOENIX—7611 W THOMAS RD (AT 75TH AVE); 623.849.7960; M-F 10-9, SA 8-9, SU 10-7

Target

"...I was surprised at how fashionable their selection is—they carry Liz Lange and other really cute selections... the price is right—especially since you'll only be wearing these clothes for a few months... great for maternity basics—T-shirts, skirts, sweaters, even maternity bras... best of all, you can do some maternity shopping while you're shopping for other household basics... shirts for $10—you can't beat that... not the most exciting or romantic maternity shopping, but once you see the prices you'll get over it... as always, Target provides the perfectly priced solution..."

Casual wear	✓	$$	Prices
Business wear	✓	❸	Product availability
Intimate apparel	✓	❸	Customer service
Nursing wear	✓	❸	Decor

WWW.TARGET.COM

PHOENIX—12602 N PARADISE VILLAGE PKY W (AT CACTUS RD); 602.953.2151; M-SA 8-10, SU 8-9; PARKING LOT

PHOENIX—16806 N 7TH ST (AT BELL RD); 602.375.1500; M-SA 8-10, SU 8-9; PARKING LOT

PHOENIX—1818 E BASELINE RD (AT 24TH ST); 602.281.1119; M-SA 8-10, SU 8-9; PARKING LOT

PHOENIX—21001 N TATUM BLVD (AT E DEER VALLEY DR); 480.419.9380; M-SA 8-10, SU 8-9; PARKING LOT

PHOENIX—2727 W AGUA FRIA FWY (AT 27TH AVE); 623.869.8070; M-SA 8-10, SU 8-9; PARKING LOT

PHOENIX—4515 E THOMAS RD (AT ARCADIA CROSSING SHOPPING CTR); 602.952.1797; M-SA 8-10, SU 8-9; PARKING LOT

PHOENIX—4734 E RAY RD (AT 48TH ST); 480.893.0588; M-SA 8-10, SU 8-9; PARKING LOT

PHOENIX—740 W CAMELBACK RD (AT 7TH AVE); 602.263.6035; M-SA 8-10, SU 8-9; PARKING LOT

PHOENIX—7409 W VIRGINIA AVE (AT 48TH ST); 480.893.9333; M-SA 8-10, SU 8-9; PARKING LOT

Northwest Valley

"lila picks"

★Motherhood Maternity

maternity

Fashion Bug

"...not the hippest collection around, but the clothes are really cheap and perfectly presentable... basics like cropped pants and babydoll shirts... plus-sizes are a 'plus' in my book... sale prices are great... check the web for coupons..."

Casual wear	✓	$$$	Prices
Business wear	✓	❸	Product availability
Intimate apparel	✓	❸	Customer service
Nursing wear	✓	❹	Decor

WWW.FASHIONBUG.COM

PEORIA—10280 N 91ST AVE (BTWN W MONROE ST AND W GOLD DUST AVE); 623.487.0907; M-SA 10-9, SU 12-6; FREE PARKING

JCPenney

"...competitive prices and a surprisingly cute selection... they carry bigger sizes that are very hard to find at other stores... much cheaper than most maternity boutiques and they always seem to have some sort of sale going on... an especially large selection of maternity jeans for plus sizes... a more conservative collection than the smaller, hipper boutiques... good for casual basics, but not much for special occasions..."

Casual wear	✓	$$	Prices
Business wear	✓	❸	Product availability
Intimate apparel	✓	❸	Customer service
Nursing wear	×	❸	Decor

WWW.JCPENNEY.COM

GLENDALE—7750 W ARROWHEAD TOWNE CTR (AT N 77TH AVE); 623.412.1121; M-F 10-9, SA 10-7, SU 11-6; PARKING LOT

PEORIA—8235 W BELL RD (AT N VALLEY POWER CTR); 623.487.9775; M-F 10-9, SA 10-7, SU 11-6; PARKING LOT

Kohl's

"...a small maternity selection but I always manage to find several items I like... our favorite shopping destination—clean, wide open aisles... not a huge amount of maternity, but if you find something the price is always right... the selection is very inconsistent but sometimes you can find nice casuals... best for the bare-bone basics like T-shirts, shorts or casual pants..."

Casual wear	✓	$$	Prices
Business wear	×	❸	Product availability
Intimate apparel	×	❸	Customer service
Nursing wear	×	❸	Decor

WWW.KOHLS.COM

GLENDALE—5408 W BELL RD (AT N 55TH AVE); 602.298.5456; M-SA 8-10, SU 10-8; FREE PARKING

PEORIA—9220 W NORTHERN AVE (AT N 91ST AVE); 623.877.0177; M-SA 8-10, SU 10-8; FREE PARKING

SURPRISE—14020 W BELL RD (AT N LITCHFIELD RD); 623.544.6330; M-SA 8-10, SU 10-8; FREE PARKING

Motherhood Maternity

"...a wide variety of styles, from business to weekend wear, all at a good price... affordable and cute... everything from bras and swimsuits to work outfits... highly recommended for those who don't want to spend a fortune on maternity clothes... less fancy and pricey than their sister stores—A Pea in the Pod and Mimi Maternity... they have frequent sales, so you just need to keep dropping in—you're bound to find something good..."

Casual wear .... ✓ | $$$ .... Prices
Business wear .... ✓ | ❹ .... Product availability
Intimate apparel .... ✓ | ❹ .... Customer service
Nursing wear .... ✓ | ❸ .... Decor

WWW.MOTHERHOOD.COM

GLENDALE—7700 W ARROWHEAD TOWNE (AT ARROWHEAD TOWNE CTR); 623.486.3888; M-SA 10-9, SU 11-6

Ross Dress For Less

"...if you don't mind looking through a lot of clothes you can find some good pieces at great prices... they sometimes have larger sizes too... totally hit or miss depending on their most recent shipment... not the most fashionable clothing, but great for that everyday, casual T-shirt or stretchy pair of pants..."

Casual wear .... ✓ | $$$ .... Prices
Business wear .... ✓ | ❸ .... Product availability
Intimate apparel .... × | ❷ .... Customer service
Nursing wear .... × | ❷ .... Decor

WWW.ROSSSTORES.COM

PEORIA—8115 W BELL RD (AT 83RD AVE); 623.486.9311; M-SA 9:30-9:30, SU 11-7; PARKING LOT

PEORIA—9460 W NORTHERN AVE (AT 91ST AVE); 623.772.1228; M-SA 9:30-9:30, SU 11-7; PARKING LOT

SURPRISE—13715 W BELL RD (AT N W POINT PKWY); 623.537.9278; M-SA 9:30-9:30, SU 11-7

Sears

"...good place to get maternity clothes for a low price... the clearance rack always has good deals and their sales are quite frequent... not necessarily super high-quality, but if you just need them for nine months, who cares... good selection of nursing bras... I love the fact that they carry maternity wear in larger sizes—I got so tired of looking in those cutesy boutiques and then being disappointed because they didn't have my size... the only place I found maternity for plus-sized women..."

Casual wear .... ✓ | $$ .... Prices
Business wear .... × | ❸ .... Product availability
Intimate apparel .... ✓ | ❸ .... Customer service
Nursing wear .... ✓ | ❸ .... Decor

WWW.SEARS.COM

GLENDALE—7780 W ARROWHEAD TOWNE CTR (AT N 77TH AVE); 623.776.4500; M-F 10-9, SA 8-9, SU 10-6

PEORIA—10140 N 91ST AVE (AT W PEORIA AVE); 623.687.2400; M-SA 8-10, SU 8-8

Target 

"...I was surprised at how fashionable their selection is—they carry Liz Lange and other really cute selections... the price is right—especially since you'll only be wearing these clothes for a few months... great for maternity basics—T-shirts, skirts, sweaters, even maternity bras... best of all, you can do some maternity shopping while you're shopping for other household basics... shirts for $10—you can't beat that... not the most exciting or romantic maternity shopping, but once you see the prices you'll get over it... as always, Target provides the perfectly priced solution..."

Casual wear	✓	$$	Prices
Business wear	✓	❸	Product availability
Intimate apparel	✓	❸	Customer service
Nursing wear	✓	❸	Decor

WWW.TARGET.COM

GLENDALE—10230 N 43RD AVE (AT FRY RD); 480.281.0008; M-SA 8-10, SU 8-9; PARKING LOT

GLENDALE—9350 W NORTHERN AVE (AT LOOP 101); 623.877.8440; M-SA 8-10, SU 8-9; PARKING LOT

PEORIA—8055 W BELL RD (AT 79TH AVE); 623.773.2172; M-SA 8-10, SU 8-9; PARKING LOT

SURPRISE—13731 W BELL RD (AT GRAND AVE); 623.975.4122; M-SA 8-10, SU 8-9; PARKING LOT

Northeast Valley

"lila picks"

★Babystyle

★Belly Boutique

★Mothers' Milk Boutique

A Pea In The Pod

"...excellent if you are looking for stylish maternity clothes and don't mind paying for them... start here for special occasions and business wear... the decor is lovely and most of the clothes are beautiful... stylish fashion solutions, but expect to pay more than at department stores... keep your eyes open for the sale rack—the markdowns can be terrific... an upscale shop that carries everything from intimates to fancy dresses... stylish, fun and non-maternity-like..."

Casual wear .... ✓ $$$$ .... Prices
Business wear .... ✓ ❹ .... Product availability
Intimate apparel .... ✓ ❹ .... Customer service
Nursing wear .... ✓ ❹ .... Decor

WWW.APEAINTHEPOD.COM

SCOTTSDALE—7014 E CAMELBACK RD (AT N GOLDWATER BLVD); 480.421.9851; M-SA 10-9, SU 11-6

Babystyle

"...compared to their web site their in-store maternity selection is more limited, but still worth checking out... the staff are really sweet and helpful... great maternity basics like pants, tops and casual wear... very fashionable stuff... an awesome range of casual and dressy maternity wear..."

Casual wear .... ✓ $$$ .... Prices
Business wear .... ✓ ❹ .... Product availability
Intimate apparel .... ✓ ❹ .... Customer service
Nursing wear .... ✓ ❹ .... Decor

WWW.BABYSTYLE.COM

SCOTTSDALE—15215 N KIERLAND BLVD (AT N 71ST ST); 480.596.9201; M-F 10-9, SA 10-7, SU 11-6; PARKING LOT

SCOTTSDALE—7014 E CAMELBACK RD (AT SCOTTSDALE RD); 480.994.5800; M-F 10-9, SA 10-7, SU 11-6; PARKING LOT

Belly Boutique

"...a little boutique that carries styles from all the hip maternity designers... they'll help you find something that looks good on you... super nice shopping experience... fun for the occasional splurge, as they have a good selection... I always thought of shopping here as a mini celebration of having such a big belly—very fun atmosphere..."

Casual wear .... ✓ $$$ .... Prices
Business wear .... ✓ ❸ .... Product availability

Intimate apparel	✓	❸	Customer service
Nursing wear	✓	❸	Decor

WWW.BELLYBOUTIQUEMATERNITY.COM

SCOTTSDALE—8787 N SCOTTSDALE RD (AT SCOTTSDALE RD); 480.596.0767; M-SA 10-6, SU 12-5

Frou Frou

Casual wear	✓	✗	Nursing wear
Business wear	✗	✓	Intimate apparel

WWW.FROUFROULIFE.COM

CAREFREE—7212 HO HUM RD (AT SPANISH VILLAGE); 480.437.9998; DAILY 11-5; PARKING LOT

Kohl's

"...a small maternity selection but I always manage to find several items I like... our favorite shopping destination—clean, wide open aisles... not a huge amount of maternity, but if you find something the price is always right... the selection is very inconsistent but sometimes you can find nice casuals... best for the bare-bone basics like T-shirts, shorts or casual pants..."

Casual wear	✓	$$	Prices
Business wear	✗	❸	Product availability
Intimate apparel	✗	❸	Customer service
Nursing wear	✗	❸	Decor

WWW.KOHLS.COM

SCOTTSDALE—8680 E RAINTREE DR (AT PIMA FWY); 480.609.9830; M-SA 8-10, SU 10-8; FREE PARKING

Macy's

"...if your local Macy's has a maternity section, you're in luck... I bought my entire pregnancy work wardrobe at Macy's... the styles are all relatively recent and the brands are well known... you can generally find some attractive dresses at very reasonable prices on their sales rack... like other large department stores, you're bound to find something that works if you dig enough... very convenient because you can get your other shopping done at the same time... the selection isn't huge, but what they have is nice..."

Casual wear	✓	$$$	Prices
Business wear	✓	❸	Product availability
Intimate apparel	✓	❸	Customer service
Nursing wear	✗	❸	Decor

WWW.MACYS.COM

SCOTTSDALE—7014 E CAMELBACK RD (AT SCOTTSDALE FASHION SQ); 480.840.0333; M-SA 10-9, SU 11-8

Motherhood Maternity

"...a wide variety of styles, from business to weekend wear, all at a good price... affordable and cute... everything from bras and swimsuits to work outfits... highly recommended for those who don't want to spend a fortune on maternity clothes... less fancy and pricey than their sister stores—A Pea in the Pod and Mimi Maternity... they have frequent sales, so you just need to keep dropping in—you're bound to find something good..."

Casual wear	✓	$$$	Prices
Business wear	✓	❹	Product availability
Intimate apparel	✓	❹	Customer service
Nursing wear	✓	❸	Decor

WWW.MOTHERHOOD.COM

SCOTTSDALE—7401 E CAMELBACK RD (AT N CIVIC CTR PL); 480.945.3916; M-SA 10-9, SU 11-6

Mothers' Milk Boutique

"...they carry a nice line of maternity wear especially the Majamas brand... best place to buy maternity bras... small selection, but knowledgeable and helpful staff... authorized Medela retailer for all of your nursing needs... nursing information and assistance too..."

Casual wear .... ✗ $$$ .... Prices
Business wear .... ✗ ❹ .... Product availability
Intimate apparel .... ✗ ❺ .... Customer service
Nursing wear .... ✓ ❹ .... Decor

WWW.MOTHERSMILKBOUTIQUE.COM

SCOTTSDALE—10816 N SCOTTSDALE RD (AT E SHEA BLVD); 480.922.4615; M-F 10-6, SA 10-5 ; PARKING LOT

Old Navy

"...the best for casual maternity clothing like stretchy T-shirts with Lycra and comfy jeans... prices are so reasonable it's ridiculous... not much for the workplace, but you can't beat the prices on casual clothes... not all Old Navy locations carry their maternity line... don't expect a huge or diverse selection... the staff is not always knowledgeable about maternity clothing and can't really help with questions about sizing... they have the best return policy—order online and return to the nearest store location... perfect for inexpensive maternity duds..."

Casual wear .... ✓ $$ .... Prices
Business wear .... ✗ ❹ .... Product availability
Intimate apparel .... ✗ ❸ .... Customer service
Nursing wear .... ✗ ❸ .... Decor

WWW.OLDNAVY.COM

SCOTTSDALE—16215 N SCOTTSDALE RD (AT E PARADISE LN); 480.998.0234; M-SA 9-9, SU 10-6

Ross Dress For Less

"...if you don't mind looking through a lot of clothes you can find some good pieces at great prices... they sometimes have larger sizes too... totally hit or miss depending on their most recent shipment... not the most fashionable clothing, but great for that everyday, casual T-shirt or stretchy pair of pants..."

Casual wear .... ✓ $$$ .... Prices
Business wear .... ✓ ❸ .... Product availability
Intimate apparel .... ✗ ❷ .... Customer service
Nursing wear .... ✗ ❷ .... Decor

WWW.ROSSSTORES.COM

SCOTTSDALE—8970 INDIAN BEND RD (AT 101); 480.951.1338; M-SA 9:30-9:30, SU 11-7; PARKING LOT

Small Change

"...bought many maternity clothes here and took in some of my daughter's clothes for consignment... buy it if you like it because it could be gone tomorrow..."

Casual wear .... ✓ $$$ .... Prices
Business wear .... ✓ ❸ .... Product availability
Intimate apparel .... ✓ ❹ .... Customer service
Nursing wear .... ✓ ❸ .... Decor

WWW.SMALLCHANGECONSIGNMENTS.COM

PARADISE VALLEY—6206 N SCOTTSDALE RD (OFF E MCDONALD DR); 480.368.9466; M-F 9:30-7, SA 9-6, SU 10-6

Target

"...I was surprised at how fashionable their selection is—they carry Liz Lange and other really cute selections... the price is right—especially

since you'll only be wearing these clothes for a few months... great for maternity basics—T-shirts, skirts, sweaters, even maternity bras... best of all, you can do some maternity shopping while you're shopping for other household basics... shirts for $10—you can't beat that... not the most exciting or romantic maternity shopping, but once you see the prices you'll get over it... as always, Target provides the perfectly priced solution... **”**

Casual wear ....✓	$$.. Prices
Business wear ....✓	❸...................... Product availability
Intimate apparel ....✓	❸......................... Customer service
Nursing wear...............................✓	❸... Decor

WWW.TARGET.COM

FOUNTAIN HILLS—16825 E SHEA BLVD (AT N TECHNOLOGY DR); 480.837.8557; M-SA 8-10, SU 8-9; PARKING LOT

SCOTTSDALE—15444 N FRANK LLOYD WRIGHT BLVD (AT 101); 480.661.7720; M-SA 9:30-9:30, SU 11-6 ; PARKING LOT

SCOTTSDALE—32351 N SCOTTSDALE RD (AT ASHLER HILLS); 480.575.7043; M-SA 8-10, SU 8-9; PARKING LOT

SCOTTSDALE—9000 E INDIAN BEND RD (AT SCOTTSDALE PAVILIONS); 480.951.4403; M-SA 8-10, SU 8-9; PARKING LOT

Southeast Valley

"lila picks"

★Baby Mother & More

★Motherhood Maternity

Baby Depot At Burlington Coat Factory

"...a surprisingly good selection of maternity clothes at great prices... staff can be hard to find so be prepared to dig... cute pants, skirts and sets... I wouldn't have thought that their selection would be as good as it is... not much other than casual items, but what they have is pretty good..."

Casual wear ✓ | $$ Prices
Business wear ✗ | ❸ Product availability
Intimate apparel ✗ | ❸ Customer service
Nursing wear ✗ | ❸ Decor

WWW.BABYDEPOT.COM

MESA—6225 E SOUTHERN AVE (AT SUPERSTITION SPRINGS BLVD); 480.325.4796; M-SA 10-9, SU 11-6; MALL PARKING

TEMPE—5000 S ARIZONA MILLS CIR (AT ARIZONA MILLS); 480.897.4700; M-SA 10-9:30, SU 11-7; MALL PARKING

Baby Mother & More

"...a nursing resource Mecca... they carry nursing support and hard-to-find breastfeeding products... staff extremely helpful and down to earth... they keep my bra size on file so I remember what I got the last time... they gave me the skills and knowledge to get my baby nursing..."

Casual wear ✗ | $$$ Prices
Business wear ✗ | ❹ Product availability
Intimate apparel ✗ | ❺ Customer service
Nursing wear ✓ | ❸ Decor

WWW.MILKSMILE.COM

MESA—1235 S GILBERT RD (AT SOUTHERN); 480.890.1870; M-SA 10-6, SU 12-4; PARKING LOT

Gap Maternity

"...the styles are very modern and attractive... the clothes are reasonably priced and wash well... comfy yet stylish basics... they have a great online resource and you can return online purchases at the store... average everyday prices, but catch a sale and you're golden... sizes run big so buy small... always a sale going on where you'll find hip items for a steal..."

Casual wear ✓ | $$$ Prices
Business wear ✓ | ❸ Product availability
Intimate apparel ✓ | ❹ Customer service

Nursing wear ✓ ❸ Decor

WWW.GAP.COM

CHANDLER—3111 W CHANDLER BLVD (AT N FEDERAL WY); 480.726.0426; M-SA 10-9, SU 11-6

JCPenney

"...competitive prices and a surprisingly cute selection... they carry bigger sizes that are very hard to find at other stores... much cheaper than most maternity boutiques and they always seem to have some sort of sale going on... an especially large selection of maternity jeans for plus sizes... a more conservative collection than the smaller, hipper boutiques... good for casual basics, but not much for special occasions..."

Casual wear	✓	$$	Prices
Business wear	✓	❸	Product availability
Intimate apparel	✓	❸	Customer service
Nursing wear	✗	❸	Decor

WWW.JCPENNEY.COM

MESA—6525 E SOUTHERN AVE (AT SUPERSTITION SPRINGS CTR); 480.832.0400; M-SA 10-9, SU 11-6; PARKING LOT

TEMPE—1140 W ELLIOT RD (AT SPORTS AUTHORITY PLAZA); 480.456.8828; M-SA 10-8, SU 10-6; PARKING LOT

Kohl's

"...a small maternity selection but I always manage to find several items I like... our favorite shopping destination—clean, wide open aisles... not a huge amount of maternity, but if you find something the price is always right... the selection is very inconsistent but sometimes you can find nice casuals... best for the bare-bone basics like T-shirts, shorts or casual pants..."

Casual wear	✓	$$	Prices
Business wear	✗	❸	Product availability
Intimate apparel	✗	❸	Customer service
Nursing wear	✗	❸	Decor

WWW.KOHLS.COM

GILBERT—1121 E BASELINE RD (AT N COOPER RD); 480.926.0290; M-SA 8-10, SU 10-8; FREE PARKING

MESA—5833 E MCKELLIPS RD (AT N RECKER RD); 480.924.8527; M-SA 8-10, SU 10-8; FREE PARKING

Macy's

"...if your local Macy's has a maternity section, you're in luck... I bought my entire pregnancy work wardrobe at Macy's... the styles are all relatively recent and the brands are well known... you can generally find some attractive dresses at very reasonable prices on their sales rack... like other large department stores, you're bound to find something that works if you dig enough... very convenient because you can get your other shopping done at the same time... the selection isn't huge, but what they have is nice..."

Casual wear	✓	$$$	Prices
Business wear	✓	❸	Product availability
Intimate apparel	✓	❸	Customer service
Nursing wear	✗	❸	Decor

WWW.MACYS.COM

MESA—4000 FIESTA MALL (OFF SOUTHERN AVE); 480.835.4500; M-SA 10-9, SU 11-8

Motherhood Maternity

"...a wide variety of styles, from business to weekend wear, all at a good price... affordable and cute... everything from bras and swimsuits

to work outfits... highly recommended for those who don't want to spend a fortune on maternity clothes... less fancy and pricey than their sister stores—A Pea in the Pod and Mimi Maternity... they have frequent sales, so you just need to keep dropping in—you're bound to find something good... ”*

Casual wear	✓	$$$	Prices
Business wear	✓	❹	Product availability
Intimate apparel	✓	❹	Customer service
Nursing wear	✓	❸	Decor

WWW.MOTHERHOOD.COM

CHANDLER—3111 W CHANDLER BLVD (AT CHANDLER FASHION CTR); 480.722.0632; M-SA 10-9, SU 11-6

MESA—1445 W SOUTHERN AVE (AT FIESTA MALL); 480.898.8942; M-SA 10-9, SU 11-6; MALL PARKING

MESA—6555 E SOUTHERN AVE (AT SUPERSTITION SPRINGS CTR); 480.854.3483; M-SA 10-9, SU 11-6

TEMPE—5000 S ARIZONA MILLS CIR (AT ARIZONA MILLS); 480.775.1818; M-SA 9-9:30, SU 11-7

Sears

“...good place to get maternity clothes for a low price... the clearance rack always has good deals and their sales are quite frequent... not necessarily super high-quality, but if you just need them for nine months, who cares... good selection of nursing bras... I love the fact that they carry maternity wear in larger sizes—I got so tired of looking in those cutesy boutiques and then being disappointed because they didn't have my size... the only place I found maternity for plus-sized women... ”

Casual wear	✓	$$	Prices
Business wear	✗	❸	Product availability
Intimate apparel	✓	❸	Customer service
Nursing wear	✓	❸	Decor

WWW.SEARS.COM

CHANDLER—3177 CHANDLER VILLAGE DR (AT CHANDLER FASHION CTR); 480.855.2800; M-F 10-9, SA 8-9, SU 10-6

MESA—1425 W SOUTHERN AVE (AT ALMA SCHOOL RD); 480.833.6767; M-F 10-9, SA 8-9, SU 10-6

Tailored For Two Maternity

“...unique maternity clothes that fit well and make you feel good... quality clothing... limited selection, but what they carry is topnotch... I found my favorite maternity jeans at this store... lots of cute clothes in smaller sizes which was great for me... ”

Casual wear	✓	$$$$	Prices
Business wear	✓	❸	Product availability
Intimate apparel	✓	❹	Customer service
Nursing wear	✓	❸	Decor

CHANDLER—2560 W CHANDLER BLVD (AT N ELLIS ST); 480.893.0465; M-F 10-7, SA 10-5, SU 11-5

Target

“...I was surprised at how fashionable their selection is—they carry Liz Lange and other really cute selections... the price is right—especially since you'll only be wearing these clothes for a few months... great for maternity basics—T-shirts, skirts, sweaters, even maternity bras... best of all, you can do some maternity shopping while you're shopping for other household basics... shirts for $10—you can't beat that... not the most exciting or romantic maternity shopping, but once you see the prices you'll get over it... as always, Target provides the perfectly priced solution... ”

Casual wear .... ✓
Business wear .... ✓
Intimate apparel .... ✓
Nursing wear............................... ✓

$$ .... Prices
❸ .... Product availability
❸ .... Customer service
❸ .... Decor

WWW.TARGET.COM

CHANDLER—2020 N ARIZONA AVE (AT WARNER RD); 480.899.7986; M-SA 8-10, SU 8-9; PARKING LOT

CHANDLER—2880 S ALMA SCHOOL RD (AT QUEEN CREEK); 480.782.1881; M-SA 8-10, SU 8-9; PARKING LOT

CHANDLER—3425 W FRYE RD (AT S PRICE RD); 480.281.0007; M-SA 8-10, SU 8-9; PARKING LOT

GILBERT—1515 E WARNER RD (AT S VAL VISTA DR); 480.892.2282; M-SA 8-10, SU 8-9

MESA—1135 S GILBERT RD (AT E SOUTHERN AVE); 480.926.3443; M-SA 8-10, SU 8-9

MESA—1525 S POWER RD (AT SUPERSTITIONS FWY); 480.396.0403; M-SA 8-10, SU 8-9; PARKING LOT

MESA—2151 N POWER RD (AT E MCKELLIPS RD); 480.830.2035; M-SA 8-10, SU 8-9; PARKING LOT

West Valley

Kohl's

"...a small maternity selection but I always manage to find several items I like... our favorite shopping destination—clean, wide open aisles... not a huge amount of maternity, but if you find something the price is always right... the selection is very inconsistent but sometimes you can find nice casuals... best for the bare-bone basics like T-shirts, shorts or casual pants..."

Casual wear	✓	$$	Prices
Business wear	×	❸	Product availability
Intimate apparel	×	❸	Customer service
Nursing wear	×	❸	Decor

WWW.KOHLS.COM

AVONDALE—1611 N DYSART RD (AT W MCDOWELL RD); 623.536.2700; M-SA 8-10, SU 10-8; FREE PARKING

Ross Dress For Less

"...if you don't mind looking through a lot of clothes you can find some good pieces at great prices... they sometimes have larger sizes too... totally hit or miss depending on their most recent shipment... not the most fashionable clothing, but great for that everyday, casual T-shirt or stretchy pair of pants..."

Casual wear	✓	$$$	Prices
Business wear	✓	❸	Product availability
Intimate apparel	×	❷	Customer service
Nursing wear	×	❷	Decor

WWW.ROSSSTORES.COM

GOODYEAR—1408 N LITCHFIELD RD (AT MCDOWELL RD); 623.535.7242; M-SA 9:30-9:30, SU 11-7; PARKING LOT

Target

"...I was surprised at how fashionable their selection is—they carry Liz Lange and other really cute selections... the price is right—especially since you'll only be wearing these clothes for a few months... great for maternity basics—T-shirts, skirts, sweaters, even maternity bras... best of all, you can do some maternity shopping while you're shopping for other household basics... shirts for $10—you can't beat that... not the most exciting or romantic maternity shopping, but once you see the prices you'll get over it... as always, Target provides the perfectly priced solution..."

Casual wear	✓	$$	Prices
Business wear	✓	❸	Product availability
Intimate apparel	✓	❸	Customer service
Nursing wear	✓	❸	Decor

WWW.TARGET.COM

GOODYEAR—1515 N LITCHFIELD RD (AT MCDOWELL RD); 623.935.3510; M-SA 8-10, SU 8-9; PARKING LOT

Online

"lila picks"

★ breastisbest.com ★ gap.com

★ maternitymall.com ★ naissancematernity.com

babiesrus.com ★★★★☆

"...their online store is surprisingly plentiful for maternity wear in addition to all of the baby stuff... they carry everything from Mimi Maternity to Belly Basics... easy shopping and good return policy... the price is right and the selection is really good..."

Casual wear ✓ ✓ Nursing wear
Business wear ✓ ✓ Intimate apparel

babycenter.com ★★★★☆

"...it's babycenter.com—of course it's good... a small but well selected maternity section... I love being able to read other people's comments before purchasing... prices are reasonable and the convenience is priceless... great customer service and easy returns..."

Casual wear ✓ ✓ Nursing wear
Business wear ✗ ✗ Intimate apparel

babystyle.com ★★★★☆

"...beautiful selection of maternity clothes... very trendy, fashionable styles... take advantage of their free shipping offers to keep the cost down... items generally ship quickly... I found a formal maternity outfit for a benefit dinner, bought it on sale and received it on time... a nice variety of things and they ship in a timely manner..."

Casual wear ✓ ✓ Nursing wear
Business wear ✓ ✓ Intimate apparel

bellablumaternity.com

Casual wear ✓ ✓ Nursing wear
Business wear ✓ ✓ Intimate apparel

breakoutbras.com

Casual wear ✗ ✓ Nursing wear
Business wear ✗ ✓ Intimate apparel

breastisbest.com ★★★★★

"...by far the best resource for purchasing good quality nursing bras online... the site is easy to use and they have an extensive online fitting guide... returns are a breeze... since they are only online you may have to try a few before you get it exactly right..."

Casual wear ✓ ✓ Nursing wear
Business wear ✗ ✓ Intimate apparel

childishclothing.com

Casual wear .... ✓ ✗ .... Nursing wear
Business wear .... ✗ ✗ .... Intimate apparel

duematernity.com ★★★★☆

"...refreshing styles... fun and hip clothing... the site is easy to navigate and use... I've ordered a bunch of clothes from them and never had a problem... everything from casual wear to fun, funky items for special occasions... prices are reasonable..."

Casual wear .... ✓ ✓ .... Nursing wear
Business wear .... ✓ ✓ .... Intimate apparel

evalillian.com

Casual wear .... ✓ ✓ .... Nursing wear
Business wear .... ✓ ✓ .... Intimate apparel

expressiva.com ★★★★½

"...the best site for nursing clothes... prices are good and their selection is terrific... lots of selection on dressy, casual, sleep, workout and even bathing suits... if you're going to shop for maternity online then be sure not to miss this cool site... good customer service—quite prompt in answering questions about my order..."

Casual wear .... ✓ ✓ .... Nursing wear
Business wear .... ✗ ✓ .... Intimate apparel

gap.com ★★★★★

"...stylish maternity clothes delivered right to your doorstep... always something worth buying... the best place for functional, comfortable and affordable maternity clothes... classic styles, not too trendy... more available online than in a store... no fancy dresses but lots of casual outfits that are cheap, look good and I don't mind parting with them after my baby is born... easy to use site and deliveries are generally prompt... you can return them to any Gap store..."

Casual wear .... ✓ ✓ .... Nursing wear
Business wear .... ✓ ✓ .... Intimate apparel

japaneseweekend.com ★★★★☆

"...pregnancy clothes that scream 'I am proud of my pregnant body'... a must for comfy, stylish stuff... they make the best maternity pants which cradle your belly as it grows... a little expensive but I lived in their pants my entire pregnancy—I definitely got my money's worth... really nice clothing that just doesn't look and feel like your traditional pregnancy wear—I still wear a couple of the outfits (my baby is now 6 months old)..."

Casual wear .... ✓ ✓ .... Nursing wear
Business wear .... ✓ ✓ .... Intimate apparel

jcpenney.com ★★★☆☆

"...competitive prices and a surprisingly cute selection... they carry bigger sizes that are very hard to find at other stores... much cheaper than most maternity boutiques and they always seem to have some sort of sale going on... an especially large selection of maternity jeans for plus sizes... a more conservative collection than the smaller, hipper boutiques... good for casual basics, but not much for special occasions..."

Casual wear .... ✓ ✓ .... Nursing wear
Business wear .... ✓ ✓ .... Intimate apparel

lizlange.com ★★★★½

"...well-designed and cute... the real buys on this site are definitely in the sale section... cute, hip selection of jeans, skirts, blouses and

bathing suits... their evening and dressy clothes are the best with wonderful fabrics and designs... easy and convenient online shopping... practical but not frumpy styles—their web site made my maternity shopping so easy... ”

Casual wear .... ✓ ✗ .... Nursing wear
Business wear .... ✓ ✗ .... Intimate apparel

maternitymall.com ★★★★★

“*...I had great luck with maternitymall.com... a large selection of vendors in all price ranges... quick and easy without having to leave my house... found everything I needed... their merchandise tends to be true to size... site is a bit hard to navigate and cluttered with ads... sale and clearance prices are fantastic...* ”

Casual wear .... ✓ ✓ .... Nursing wear
Business wear .... ✓ ✓ .... Intimate apparel

mommygear.com

Casual wear .... ✓ ✓ .... Nursing wear
Business wear .... ✗ ✓ .... Intimate apparel

momsnightout.com

“*...for that fashionable-not-frumpy fancy occasion dress... beautiful store with gorgeous selection of dresses from cocktail to bridal... one on one attention... expensive but worth it...* ”

Casual wear .... ✗ ✗ .... Nursing wear
Business wear .... ✓ ✗ .... Intimate apparel

motherhood.com ★★★★☆

“*...a wide variety of styles, from business to weekend wear—all at a good price... affordable and cute... everything from bras and swimsuits to work outfits... highly recommended for those who don't want to spend a fortune on maternity clothes... less fancy and pricey than their sister stores—A Pea in the Pod and Mimi Maternity... they have frequent sales, so you just need to keep dropping in—you're bound to find something good...* ”

Casual wear .... ✓ ✓ .... Nursing wear
Business wear .... ✓ ✓ .... Intimate apparel

motherwear.com ★★★★½

“*...excellent selection of cute and practical nursing clothes at reasonable prices... sign up for their e-mail newsletter for great offers, including free shipping... top quality clothes... decent selection of hard to find plus sizes... golden return policy, you can return any item (even used!) you aren't 100% happy with... they sell the only nursing tops I could actually wear outside the house... cute styles that aren't frumpy... so easy... pricey but worth it for the quality... top notch customer service...* ”

Casual wear .... ✗ ✓ .... Nursing wear
Business wear .... ✗ ✓ .... Intimate apparel

naissancematernity.com ★★★★★

“*...the cutest maternity clothes around... hip and funky clothes for the artsy, well-dressed mom to be... their site is easy to navigate... if you can't make it down to the actual store in LA, just go online... clothes that make you look and feel sexy... it ain't cheap but you will look marvelous and the clothes will grow with you... web site is great and their phone order service was incredible...* ”

Casual wear .... ✓ ✗ .... Nursing wear
Business wear .... ✓ ✗ .... Intimate apparel

nordstrom.com

"...now that they don't carry maternity in stores anymore, this is the only way to get any maternity from Nordstrom... overpriced but nice... makes returns harder, since you have to ship everything instead of just going back to a store... they carry Cadeau, Liz Lange, Belly Basics, etc... nice stuff, not so nice prices..."

Casual wear ✓ ✓ Nursing wear
Business wear ✓ ✓ Intimate apparel

oldnavy.com

★★★★☆

"...since not all Old Navy stores carry maternity clothes, this is the easiest way to go... just like their regular clothes, the maternity selection is great for casual wear... cheap, cheap, cheap... the quality is good and the price is definitely right... frequent sales make great prices even better..."

Casual wear ✓ ✓ Nursing wear
Business wear ✗ ✗ Intimate apparel

onehotmama.com

★★★½☆

"...you'll find many things you must have... cool and very nice clothing... they carry everything from underwear and tights to formal dresses... you can find some real bargains online... super fast shipping... also, lots of choices for nursing and get-back-in-shape wear..."

Casual wear ✓ ✓ Nursing wear
Business wear ✓ ✓ Intimate apparel

showeryourbaby.com

Casual wear ✓ ✓ Nursing wear
Business wear ✗ ✓ Intimate apparel

target.com

★★★★☆

"...lots of Liz Lange at very fair prices... the selection is great and it's so easy to shop online—we bought most of our baby gear here and I managed to slip in a couple of orders for some maternity wear too... maternity shirts for $10—where else can you find deals like that..."

Casual wear ✓ ✓ Nursing wear
Business wear ✓ ✓ Intimate apparel

activities & outings

Central Phoenix

"lila picks"

★Desert Botanical Garden

★Great Arizona Puppet Theater

★Imagination Avenue

All The Hands

"...we absolutely loved this place... the staff was extremely helpful and were very patient with my young children (2 and 4)... they have a little gated area full of toys for younger children so you can get some work done while they play... great spot for a birthday party for older children... they also have ladies' night out evenings..."

Customer service........................❸ $$$.......................................Prices

WWW.ALLTHEHANDS.COM

PHOENIX—3375 E SHEA BLVD (AT SR 51); 602.493.1604; M-SA 11-9, SU 12-7

Arizona Doll & Toy Museum

★★½☆☆

"...dolls as far as the eye can see... the exhibits are really well done, but my daughter found it frustrating that she couldn't touch and play with them... probably more exciting for girls than for boys... it's only $3 for adults ..."

Customer service........................❸ $$.......................................Prices

Age range....................2 yrs and up

WWW.AZCAMA.COM/MUSEUMS/DOLL&TOY.HTM

PHOENIX—7TH ST (AT MONROE); 602.253.9337; T-SA 10-4, SU 12-4; PARKING GARAGE

Arizona Science Center

"...older kids would probably enjoy this more, however I found that my pre-school aged children enjoyed all the interactive exhibits... from time to time there are exhibits geared toward younger children... planetarium, big screen movies... very educational, fabulous exhibits... the perfect outing for young and old alike... they even have an evening for adults only... general admission is $9, movies and planetarium are extra..."

Customer service........................❹ $$.......................................Prices

Age range....................3 yrs and up

WWW.AZSCIENCE.ORG

PHOENIX—600 E WASHINGTON ST (AT HERITAGE AND SCIENCE PARK); 602.716.2000; OPEN DAILY 10-7; GARAGE PARKING

Arizona Sunrays

"...their Kindergym program is fun and totally age appropriate... lots of climbing, rolling and jumping... my daughter loves being around all the big, 'real' gymnasts... the teachers are fun and also throw a great

party... the best part is that kids can keep 'training' here as they get older... foam pits and lots of fun equipment to climb on..."

Customer service .... ❸ $$$ .... Prices
Age range .... 18 mths and up
WWW.ARIZONASUNRAYS.COM

PHOENIX—3110 E THUNDERBIRD RD (AT 31ST ST); 602.992.5790; CHECK SCHEDULE ONLINE

As You Wish Pottery

WWW.ASYOUWISHPOTTERY.COM

PHOENIX—21001 N TATUM BLVD (AT E DEER VALLEY RD); 480.585.0041; M-TH 10-9, F-SA 10-10, SU 12-6

PHOENIX—3009 W AGUA FRIA FWY (AT 1-17 & LOOP 101); 623.587.7700; M-TH 10-9, F-SA 10-10, SU 12-6

PHOENIX—4905 E RAY RD (AT AMC 24 CENTER); 480.753.9500; M-TH 10-9, F-SA 10-10, SU 12-6

Barnes & Noble

"*...wonderful weekly story times for all ages and frequent author visits for older kids... lovely selection of books and the story times are fun and very well done... they have evening story times—we put our kids in their pjs and come here as a treat before bedtime... they read a story, and then usually have a little craft or related coloring project... times vary by location so give them a call...*"

Customer service .... ❹ $ .... Prices
Age range .... 6 mths to 6 yrs
WWW.BARNESANDNOBLE.COM

PHOENIX—10235 N METRO PKWY E (AT METRO CTR); 602.678.0088; CALL FOR SCHEDULE

PHOENIX—2073 E CAMELBACK RD (AT N 20TH ST); 602.957.2001; CALL FOR SCHEDULE

PHOENIX—21001 N TATUM BLVD (AT DEER VALLEY DR); 480.538.8520; CALL FOR SCHEDULE

PHOENIX—2501 W HAPPY VALLEY RD (AT I-17); 623.780.3300; CALL FOR SCHEDULE

PHOENIX—4847 E RAY RD (AT S 48TH ST); 480.940.7136; CALL FOR SCHEDULE

PHOENIX—7030 E GREENWAY PKWY (AT N KIERLAND BLVD); 480.948.8551; CALL FOR SCHEDULE

Borders Books

"*...very popular weekly story time held in most branches (check the web site for locations and times)... call before you go since they are very popular and get extremely crowded... kids love the unique blend of songs, stories and dancing... Mr. Hatbox's appearances are a delight to everyone (unfortunately he doesn't make appearances at all locations)... large children's section is well categorized and well priced... they make it fun for young tots to browse through the board-book section by hanging toys around the shelves... the low-key cafe is a great place to have coffee with your baby and leaf through some magazines...*"

Customer service .... ❹ $ .... Prices
Age range .... 6 mths to 6 yrs
WWW.BORDERSSTORES.COM

PHOENIX—4555 E CACTUS RD (AT PARADISE VALLEY & N TATUM BLVD); 602.953.9699; CALL FOR SCHEDULE

PHOENIX—7000 E MAYO BLVD (AT N SCOTTSDALE RD); 480.513.8848; CALL FOR SCHEDULE

activities & outings

PHOENIX—BILTMORE FASHION PARK (ON N 24TH ST AT E CAMELBACK RD); 602.957.6660; CALL FOR SCHEDULE

Castles N Coasters

"...coasters and rides for big kids and a carousel for the little ones... my 2 year old also likes the mini golf... lots of junk food so if you want to eat healthy you should bring your own food... good for birthday parties... I used to go here when I was little and I love coming here with my kids... it gets crowded so make sure you hang on to your babes... parking is weird, but manageable... a nice place to take the family and also a good place for Mom and Dad to go for a date night..."

Customer service........................❸ $$$......................................Prices
Age range....................2 yrs and up

WWW.CASTLESNCOASTERS.COM

PHOENIX—9445 N METRO PKWY E (AT METRO CTR); 602.997.7575; DAILY 10-9 CALL; FREE PARKING

Creative Youth Theatre

"...wonderful community theater productions... what a great role model for the young kids—to see older kids being creative and confident... my kid are too young to participate, but we go see the shows because they are so well done... awesome family theater..."

Customer service........................❸ $$$......................................Prices
Age range....................3 yrs and up

WWW.CREATIVEYOUTHTHEATRE.ORG

PHOENIX—3039 W PEORIA AVE (AT N 31ST AVE); 623.363.8385; CHECK SCHEDULE ONLINE; STREET PARKING

Desert Botanical Garden

"...what a wonderful place to see desert nature... they even have a tour that highlights plants that can be eaten... right next to the Phoenix Zoo so you get two adventures in one day... a lovely mommy and me walk... great seasonal activities including the Butterfly House, native American crafts... during the summer it is way too hot to walk through during the day, but an early evening stroll is lovely... also jazz during summer evenings... gorgeous in late fall or early spring... $9 for adults; under 3 free..."

Customer service........................❹ $$..Prices
Age range....................2 yrs and up

WWW.DBG.ORG

PHOENIX—1201 N GALVIN PKWY (AT E MCDOWELL RD); 480.941.1217; CHECK SCHEDULE ONLINE; FREE PARKING

Enchanted Island

"...fun, fun, fun... carousel, steam train, car rides—my kids love coming here and hate leaving... we attended a birthday party here and it was a blast... this place is fun for kids and can be absolutely exhausting for adults—everyone needs a nap after spending the day here... single ticket is only $1 and an all day pass $10..."

Customer service........................❸ $$$......................................Prices
Age range...............6 mths to 12 yrs

WWW.ENCHANTEDISLAND.COM

PHOENIX—1202 W ENCANTO BLVD (AT 12TH AVE); 602.254.1200; CHECK SCHEDULE ONLINE; FREE PARKING

Great Arizona Puppet Theater

"...a terrific place for young children—puppet shows that include classics like Cinderella... the puppets are amazing and after the show they show you how the puppets work... sometimes they have a table

set up where children can make their own puppets before the show starts... they also have shows just for adults... terrific gift shop—many unique items... a great place to go during the hot summer months... make reservations—many of the shows sell out... $8 for adults and free for 2 and under... ❞

Customer service .... ❺ $ .... Prices
Age range .... 18 mths and up

WWW.AZPUPPETS.ORG

PHOENIX—302 W LATHAM ST (AT 3RD AVE); 602.262.2050; CALL FOR SHOWTIMES; FREE PARKING

Hall of Flame Museum of Firefighting

❝*...fire engines, fire men outfits, pictures and movies about fire... geared toward older kids—my daughter got bored pretty quickly... a neat glimpse into the history of fire fighting... lots of hardware to look at and even touch... $6 for adults, kids under 3 are free...* ❞

Customer service .... ❸ $$$ .... Prices
Age range .... 2 yrs and up

WWW.HALLOFFLAME.ORG

PHOENIX—600 E WASHINGTON ST (AT 7TH ST); 602.275.3473; M-SA 9-5, SU 12-4; PARKING LOT

Harkins Theatres

❝*...big movie complex throughout the Valley that has inexpensive movies for children during the summer... some locations offer childcare during the movies, however your child has to be potty trained... good place to send your kids off with the babysitter for a few hours... a great way to see those kids classics on the big screen again...* ❞

Customer service .... ❸ $ .... Prices
Age range .... 3 yrs and up

WWW.HARKINSTHEATRES.COM

PHOENIX—5705 N 19TH AVE (AT CHRIS-TOWN MALL); 602.249.2844; CALL FOR SHOWTIMES; FREE PARKING

Heard Museum

❝*...a fantastic collection of Native American art... not really geared toward young children, so we tend to keep our visits short... nice place to stroll with a baby because it's nice and quiet... good way to get out of the house especially during the hot summer months... very educational for older kids... $10 for adults and free for kids under 3...* ❞

Customer service .... ❸ $$$ .... Prices
Age range .... 2 yrs and up

WWW.HEARD.ORG

PHOENIX—2301 N CENTRAL AVE (AT ENCANTO BLVD); 602.252.8848; DAILY 9:30-5

Herberger Theater Center

❝*...an amazing place to introduce your little one to live performances... they usually showcase kid's classics like Wizard of Oz at some point throughout the season... many youth theaters perform too—their admission prices are a little cheaper...* ❞

Customer service .... ❸ $$$ .... Prices
Age range .... 3 yrs and up

WWW.HERBERGERTHEATER.ORG

PHOENIX—222 E MONROE ST (AT 3RD ST); 602.254.7399; CHECK SCHEDULE ONLINE

Hubbard Family Swim School ★★★★☆

"...great and very popular place for swim classes for young babies and toddlers... indoor pool with 90 degree water... birthday parties here are a blast—they let you take out the floaties and everybody wears themselves out for a good nap... bring your own food—the concession stand is pretty standard..."

Customer service....................❹ $$$....................Prices
Age range.................6 mths and up
WWW.HUBBARDSPORTS.COM
PHOENIX—13832 N 32ND ST (AT E THUNDERBIRD RD); 602.971.4044; CHECK SCHEDULE ONLINE; FREE PARKING

Imagination Avenue ★★★★★

"...my child loves this place... a great indoor play center... really cute pretend town with a movie theater, hospital, home depot and fire station as well as a small jumping castle and cars... they even have a separate area for infants... a small cafe for food and espresso... it's very clean and the staff requests that everybody use wipes and antibacterial cream before entering... make sure you bring a pair socks for yourself and your children or you will have to purchase them... colorful place—a wonderful backdrop for creative play... weekends are usually booked for parties so call before you go... you can rent the facility for private parties..."

Customer service....................❹ $....................Prices
Age range................6 mths to 6 yrs
WWW.IMAGINATIONAVENUE.US
PHOENIX—10610 N 32ND ST (AT SHEA); 602.765.3192; T-F 10-2, SA 10-5; FREE PARKING

Japanese Friendship Garden ★★★½☆

"...a nice stroll with a sleeping baby (strollers are allowed)... it's meant to be a tranquil, quiet place so not ideal for children who want to run around... huge goldfish and tortoises... the tea ceremony is fun, but unfortunately my kids don't like tea... $1 for adults; free for kids..."

Customer service....................❸ $$$....................Prices
Age range.................6 mths and up
WWW.ASAHI-NET.OR.JP/~UW7G-BWR/GARDEN/GARDEN.HTM
PHOENIX—1125 N 3RD AVE (IN MARGARET T HANCE PARK); 602.262.6412; FREE PARKING

Jeepers ★★★★☆

"...they have a ton of video games and a few rides—flying bananas, bumper cars, Himalaya, monkey barrels and a train... plus, a tube for climbing and crawling... you can buy a wristband for unlimited use of the rides... awesome birthday parties... the snack bar serves up pizza, hot dogs and other 'standard' amusement park fare..."

Customer service....................❸ $$....................Prices
Age range.................2 yrs to 12 yrs
WWW.JEEPERS.COM
PHOENIX—4961 BELL RD (AT N TATUM BLVD); 602.439.9200; M-TH 10-9, F-SA 10-10, SU 11-8; FREE PARKING

Music Together ★★★★½

"...the best mom and baby classes out there... music, singing, dancing—even instruments for tots to play with... liberal make-up policy, great venues, take home books, CDs and tapes which are different each semester... it's a national franchise so instructors vary and have their own style... different age groups get mixed up which makes it a good learning experience for all involved... the highlight of

our week—grandma always comes along... be prepared to have your tot sing the songs at home, in the car—everywhere...”

Customer service .... ❹ $$$ .... Prices

Age range .... 2 mths to 5 yrs

WWW.MUSICTOGETHER.COM

PHOENIX—2 LOCATIONS IN PHOENIX (3241 E SHEA BLVD); 602.363.8202; CALL FOR SCHEDULE

Phoenix Art Museum ★★★☆☆

“...definitely better for older kids—it is an art museum after all... perfect for a stroll with a sleeping baby... my boy can usually handle about an hour of looking at exhibits before he loses interest... some of their weekend 'arts and crafts' activities are fun for the whole family... $9 for adults and free for kids under 3...”

Customer service .... ❸ $$$ .... Prices

Age range .... 5 yrs and up

WWW.PHXART.ORG

PHOENIX—1625 N CENTRAL AVE (AT MCDOWELL RD); 602.257.1222; T-SU 10-5, TH 10-9

Phoenix Zoo ★★★★☆

“...the most informative, educational, convenient place to introduce kids to the life and habitats of animals... get a membership—it's well worth the money (starts at $45 per year)... always fun for kids... take the train—it's a fun, fast way to get around the park... my kids like the playgrounds and love the petting zoo (goats, sheep etc.)... the summer camps are awesome... they keep improving the zoo—we come back every year... $14 for adults; under 2 free...”

Customer service .... ❹ $$ .... Prices

Age range ....6 mths and up

WWW.PHOENIXZOO.ORG

PHOENIX—455 N GALVIN PKWY (OFF VAN BUREN ST); 602.273.1341; CHECK SCHEDULE ONLINE; LOT PARKING

Place Music Academy ★★★☆☆

“...music education and fun for all ages... parent participation classes for the really little ones and more independent groups for the older ones... topnotch instruction—the teachers know how to teach and make it fun at the same time...”

Customer service .... ❸ $$$ .... Prices

Age range .... 12 mths and up

WWW.PLACEMUSIC.COM

PHOENIX—10240 N 27TH AVE (AT METRO CENTER); 602.678.5850; CHECK SCHEDULE ONLINE

Pump It Up ★★★★☆

“...huge warehouse type buildings filled with a variety of bounce houses and inflatable obstacle courses... colorful, padded slides and bouncers... the birthday party I went to was a blast—kids and adults were having way too much fun... they have an open gym a couple of days a week for $5 per tot—a great way to jump around and burn off some energy... $200-$250 for a really easy party that will have everybody smiling...”

Customer service .... ❹ $$ .... Prices

Age range .... 2 yrs to 12 yrs

WWW.PUMPITUPPARTY.COM

PHOENIX—22515 N 18TH DR (AT N 19TH AVE); 623.434.7867; CHECK SCHEDULE ONLINE

The Teeter House

WWW.THETEETERHOUSE.COM

PHOENIX—622 E ADAMS ST (AT N 7TH ST); 602.252.4682; CALL FOR SCHEDULE

Toy Town Playcenter

"...owner is super nice and very knowledgeable about different mom's groups... very nice and clean... nice snack bar with a variety of items to choose from (no outside food allowed)... I really liked that is in a space small enough that I can see my children at all times and be able to relax and read a magazine... afternoon is the best time to go because it's not so crowded..."

Customer service........................❸ $$$......................................Prices

WWW.AZTOYTOWN.COM

PHOENIX—12020 S WARNER ELLIOT LOOP (AT EQUESTRIAN TRL); 480.496.4393; M-F 9-3; PARKING LOT

Valley Youth Theatre

"...theater the way it was meant to be for kids... all the classics—Charlie Brown, Wizard of Oz, Snow White... my kids love coming here (and they even manage to sit still for the entire show)... an easy, fun outing that's different than going to the movies... the quality of the shows varies, but my kids love them all anyway..."

Customer service........................❸ $$$......................................Prices

Age range....................2 yrs and up

WWW.VYT.COM

PHOENIX—525 N 1ST ST (AT E FILLMORE ST); 602.253.8188; CHECK SCHEDULE ONLINE; FREE PARKING

Washington Adult Center

"...an amazing array of programs for both children and adults... what an amazing resource in our own back yard... arts and crafts, dance, music... the quality of the programs varies, but you're definitely going to find something you'll like... great deals since the classes are relatively inexpensive..."

Customer service........................❸ $$$......................................Prices

Age range....................2 yrs and up

PHOENIX—2240 W CITRUS WY (AT N 23RD AVE); 602.262.6971; M-TH 9-9, F 9-10, SA 9-12

Waterworld Safari

"...fun for all ages—little ones can splash in the shallow pools, while older children can go crazy on the slides... I always wonder who has more fun here—my kids or my husband... bring lots of sun block and hats for the little ones... snacks are expensive so bring your own... $20 for adults, kids under 6 are free..."

Customer service........................❸ $$$......................................Prices

Age range.................6 mths and up

WWW.GOLFLAND.COM

PHOENIX—4243 W PINNACLE PEAK RD (AT TATUM BLVD); 623.581.1947; M-TH 10-8, F-SA 10-9, SU 11-7

Westcor Kids Club

WWW.WESTCOR.COM

PHOENIX—4568 E CACTUS RD (AT PARADISE VALLEY MALL); 602.996.8846; 1ST M 11AM; MALL PARKING

PHOENIX—7611 W THOMAS RD (AT S END OF DESERT SKY MALL); 623.245.1400; TH 6:30PM; MALL PARKING

PHOENIX—9617 N METRO PKWY (AT METROCENTER); 602.997.8797; 1ST T 6PM; MALL PARKING

YMCA

"...most of the Ys in the area have classes and activities for kids... swimming, gym classes, dance—even play groups for the really little ones... ... some facilities are nicer than others, but in general their programs are worth checking out... prices are more than reasonable for what is offered... the best bang for your buck... they have it all—great programs that meet the needs of a diverse range of families... check out their camps during the summer and school breaks..."

Customer service .... ❹ $$ .... Prices

Age range ....3 mths and up

WWW.VALLEYYMCA.ORG

PHOENIX—1030 E LIBERTY LN (AT S DESERT FOOTHILLS PKWY); 480.460.3959; CHECK SCHEDULE ONLINE

Northwest Valley

"lila picks"

★Build-A-Bear Workshop

★Music Together

Arrowhead Spinetts Gymnastics

"...wonderful parent/tot classes... music, rolling and tumbling... fantastic programs that enhance coordination, balance and self-esteem... we've met so many fun parents here—my daughter loves it... the highlight of our week... we love their equipment—ball pit, rope swing, padded floors... easy birthday party... "

Customer service........................❸ $$$..Prices
Age range....................2 yrs and up
WWW.ARROWHEADGYMNASTICSAZ.COM

PEORIA—19085 N 83RD AVE (AT W UNION HILLS RD); 623.825.4777; M-TH 3:30-8, SA 10-12

Barnes & Noble

"...wonderful weekly story times for all ages and frequent author visits for older kids... lovely selection of books and the story times are fun and very well done... they have evening story times—we put our kids in their pjs and come here as a treat before bedtime... they read a story, and then usually have a little craft or related coloring project... times vary by location so give them a call... "

Customer service........................❹ $ ....Prices
Age range................ 6 mths to 6 yrs
WWW.BARNESANDNOBLE.COM

PEORIA—7685 W BELL RD (AT ARROWHEAD TOWNE CTR); 623.487.9022; CALL FOR SCHEDULE

SURPRISE—13719 W BELL RD (AT N L:ITCHFIELD RD); 623.544.4435; CALL FOR SCHEDULE

Borders Books

"...very popular weekly story time held in most branches (check the web site for locations and times)... call before you go since they are very popular and get extremely crowded... kids love the unique blend of songs, stories and dancing... Mr. Hatbox's appearances are a delight to everyone (unfortunately he doesn't make appearances at all locations)... large children's section is well categorized and well priced... they make it fun for young tots to browse through the board-book section by hanging toys around the shelves... the low-key cafe is a great place to have coffee with your baby and leaf through some magazines... "

Customer service........................❹ $ ....Prices
Age range................ 6 mths to 6 yrs
WWW.BORDERSSTORES.COM

GLENDALE—7320 W BELL RD (AT N 75TH AVE); 623.487.9110; CALL FOR SCHEDULE

Build-A-Bear Workshop

"...design and make your own bear—it's a dream come true... the most cherished toy my daughter owns... they even come with birth certificates... the staff is fun and knows how to play along with the kids' excitement... the basic stuffed animal is only about $15, but the extras add up quickly... great for field trips, birthdays and special occasions... how darling—my nephew is 8 years old now, and still sleeps with his favorite bear..."

Customer service .... ❹ $$$ .... Prices
Age range .... 3 yrs and up

WWW.BUILDABEAR.COM

GLENDALE—7700 W ARROWHEAD TOWNE CTR DR (AT ARROWHEAD TOWNE CTR); 623.773.3964; M-SA 10-9, SU 11-6; FREE PARKING

Desert Schools Coyotes Center

WWW.DESERTSCHOOLSCOYOTESCENTER.COM

PEORIA—15829 N 83RD AVE (AT PEORIA SPORTS COMPLEX); 623.334.1200; CHECK SCHEDULE ONLINE

Gymboree Play & Music

"...we've done several rounds of classes with our kids and they absolutely love it... colorful, padded environment with tons of things to climb and play on... a good indoor place to meet other families and for kids to learn how to play with each other... the equipment and play areas are generally neat and clean... an easy birthday party spot... a guaranteed nap after class... costs vary, so call before showing up..."

Customer service .... ❹ $$$ .... Prices
Age range .... birth to 5 yrs

WWW.GYMBOREE.COM

GLENDALE—4920 W THUNDERBIRD (CAMPUS VLG W); 480.596.6909; CHECK SCHEDULE ONLINE; FREE PARKING

Historic Sahuaro Ranch

"...nice for a stroll with or without kids... not much to 'do' other than walk around and look at the old buildings... the huge peacocks were the highlight of the day... best of all it's free to check out..."

Customer service .... ❸ $$$ .... Prices
Age range .... 3 yrs and up

WWW.SAHUARORANCH.ORG

GLENDALE—9802 N 59TH AVE (AT W MOUNTAIN VIEW RD); 623.930.4200; W-SA, 10-2; FREE PARKING

Music Together

"...the best mom and baby classes out there... music, singing, dancing—even instruments for tots to play with... liberal make-up policy, great venues, take home books, CDs and tapes which are different each semester... it's a national franchise so instructors vary and have their own style... different age groups get mixed up which makes it a good learning experience for all involved... the highlight of our week—grandma always comes along... be prepared to have your tot sing the songs at home, in the car—everywhere..."

Customer service .... ❹ $$$ .... Prices
Age range .... 2 mths to 5 yrs

WWW.MUSICTOGETHER.COM

ANTHEM—623.374.9509; CALL FOR SCHEDULE

PEORIA—8815 W PEORIA (AT N 91ST ST); 602.363.8202; CALL FOR SCHEDULE

Teacher Lynda's Swim School ★★★☆☆

"...the staff is really good here... swim classes for infants on up... my 2 year old can now swim under water and doesn't freak out about water in his eyes... not cheap, but the instructors are really worth it... I feel much more relaxed being around water with my toddler..."

Customer service........................❸ $$$..Prices

Age range.................6 mths and up

WWW.TEACHERLYNDA.COM

PEORIA—8853 N 78TH AVE (OFF OLIVE AVE); 623.935.4878; CALL FOR SCHEDULE; FREE PARKING

USA's The Great Skate

WWW.USAGREATSKATE.COM

GLENDALE—10054 N 43RD AVE (AT W PEORIA AVE); 623.842.1182; CHECK SCHEDULE ONLINE

Westcor Kids Club

WWW.WESTCOR.COM

GLENDALE—7700 W ARROWHEAD TOWNE CTR (AT ARROWHEAD TOWNE CTR); 623.979.7777; W 10AM; MALL PARKING

Western Area Regional Park Aquatic Playground ★★★☆☆

"...8,500-square-foot aquatic playground features nearly 30 different nozzles and buckets, from cattails to ground geysers..."

Customer service........................❸ $ ....Prices

Age range.................6 mths and up

WWW.CI.GLENDALE.AZ.US/PARKSANDRECREATION/CLASSESANDPROGRAMS/AQUATICS.CFM

GLENDALE—N 83RD AVE (AT W BETHANY HOME RD); 623.930.2833; CHECK SCHEDULE ONLINE

Northeast Valley

"lila picks"

- ★Barnes & Noble
- ★Gymboree Play & Music
- ★Health World Children's Museum
- ★McCormick-Stillman Railroad Park

AZ on the Rocks

WWW.AZONTHEROCKS.COM

SCOTTSDALE—16447 N 91ST ST (AT E BABIA ST); 480.502.9777; M W F 3-10, T TH 6-7, SA-SU 9-7

Barnes & Noble

"...wonderful weekly story times for all ages and frequent author visits for older kids... lovely selection of books and the story times are fun and very well done... they have evening story times—we put our kids in their pjs and come here as a treat before bedtime... they read a story, and then usually have a little craft or related coloring project... times vary by location so give them a call..."

Customer service .... ❹ $.. Prices

Age range .... 6 mths to 6 yrs

WWW.BARNESANDNOBLE.COM

SCOTTSDALE—10500 N 90TH ST (AT SHEA BLVD); 480.391.0048; CALL FOR SCHEDULE

SCOTTSDALE—8919 E INDIAN BEND RD (AT N PIMA RD); 480.443.4909; CALL FOR SCHEDULE

Borders Books

"...very popular weekly story time held in most branches (check the web site for locations and times)... call before you go since they are very popular and get extremely crowded... kids love the unique blend of songs, stories and dancing... Mr. Hatbox's appearances are a delight to everyone (unfortunately he doesn't make appearances at all locations)... large children's section is well categorized and well priced... they make it fun for young tots to browse through the board-book section by hanging toys around the shelves... the low-key cafe is a great place to have coffee with your baby and leaf through some magazines..."

Customer service .... ❹ $.. Prices

Age range .... 6 mths to 6 yrs

WWW.BORDERSSTORES.COM

SCOTTSDALE—7135 E CAMELBACK RD (AT N SCOTTSDALE RD); CALL FOR SCHEDULE

Build-A-Bear Workshop

"...design and make your own bear—it's a dream come true... the most cherished toy my daughter owns... they even come with birth certificates... the staff is fun and knows how to play along with the kids' excitement... the basic stuffed animal is only about $15, but the extras add up quickly... great for field trips, birthdays and special occasions... how darling—my nephew is 8 years old now, and still sleeps with his favorite bear..."

Customer service........................❹ $$$...................................... Prices

Age range.....................3 yrs and up

WWW.BUILDABEAR.COM

SCOTTSDALE—7014 E CAMELBACK RD (AT SCOTTSDALE FASHION SQUARE); 480.946.2327; M-SA 10-9, SU 11-6; FREE PARKING

Cactus Park

"...something to do for all ages... playground, pool and fitness center... the playground is clean and big... the bathrooms are clean as well... climbing equipment and swings for a variety of ages and abilities... a good place to meet and network with other parents who have kids the same age as yours... the pool only costs $2 per visit..."

Customer service........................❹ $$.. Prices

Age range.................6 mths and up

WWW.SCOTTSDALEAZ.GOV/PARKS/CACTUS

SCOTTSDALE—7202 E CACTUS RD (AT SCOTTSDALE RD); 480.312.7961; SUNRISE TO10:30; FREE PARKING

Crackerjax Family Fun & Sports

"...an entertainment complex appropriate for older kids... too loud and blaring for the really little ones... bumper boats, go-carts, indoor arcade... greasy food... everyone is friendly and there are lots of school-age kids and teens running around..."

Customer service........................❹ $$.. Prices

Age range.....................2 yrs and up

WWW.CRACKERJAX.COM

SCOTTSDALE—16001 N SCOTTSDALE RD (AT E FRANK LLOYD WRIGHT BLVD); 480.998.2800; DAILY 10-10; FREE PARKING

Do, Re, Mi, School of the Arts

WWW.DOREMISCHOOL.COM

SCOTTSDALE—8050 E MOUNTAIN VIEW RD (AT N HAYDEN RD); 480.451.8233

Fiddlesticks Family Fun Park

"...a huge play land for kids... definitely more to do for bigger kids... go-carts, miniature golf, video arcade... way to much stimulation for little brains—be prepared for a meltdown when you go and a nap in the car on the way home... you pay per ride..."

Customer service........................❸ $$$...................................... Prices

WWW.FIDDLESTICKSAZ.COM

SCOTTSDALE—8800 E INDIAN BEND RD (AT N PIMA RD); 480.951.6060; HOURS VARY, CALL FOR SCHEDULE

Fountain Hills Fountain

WWW.CI.FOUNTAIN-HILLS.AZ.US/

FOUNTAIN HILLS—12925 N SAGUARO BLVD (OFF PALISADES BLVD); 480.816.5252; DAILY 9-9

Girly Girlz

WWW.GIRLY-GIRLZ.COM/

SCOTTSDALE—15425 N SCOTTSDALE RD (AT THE SHOPS AT ZOCALLO); 480.998.4832

Gymboree Play & Music

"...we've done several rounds of classes with our kids and they absolutely love it... colorful, padded environment with tons of things to climb and play on... a good indoor place to meet other families and for kids to learn how to play with each other... the equipment and play areas are generally neat and clean... an easy birthday party spot... a guaranteed nap after class... costs vary, so call before showing up..."

Customer service .... ❹ $$$ .... Prices

Age range .... birth to 5 yrs

WWW.GYMBOREE.COM

SCOTTSDALE—7000 E SHEA BLVD (AT SCOTTSDALE PROMENADE); 480.596.6909; CHECK SCHEDULE ONLINE; FREE PARKING

Health World Children's Museum

"...exhibits that promote health and safety for children... wonderful for young and old—I learned a lot... tots can play with the shopping cart to buy fake food, milk a cow, go down the tree slide, check out a real ambulance... my daughter's favorite was the real bee hive... fake train ride with movie... a great rainy day and summer outing... $7 per person; under 2 free..."

Customer service .... ❹ $$ .... Prices

Age range .... 2 yrs and up

WWW.HEALTHWORLDMUSEUM.ORG

SCOTTSDALE—22401 N LOS CABALLOS DR (AT E LOS GATOS DR); 480.513.8100; F 10-8, SA-TH 10-3

Jewish Community Center

"...programs vary from facility to facility, but most JCCs have outstanding early childhood programs... everything from mom and me music classes to arts and crafts for older kids... a wonderful place to meet other parents and make new friends... class fees are cheaper (if not free) for members, but still quite a good deal for nonmembers... a superb resource for new families looking for fun..."

Customer service .... ❹ $$$ .... Prices

Age range ....3 mths and up

WWW.VOSJCC.ORG

SCOTTSDALE—12701 N SCOTTSDALE RD (AT E SWEETWATER AVE); 480.483.7121; CALL FOR SCHEDULE

Kierland Commons

"...wonderful shopping for children... nice, expensive, but generally child-friendly stores... they have a small, but fun water play area—children must wear a swimsuit to play in the fountain..."

Customer service .... ❸ $$$ .... Prices

WWW.KIERLANDCOMMONS.COM

SCOTTSDALE—15044 N SCOTTSDALE RD (AT E GREENWAY PKWY); 480.348.1577; M-SA 10-8, SU 12-6

MacDonald's Ranch

WWW.MACDONALDSRANCH.COM

SCOTTSDALE—26540 N SCOTTSDALE RD (AT E JOMAX RD); 480.585.0239

McCormick-Stillman Railroad Park

"...train rides, carousel and playgrounds—it's every toddler's dream outing... the playground has different structures for different age groups... they also have water misters to run through and pretend construction equipment to dig in the sand with... there is a wonderful train store as well as a miniature train exhibit run by a train enthusiast club... a caboose serves inexpensive lunch and ice cream... great for birthday parties... $1 per ride and kids under 3 ride free... my boy goes nuts over the real steam engines... beautiful when the train is running at night... a nice place for a picnic, but it can get pretty crowded... the hard part is getting your kids to leave..."

Customer service........................❹ $ .... Prices

Age range................. 6 mths and up

WWW.THERAILROADPARK.COM

SCOTTSDALE—7301 E INDIAN BEND RD (AT SCOTTSDALE RD); 480.312.2312; CHECK ONLINE; FREE PARKING

Music Together

"...the best mom and baby classes out there... music, singing, dancing—even instruments for tots to play with... liberal make-up policy, great venues, take home books, CDs and tapes which are different each semester... it's a national franchise so instructors vary and have their own style... different age groups get mixed up which makes it a good learning experience for all involved... the highlight of our week—grandma always comes along... be prepared to have your tot sing the songs at home, in the car—everywhere..."

Customer service........................❹ $$$...................................... Prices

Age range................ 2 mths to 5 yrs

WWW.MUSICTOGETHER.COM

SCOTTSDALE—602.363.8202; CALL FOR SCHEDULE

SCOTTSDALE—10810 E VIA LINDA ; 480.688.9597; CALL FOR SCHEDULE

My Gym Children's Fitness Center

"...a wonderful gym environment for parents with babies and older tots... classes range from tiny tots to school-aged children and the staff is great about making it fun for all ages... equipment and facilities are really neat—ropes, pulleys, swings, you name it... the kind of place your kids hate to leave... the staff's enthusiasm is contagious... great for memorable birthday parties... although it's a franchise, each gym seems to have its own individual feeling... awesome for meeting playmates and other parents..."

Customer service........................❹ $$$...................................... Prices

Age range................ 3 mths to 9 yrs

WWW.MY-GYM.COM

SCOTTSDALE—7341 N VIA PASEO DEL SUR (AT PASEO VILLAGE SHOPPING CTR); 480.483.5936; CHECK SCHEDULE ONLINE

Palomino Branch Public Library

"...offers fun activities for children...'Babytime' is for newborns through 12 mos. ,offers short stories and songs... 'Time for 1's and 2's' offers stories and and fingerplay... 'Shake Rattle and Roll' is music and singing for children of all ages... 'Preschool Adventures' is for 3-5 year olds and offers stories and music...nice way to meet other moms... check web site for times..."

Customer service........................❸ $ .... Prices

HTTP://LIBRARY.CI.SCOTTSDALE.AZ.US

SCOTTSDALE—12575 E VIA LINDA (AT N 126TH ST); 480.312.6100; CHECK SCHEDULE ONLINE; PARKING AVAILABLE

Pump It Up

"...huge warehouse type buildings filled with a variety of bounce houses and inflatable obstacle courses... colorful, padded slides and bouncers... the birthday party I went to was a blast—kids and adults were having way too much fun... they have an open gym a couple of days a week for $5 per tot—a great way to jump around and burn off some energy... $200-$250 for a really easy party that will have everybody smiling..."

Customer service .... 4 $$ .... Prices
Age range .... 2 yrs to 12 yrs

WWW.PUMPITUPPARTY.COM

SCOTTSDALE—9378 E BAHIA DR (AT N 94TH ST); 480.425.7867; M W TH 10-11

Rawhide Wild West Town

"...a real surprise—they have camels, burros and horses to ride... a train, stagecoach and lots of other 'wild west' things to climb on... no charge to come in and hang out—just to get on the rides... a quirky western-themed park with hay rides, gunfight shows and petting zoo... they always do something special for each holiday... moving to Wild Horse Pass, just south of Phoenix, in December 2005—check their web site for details..."

Customer service .... 4 $$ .... Prices
Age range .... 2 yrs and up

WWW.RAWHIDE.COM

SCOTTSDALE—23023 N SCOTTSDALE RD (AT E PINNACLE PEAK RD); 480.502.5600; CHECK SCHEDULE ONLINE; FREE PARKING

Scottsdale Civic Center

"...tons to do in the area, so you might as well stop by the spray fountain... great fun, especially when it's hot (bring a change of clothes)... you can have breakfast at the Orange Table restaurant and afterwards let the kids play in the fountain... water shoots up from the ground intermittently... great, free fun..."

Customer service .... 3 $ .... Prices
Age range .... 12 mths and up

WWW.SCOTTSDALEAZ.GOV/PARKS/SCOTTSDALEMALL/DEFAULT.ASP

SCOTTSDALE—3839 N DRINKWATER BLVD (AT SCOTTSDALE MALL); 480.874.4607; CHECK SCHEDULE ONLINE

Temple Beth Israel

"...a drop-in Friday morning play group for tots run by the Rabbi's wife... lots of toys, puppets, parachute play, and music (the Rabbi stops by with his guitar)... includes pre-Shabbat candle lighting and challah... mostly moms and kids aged birth-to-2 years... free your first time, $7 for members/$9 for nonmembers thereafter..."

Customer service .... 5 $$ .... Prices
Age range .... 6 mths to 5 yrs

WWW.TEMPLEBETHISRAEL.ORG

SCOTTSDALE—10460 N 56TH ST (AT E SHEA BLVD); 480.951.0323; CHECK SCHEDULE ONLINE

Xtreme Gymnastics

"...parents and babies have so much fun... everyone is so positive and encouraging here... circle time, obstacle courses... lots of bouncy and

activities & outings

padded things to climb on... take their free trial class to check it out..."

Customer service........................❸ $$$..Prices

Age range............... 12 mths and up

WWW.XTREMEGYMNASTICS.COM

SCOTTSDALE—15821 N 79TH ST (AT N GREENWAY HAYDEN LOOP); 480.596.3543; CALL FOR SCHEDULE

Southeast Valley

"lila picks"

- ★ Arizona Museum For Youth
- ★ Borders Books
- ★ Changing Hands Bookstore
- ★ The Little Gym

Arizona Museum for Youth

"...a lovely museum experience for children... half of the museum is an interactive gallery and has small art stations to make crafts pertaining to the exhibit... other half of the museum is called Artville and is a small pretend town... small area just for infants... so nicely designed for infants through school age kids... nice clean bathrooms... friendly staff and nice gift shop... kids can pretend to cook, grow a garden, fish, play basketball—even be like a monkey jumping on the bed... can't beat the price—$3.50 and infants are free... a staple visit for when our friends come to town..."

Customer service .... ❹ $ .... Prices
Age range .... 6 mths to 12 yrs

WWW.CI.MESA.AZ.US/AMFY

MESA—35 N ROBSON ST (AT W MAIN ST); 480.644.2467; CHECK SCHEDULE ONLINE; PARKING AVAILABLE

Arrowhead Meadows Pool

"...newly renovated and beautiful... a pool for adults and a zero depth splash pool for tots... water slide, lazy river and lots of grass to sit and watch... a wonderful day out..."

Customer service .... ❸ $$$ .... Prices
Age range ....6 mths and up

WWW.CHANDLERAZ.ORG

CHANDLER—1475 E ERIE ST (OFF N ALMA SCHOOL RD); 480.732.1064; CHECK SCHEDULE ONLINE

As You Wish Pottery

WWW.ASYOUWISHPOTTERY.COM

MESA—1649 S STAPLEY (AT US 60); 480.539.8400; M-TH 10-9, F-SA 10-10, SU 12-6

Barnes & Noble

"...wonderful weekly story times for all ages and frequent author visits for older kids... lovely selection of books and the story times are fun and very well done... they have evening story times—we put our kids in their pjs and come here as a treat before bedtime... they read a story, and then usually have a little craft or related coloring project... times vary by location so give them a call..."

Customer service........................❹ $ .... Prices
Age range................ 6 mths to 6 yrs

WWW.BARNESANDNOBLE.COM

CHANDLER—3111 W CHANDLER BLVD (AT CHANDLER FASHION CTR); 480.792.1312; CALL FOR SCHEDULE

GILBERT—3807 S GILBERT RD (AT E ELLIOT RD); 480.917.0301; CALL FOR SCHEDULE

MESA—1758 S VAL VISTA DR (AT SUPERSTITION FWY); 480.545.8507; CALL FOR SCHEDULE

Basha Library ★★★☆☆

"...offers story times for infants, toddlers and preschool age children... family movie nights... sign language story time... music and lots of fun activities for all ages... check web site or call for monthly events..."

Customer service........................❸ $$$...................................... Prices

WWW.CHANDLERLIBRARY.ORG

CHANDLER—5999 S VAL VISTA DR (AT E RIGGS RD); 480.782.2850; CALL FOR SCHEDULE; FREE PARKING

Borders Books ★★★★★

"...very popular weekly story time held in most branches (check the web site for locations and times)... call before you go since they are very popular and get extremely crowded... kids love the unique blend of songs, stories and dancing... Mr. Hatbox's appearances are a delight to everyone (unfortunately he doesn't make appearances at all locations)... large children's section is well categorized and well priced... they make it fun for young tots to browse through the board-book section by hanging toys around the shelves... the low-key cafe is a great place to have coffee with your baby and leaf through some magazines..."

Customer service........................❹ $ .... Prices
Age range................ 6 mths to 6 yrs

WWW.BORDERSSTORES.COM

CHANDLER—CHANDLER PAVILIONS (AT N 54TH ST & W RAY RD); 480.961.4915; CALL FOR SCHEDULE

MESA—1361 S ALMA SCHOOL RD (AT FIESTA MALL); 480.833.2244; CALL FOR SCHEDULE

TEMPE—699 S MILL AVE (AT E UNIVERSITY DR); 480.921.8659; CALL FOR SCHEDULE

BounceU ★★★☆☆

"...they will host a really fun party for you... their rooms are packed with those big blowup bouncy things that you see at fairgrounds... they'll also organize the food—makes for an easy and pretty seamless party..."

Customer service........................❹ $$.. Prices
Age range................. 2 yrs to 10 yrs

WWW.BOUNCEU.COM

MESA—1166 S GILBERT RD (AT E SOUTHERN AVE); 480.632.9663; BY RESERVATION ONLY

Build-A-Bear Workshop ★★★½☆

"...design and make your own bear—it's a dream come true... the most cherished toy my daughter owns... they even come with birth certificates... the staff is fun and knows how to play along with the kids' excitement... the basic stuffed animal is only about $15, but the extras add up quickly... great for field trips, birthdays and special occasions... how darling—my nephew is 8 years old now, and still sleeps with his favorite bear..."

Customer service........................❹ $$$...................................... Prices

Age range .... 3 yrs and up

WWW.BUILDABEAR.COM

CHANDLER—3111 W CHANDLER BLVD (AT CHANDLER FASHION CTR); 480.821.5800; M-SA 10-9, SU 11-6; FREE PARKING

Changing Hands Bookstore

"...a great, eclectic bookstore with just about every topic you can think of... a nice selection of new and used books and unique gifts... offers summer classes in writing, Spanish, scrapbooking and arts and crafts... events such as storytelling with costumed characters and animal tales with live creatures from the zoo... lots of book signings... be sure to sign up for their monthly e-newsletter... there is a cafe connected to the store that has yummy food and baked goods... friendly atmosphere..."

Customer service .... ❹ $$ .... Prices

Age range .... 6 mths to 5 yrs

WWW.CHANGINGHANDS.COM

TEMPE—6428 S MCCLINTOCK DR (AT E GUADALUPE RD); 480.730.0205; M-F 10-9, SA 9-9, SU 10-7; FREE PARKING

Childsplay

"...great original performances... kids just stare with their mouths open... these guys are great at what they do... convenient show times make it an easy trip with kids..."

Customer service .... ❸ $$ .... Prices

Age range .... 4 yrs and up

WWW.CHILDSPLAYAZ.ORG

TEMPE—132 E 6TH ST (AT MYRTLE AVE); 480.350.8101; CHECK SCHEDULE ONLINE; FREE PARKING

Chuck E Cheese's

"...lots of games, rides, playrooms and very greasy food... the kids can play and eat and parents can unwind a little... a good rainy day activity... the kids love the food, but it's a bit greasy for adults... always crowded and crazy—but that's half the fun... can you ever go wrong with pizza, games and singing?... although they do have a salad bar for adults, remember, you're not going for the food—you're going because your kids will love it... just about the easiest birthday party around—just pay money and show up..."

Customer service .... ❸ $$ .... Prices

Age range .... 12 mths to 7 yrs

WWW.CHUCKECHEESE.COM

MESA—856 S ALMA SCHOOL RD (AT W 8TH AVE); 480.834.9322; SU-TH 9-10, F-SA 9-11

Desert Schools Coyotes Center

WWW.DESERTSCHOOLSCOYOTESCENTER.COM

CHANDLER—7225 W HARRISON ST (AT N 56TH ST); 480.598.9400; CHECK SCHEDULE ONLINE

Dugans Dairy Farm

"...a really neat tour... now my girls really know where milk comes from... no strollers allowed inside so be ready to carry your kid at least part of the way... lots of tractors for boys to gawk at... only $5 per person... fun and educational..."

Customer service .... ❸ $$$ .... Prices

Age range .... 3 yrs and up

WWW.DUGANSDAIRY.COM

CHANDLER—2481 S DOBSON RD (AT CHUPAROSA PARK); 480.899.8795; CHECK SCHEDULE ONLINE; FREE PARKING

East Valley Children's Theatre

"...although the really little kids can't participate, their performances are great fun for toddlers to watch... community theater at its best—the quality of the shows varies, but it's always a fun outing with my girls..."

Customer service........................❹ $$$....................................Prices
Age range....................8 yrs and up

WWW.EVCT.ORG

MESA—6640 E TONTO ST (AT N 66TH PL); 480.756.3828; M-F 9-5

Fiddlesticks Family Fun Park

"...a huge play land for kids... definitely more to do for bigger kids... go-carts, miniature golf, video arcade... way to much stimulation for little brains—be prepared for a meltdown when you go and a nap in the car on the way home... you pay per ride..."

Customer service........................❸ $$$....................................Prices
Age range....................2 yrs and up

WWW.FIDDLESTICKSAZ.COM

TEMPE—1155 W ELLIOTT RD (AT SPORTS AUTHORITY PL); 480.961.0800; HOURS VARY, CALL FOR SCHEDULE

Folley Pool

"...a nice big pool... I love watching my kids jump off the diving boards—they are giddy with excitement... nice wading pool and water playground with water spraying in all directions... nice and shallow so it's easy for me to swim with my baby..."

Customer service........................❸ $$$....................................Prices
Age range.................6 mths and up

WWW.CHANDLERAZ.ORG

CHANDLER—600 E FAIRVIEW (OFF S BOGLE AVE); 480.732.1063; CHECK SCHEDULE ONLINE

Girly Girlz Tea & Trinkets

WWW.GIRLY-GIRLZ.COM/

MESA—3426 E BASELINE (AT DANA PARK SHOPPES); 480.503.4832

Golfland Sunsplash

"...part of the Golfland chain of miniature golf and amusement centers... fun place to spend a day in the summer... arcade, outdoor pool, slides, bumper boats and race cars... be attentive with your little ones as this a popular hangout for older kids and teenagers..."

Customer service........................❸ $$$....................................Prices

WWW.GOLFLAND.COM

MESA—155 W HAMPTON AVE (AT COUNTRY CLUB DR); 480.834.8319; M-F 8:30-5; PARKING LOT

Gymboree Play & Music

"...we've done several rounds of classes with our kids and they absolutely love it... colorful, padded environment with tons of things to climb and play on... a good indoor place to meet other families and for kids to learn how to play with each other... the equipment and play areas are generally neat and clean... an easy birthday party spot... a guaranteed nap after class... costs vary, so call before showing up..."

Customer service........................❹ $$$....................................Prices
Age range....................birth to 5 yrs

WWW.GYMBOREE.COM

AHWATUKEE—4025 E CHANDLER BLVD (AT MOUNTAINSIDE PLZ); 480.963.1756; CHECK SCHEDULE ONLINE

CHANDLER—2160 W CHANDLER BLVD (AT BOULEVARD CTR); 480.894.9611; CHECK SCHEDULE ONLINE; FREE PARKING

MESA—5654 E MAIN ST (AT VELDA ROSE CTR); 480.632.9022; CHECK SCHEDULE ONLINE; FREE PARKING

Jeepers

"...they have a ton of video games and a few rides—flying bananas, bumper cars, Himalaya, monkey barrels and a train... plus, a tube for climbing and crawling... you can buy a wristband for unlimited use of the rides... awesome birthday parties... the snack bar serves up pizza, hot dogs and other 'standard' amusement park fare..."

Customer service .... ❸ $$ .... Prices

Age range .... 2 yrs to 12 yrs

WWW.JEEPERS.COM

MESA—2726 S ALMA SCHOOL RD (AT W GUADALUPE RD); 480.820.8300; M-TH 10-9, F-SA 10-10, SU 11-8; FREE PARKING

Jewish Community Center

"...programs vary from facility to facility, but most JCCs have outstanding early childhood programs... everything from mom and me music classes to arts and crafts for older kids... a wonderful place to meet other parents and make new friends... class fees are cheaper (if not free) for members, but still quite a good deal for nonmembers... a superb resource for new families looking for fun..."

Customer service .... ❹ $$$ .... Prices

Age range .... 3 mths and up

WWW.EVJCC.ORG

TEMPE—1521 S INDIAN BEND RD (AT E GRANADA DR); 480.897.0588; CHECK SCHEDULE ONLINE

Kiwanis Park Recreation Center

"...a nice place to relax... they also have lots of activities and classes for children... good swimming lessons—our baby really enjoyed the water and the girl teaching the class was great... you can feed ducks and have a picnic... perfect on a hot day—plenty of water to cool off in..."

Customer service .... ❹ $ .... Prices

Age range .... 6 mths and up

WWW.TEMPE.GOV/PKREC/KRC

TEMPE—6111 S ALL AMERICAN WY (AT KIWANIS PARK); 480.350.5201; CHECK SCHEDULE ONLINE; PARKING AVAILABLE

Little Gym, The

"...a well thought-out program of gym and tumbling geared toward different age groups... a clean facility, excellent and knowledgeable staff... we love the small-sized gym equipment and their willingness to work with kids with special needs... activities are fun and personalized to match the kids' age... great place for birthday parties with a nice party room—they'll organize and do everything for you..."

Customer service .... ❹ $$$ .... Prices

Age range .... 4 mths to 12 yrs

WWW.THELITTLEGYM.COM

CHANDLER—6125 W CHANDLER BLVD (AT KYRENE VLG SHOPPING CTR); 480.705.8040; CALL FOR SCHEDULE; FREE PARKING

Makutu's Island

“...a nice alternative when it's scorching hot outside... really big place... has a cafe with a variety of food to eat... remember to bring socks... a fun place for playing with your kids—some areas are big enough for adults to crawl into... surprisingly clean... lots of colorful tubes and pipes and the whole floor is padded... birthday parties are totally coordinated by the staff which lets mom and dad actually enjoy the party... the best indoor playroom in town...”

Customer service........................❹ $$$..Prices

Age range...............6 mths to 12 yrs

WWW.MAKUTUSISLAND.COM

CHANDLER—6919 W RAY RD (AT 56TH ST); 480.893.0106; SU-TH 10-7, F-SA 10-9 ; FREE PARKING

Mesa Art Center

“...beautiful new facility offering performing arts, visual arts and arts education...check web site or call to see if there are any performances or classes geared toward younger children...nice place to walk around and see the gardens ...”

Customer service........................❸ $$$..Prices

Age range....................3 yrs and up

WWW.MESAARTSCENTER.COM

MESA—155 N CENTER ST (AT 1ST ST); 480.644.6500; CHECK SCHEDULE ONLINE

Music Together

“...the best mom and baby classes out there... music, singing, dancing—even instruments for tots to play with... liberal make-up policy, great venues, take home books, CDs and tapes which are different each semester... it's a national franchise so instructors vary and have their own style... different age groups get mixed up which makes it a good learning experience for all involved... the highlight of our week—grandma always comes along... be prepared to have your tot sing the songs at home, in the car—everywhere...”

Customer service........................❹ $$$..Prices

Age range................ 2 mths to 5 yrs

WWW.MUSICTOGETHER.COM

CHANDLER—623.374.9509; CALL FOR SCHEDULE

CHANDLER—4500 S BASHA RD (OFF S ALMA SCHOOL RD); 480.699.6871; CALL FOR SCHEDULE

GILBERT—623.374.9509; CALL FOR SCHEDULE

Pecos Pool

Age range.................3 mths and up

AHWATUKEE—17010 S 48TH ST (AT E PECOS RD); 602.534.9255; CALL FOR SCHEDULE

Place Music Academy

“...music education and fun for all ages... parent participation classes for the really little ones and more independent groups for the older ones... topnotch instruction—the teachers know how to teach and make it fun at the same time...”

Customer service........................❸ $$$..Prices

Age range............... 12 mths and up

WWW.PLACEMUSIC.COM

MESA—1220 S ALMA SCHOOL RD (AT W SOUTHERN AVE); 602.678.5850; CHECK SCHEDULE ONLINE

Play In Place

"...costumes, play kitchens, cars—lots for kids to go crazy over... the hardest part is leaving without anyone crying... an easy birthday party—they do most of the work and you just show up... play session is about $7 per kid..."

Customer service .... ❸ $ .... Prices
Age range .... 6 mths to 6 yrs
WWW.PLAYINPLACECENTER.COM
GILBERT—655 N GILBERT RD (AT E OLIVE AVE); 480.892.4122; M-F 9-12; FREE PARKING

Pump It Up

"...huge warehouse type buildings filled with a variety of bounce houses and inflatable obstacle courses... colorful, padded slides and bouncers... the birthday party I went to was a blast—kids and adults were having way too much fun... they have an open gym a couple of days a week for $5 per tot—a great way to jump around and burn off some energy... $200-$250 for a really easy party that will have everybody smiling..."

Customer service .... ❹ $$ .... Prices
Age range .... 2 yrs to 12 yrs
WWW.PUMPITUPPARTY.COM
TEMPE—1325 W AUTO DR (AT S HARDY DR); 480.940.7867; CHECK SCHEDULE ONLINE

Schnepf Farms

"...fun and more importantly educational... there's so much to do out here—interact with animals, learn how vegetables grow, baking, playing... the kids club is a great way to expose your children to the wonders of nature... very well organized and a great family outing... pick your own fruits and vegetables, go home and enjoy a delicious meal..."

Customer service .... ❸ $$$ .... Prices
Age range ....6 mths and up
WWW.SCHNEPFFARMS.COM
QUEEN CREEK—22601 E CLOUD RD (AT E RIGGS RD); 480.987.3100; CHECK SCHEDULE ONLINE

Southeast Regional Library

"...offers Spanish classes for children...puppet shows, movie nights, story time and arts and crafts...call for registration information or visit web site+D85..."

Customer service .... ❸ $ .... Prices
Age range ....6 mths and up
WWW.CI.GILBERT.AZ.US/LIBRARY
GILBERT—775 N GREENFIELD RD (AT GUADALUPE RD); 480.539.5100; M-TH 9-9, F-SA 9-5, SU 1-5; FREE PARKING

Southwest Museum Foundation

"...a great museum with lots to look at... the dinosaur exhibit is very popular with the little people... nicely air conditioned in the summer... one of the best museums in the Valley—the renovations have tripled its size... dinosaurs, rocks, paintings, Arizona history, Mexican history, etc... $6 for adults; under 2 free..."

Customer service .... ❹ $ .... Prices
Age range .... 2 yrs and up
WWW.CITYOFMESA.ORG/SWMUSEUM/INFO.ASP

MESA—53 N MACDONALD MESA (AT W MAIN ST); 480.898.0907; T-SA 10-5, SU 1-5; FREE PARKING

Tempe Historical Museum

"...not really interesting for little kids... it's a nice museum, but my 3 year old got bored pretty quickly... lots of natural history and Tempe history here... admission is free..."

Customer service........................❸ $$$.....................................Prices
Age range....................4 yrs and up

WWW.TEMPE.GOV/MUSEUM

TEMPE—809 E SOUTHERN AVE (AT S RURAL RD); M-TH 10-5, SA 10-5, SU 1-5

USA Skateland

WWW.USA-SKATING.COM

CHANDLER—1101 W RAY RD (AT N ALMA SCHOOL RD); 480.917.9444; CHECK SCHEDULE ONLINE

MESA—7 E SOUTHERN AVE (AT S MESA DR); 480.833.7775; CHECK SCHEDULE ONLINE

Westcor Kids Club

WWW.WESTCOR.COM

MESA—1445 W SOUTHERN AVE (AT FIESTA MALL); 480.833.5587; 2ND & 4TH M 10AM; MALL PARKING

MESA—6555 E SOUTHERN AVE (AT SUPERSTITION SPRINGS CENTER); 480.832.0212; TH 10AM; MALL PARKING

YMCA

"...most of the Ys in the area have classes and activities for kids... swimming, gym classes, dance—even play groups for the really little ones... ... some facilities are nicer than others, but in general their programs are worth checking out... prices are more than reasonable for what is offered... the best bang for your buck... they have it all—great programs that meet the needs of a diverse range of families... check out their camps during the summer and school breaks..."

Customer service........................❹ $$.......................................Prices
Age range.................3 mths and up

WWW.VALLEYYMCA.ORG

MESA—207 N MESA DR (AT E 2ND ST); 480.969.8166; CHECK SCHEDULE ONLINE

TEMPE—7070 S RURAL RD (AT E BELL DE MAR DR); 480.730.4523; CHECK SCHEDULE ONLINE; FREE PARKING

West Valley

"lila picks"

★Wildlife World Zoo

Barnes & Noble

"...wonderful weekly story times for all ages and frequent author visits for older kids... lovely selection of books and the story times are fun and very well done... they have evening story times—we put our kids in their pjs and come here as a treat before bedtime... they read a story, and then usually have a little craft or related coloring project... times vary by location so give them a call..."

Customer service .... ❹ $ .... Prices

Age range .... 6 mths to 6 yrs

WWW.BARNESANDNOBLE.COM

GOODYEAR—1446 N LITCHFIELD RD (AT MCDOWELL RD); 623.935.0128; CALL FOR SCHEDULE

Borders Books

"...very popular weekly story time held in most branches (check the web site for locations and times)... call before you go since they are very popular and get extremely crowded... kids love the unique blend of songs, stories and dancing... Mr. Hatbox's appearances are a delight to everyone (unfortunately he doesn't make appearances at all locations)... large children's section is well categorized and well priced... they make it fun for young tots to browse through the board-book section by hanging toys around the shelves... the low-key cafe is a great place to have coffee with your baby and leaf through some magazines..."

Customer service .... ❹ $ .... Prices

Age range .... 6 mths to 6 yrs

WWW.BORDERSSTORES.COM

AVONDALE—10100 W MCDOWELL RD (AT N 99TH AVE); 623.478.9880; CALL FOR SCHEDULE

Music Together

"...the best mom and baby classes out there... music, singing, dancing—even instruments for tots to play with... liberal make-up policy, great venues, take home books, CDs and tapes which are different each semester... it's a national franchise so instructors vary and have their own style... different age groups get mixed up which makes it a good learning experience for all involved... the highlight of our week—grandma always comes along... be prepared to have your tot sing the songs at home, in the car—everywhere..."

Customer service .... ❹ $$$ .... Prices

Age range .... 2 mths to 5 yrs

WWW.MUSICTOGETHER.COM

LITCHFIELD PARK—623.935.5313; CALL FOR SCHEDULE

LITCHFIELD PARK—1157 E ACACIA CIRCLE (AT CAMELBACK PARK); 623.935.5313; CALL FOR SCHEDULE

Wildlife World Zoo

“...this zoo is unique because they let you feed the giraffes and some of the birds... a very 'hands on' zoo which makes all the difference with little children... the perfect place to spend family time—it's educational too... the train ride was fun and the animals are fairly close... the zoo is laid out nicely and the yearly passes are a great idea—one pass pays for itself on the second visit... regular admission: adults $15, 2 and under free...”

Customer service........................❹ $$..Prices
Age range.................6 mths and up

WWW.WILDLIFEWORLD.COM

LITCHFIELD PARK—16501 W NORTHERN AVE (AT ESTRELLA PKWY); 623.935.9453; DAILY 9-5

parks & playgrounds

Central Phoenix

"lila picks"

★Cortez Park

★Encanto Park

★Steele Indian School Park

Acoma Park

"...this park is alright to take the kids to run around... it's in a residential neighborhood, so traffic surrounding the park isn't so bad... there's an exercise course, picnic area, playground, and soccer..."

Equipment/play structures............❹ ❹..............................Maintenance

WWW.PHOENIX.GOV/PRL/PARKSMAIN.HTML

PHOENIX—39TH AVE (AT W ACOMA DR); 602.262.6575

Altadena Park

"...nice small park... playground, picnic area, and a spray pad..."

Equipment/play structures............❸ ❸..............................Maintenance

WWW.PHOENIX.GOV/PRL/PARKSMAIN.HTML

PHOENIX—ALTADENA AVE (AT N 37TH AVE); 602.262.6696

Buffalo Ridge Park

"...basketball, playground, restrooms, and softball field... playground is fairly clean, but needs better shade..."

Equipment/play structures............❸ ❸..............................Maintenance

WWW.PHOENIX.GOV/PRL/PARKSMAIN.HTML

PHOENIX—E WESCOTT DR (AT 16TH ST); 602.262.6696

Cactus Park

"...I like the play area and my son loves to feed the ducks and geese that have made this park home... there are tennis courts, and a pool that offers lessons during the summer months... basic park w/lots of grass/room for pets, leashed of course... slides, swings and climbing equipment... basic pool..."

Equipment/play structures............❹ ❹..............................Maintenance

WWW.PHOENIX.GOV/PRL/PARKSMAIN.HTML

PHOENIX—3801 W CACTUS RD (BTWN 37TH AND 39TH AVES); 602.262.6575

Cashman Park

"...a smaller park, but it works... shaded playground, ramadas with tables/grills, two lit basketball courts, two lit sand volleyball courts, a playfield, restrooms and drinking fountain..."

Equipment/play structures............❸ ❸..............................Maintenance

WWW.PHOENIX.GOV/PRL/PARKSMAIN.HTML

PHOENIX—22222 N 44TH ST (AT N 44TH ST)

Central Park

"...ball field, basketball, picnic area, playground, recreation building, restrooms, spray pad, volleyball... nice park, but could use more shade..."

Equipment/play structures .... ❸ ❹ .... Maintenance

WWW.PHOENIX.GOV/PRL/PARKSMAIN.HTML

PHOENIX—1202 S 3RD ST (AT E BUCKEYE RD); 602.262.6798

Cholla Cove Park

"...you will see every kind of dog at this park... a sleepy little off-the-beaten path park... never very crowded... has monkey bars with slides, swings for babies and older kids, a basketball court, beach volleyball court and open grassy field... frequented mostly by neighborhood kids and dog walkers... see the occasional Dad practicing sports with his kids... not as big as Cactus Park, but a nice, secret find for the area... most people don't seem to know about this place..."

Equipment/play structures .... ❸ ❸ .... Maintenance

WWW.PHOENIX.GOV/PARKS/PARK41.HTML

PHOENIX—4121 E LUPINE AVE (AT N 41ST AVE); 602.262.6696

Coronado Park

WWW.PHOENIX.GOV/PRL/PARKSMAIN.HTML

PHOENIX—CORONADO RD (AT N 12TH ST); 602.256.3220

Cortez Park

"...a fun place to feed the ducks... nice size playground too for all ages... the location is starting to get a bit iffy, but the playground is large and fun and families bring their children after school on weekdays... this park is super clean, and there are always available swings and slides for the kids..."

Equipment/play structures .... ❹ ❹ .... Maintenance

WWW.PHOENIX.GOV/PRL/PARKSMAIN.HTML

PHOENIX—N 35TH AVE (AT DUNLAP AVE); 602.262.6575

Desert Horizon Park

"...wonderful place to meet other parents... baseball, basketball, exercise course, picnic area, playground, restrooms, softball, volleyball, ramadas..."

Equipment/play structures .... ❸ ❸ .... Maintenance

WWW.PHOENIX.GOV/PRL/PARKSMAIN.HTML

PHOENIX—16002 N 56TH ST (E PARADISE LN); 602.262.6696

Desert West Park

"...awesome park... if you love to skateboard this is a great place to go... plethora of activities to sign kids up for... great play area... skate park basketball courts inside and out... lake and baseball diamonds... staff friendly and from the neighborhood... they know the kids by name if they come in often... ..."

Equipment/play structures .... ❹ ❹ .... Maintenance

WWW.PHOENIX.GOV/PRL/PARKSMAIN.HTML

PHOENIX—6602 W ENCANTO BLVD (AT N 65TH ST); 602.495.3700

El Oso Park

"...amphitheater, archery range, basketball, picnic area and ramada, playground, restrooms, soccer, softball, sand volleyball court, sprinkler... not in the best area, but lots of space..."

Equipment/play structures .... ❹ ❸ .... Maintenance

WWW.PHOENIX.GOV/PRL/PARKSMAIN.HTML

PHOENIX—75TH AVE (AT OSBORN RD); 602.262.4539

Encanto Park

"...such a cool park—they even have a little amusement park for kids ages 1 to 5... the best part is Enchanted Island with a train, carousel and carnival rides and open on weekends and holidays... the main park has 2 playgrounds and paddleboats on the lake... great place to have a birthday party... love the park entertainment... during the summer the amusement park is only open on the weekends in the evenings..."

Equipment/play structures........... ❹ ❸ .... Maintenance

WWW.PHOENIX.GOV/PRL/PARKSMAIN.HTML

PHOENIX—15TH AVE (AT W ENCANTO BLVD); 602.261.8993

Granada Park

"...love the pond, although the geese are a little aggressive... tons of room to run... lots of dogs... elevated city park, I'm told you can see a great fireworks show from there... nice lake, quiet park..."

Equipment/play structures........... ❹ ❹ .... Maintenance

WWW.PHOENIX.GOV/PRL/PARKSMAIN.HTML

PHOENIX—6505 N 20TH ST (AT E STELLA LN); 602.262.6696

Horse Lovers Park

"...three arenas with a picnic area... very fun if you like riding horses or watching them... there's also special events like hayrides, kid rodeos, and trail rides put on by Park and Rec..."

Equipment/play structures........... ❸ ❺ .... Maintenance

HTTP://PHOENIX.GOV/PARKS/PHXEQUCT.HTML

PHOENIX—19224 N TATUM BLVD (14 MI N OF BELL RD)

Hoshoni Park

"...small neighborhood park... nice playground equipment... lots of space to run... basketball and volleyball, no baseball field..."

Equipment/play structures........... ❹ ❸ .... Maintenance

WWW.PHOENIX.GOV/PRL/PARKSMAIN.HTML

PHOENIX—39TH AVE (AT BUTLER DR); 602.262.6575

Indian Bend Park

"...a really beautiful park... lots to see and very peaceful as well as educational... basketball court, picnic tables/grills, tennis courts..."

Equipment/play structures........... ❸ ❺ .... Maintenance

WWW.PHOENIX.GOV/PRL/PARKSMAIN.HTML

PHOENIX—37TH PL (AT E THUNDERBIRD RD); 602.262.6696

Japanese Friendship Garden

"...a lovely peaceful garden to stroll through, my children love the koi pond...check web site for schedule..."

Equipment/play structures........... ❸ ❸ .... Maintenance

WWW.ASAHI-NET.OR.JP/~UW7G-BWR/GARDEN/GARDEN.HTM

PHOENIX—1125 N 3RD AVE (IN MARGARET T HANCE PARK); 602.262.6412; FREE PARKING

Madison Park

WWW.PHOENIX.GOV/PRL/PARKSMAIN.HTML

PHOENIX—16TH ST (AT GLENROSA AVE); 602.495.0215

Margaret T. Hance Park

"...I love this park, it is beautiful!..."

Equipment/play structures........... ❹ ❹ .... Maintenance

WWW.PHOENIX.GOV/PRL/PARKSMAIN.HTML

PHOENIX—1134 N CENTRAL AVE (AT E PORTLAND ST); 602.534.2406

Marivue Park

WWW.PHOENIX.GOV/PRL/PARKSMAIN.HTML

PHOENIX—N 55TH AVE (AT W OSBORN RD); 602.262.4539

Mercury Mine Basin

"...clean playground... large grassy picnic area in the center and a nice oval shape walking path...I like it because it is very open and I can see my children from all parts of the park... parking is a pain since you can't park on the street until after 6pm..."

Equipment/play structures .... ❸ ❸ .... Maintenance

WWW.PHOENIX.GOV/PRL/PARKSMAIN.HTML

PHOENIX—3335 E MOUNTAIN VIEW RD (AT N 32ND ST); 602.262.6696

Moon Valley Park

"...basketball, exercise course, gazebo, playground, ramada, and picnic area, restrooms, soccer, tennis, volleyball..."

Equipment/play structures .... ❹ ❹ .... Maintenance

WWW.PHOENIX.GOV/PRL/PARKSMAIN.HTML

PHOENIX—7TH AVE (AT CORAL GABLES DR); 602.262.6575

Mountain View Park

"...lots of homeless people make their home here... not really a place for families to go..."

Equipment/play structures .... ❸ ❸ .... Maintenance

WWW.PHOENIX.GOV/PRL/PARKSMAIN.HTML

PHOENIX—7TH AVE (AT W CINNABAR AVE); 602.262.6575

Norton Park

"...plenty of facilities there, but this park in the heart of Sunnyslope is not really a safe place for families to hang out..."

Equipment/play structures .... ❷ ❷ .... Maintenance

WWW.PHOENIX.GOV/PRL/PARKSMAIN.HTML

PHOENIX—1224 E HATCHER RD (AT N 12TH PL); 602.262.6696

Orme Park

WWW.PHOENIX.GOV/PRL/PARKSMAIN.HTML

PHOENIX—47TH AVE (AT OSBORN RD); 602.262.4539

Palma Park

"...the park itself is pretty big, but the playground there is small... the park is known more for soccer and basketball... restrooms are hardly ever open..."

Equipment/play structures .... ❸ ❸ .... Maintenance

WWW.PHOENIX.GOV/PRL/PARKSMAIN.HTML

PHOENIX—N 12TH ST (AT E DUNLAP AVE); 602.262.6696

Papago Park

HTTP://PHOENIX.GOV/PARKS/PAPAGO.HTML

PHOENIX—GALVIN PKWY (E VAN BUREN ST); 602.256.3220

Paradise Valley Park

"...lots of activities offered here at the park and community center/pool... the pool has areas for the young ones to play in, and offers a lot of activities for young children in the summertime—be sure to check their calendar..."

Equipment/play structures .... ❹ ❹ .... Maintenance

WWW.PHOENIX.GOV/PRL/PARKSMAIN.HTML

PHOENIX—17642 N 40TH ST (AT PARADISE VALLEY PARK); 602.262.6696

Patriots Square Park

"...a great place to get away from the office on those nice weather days... there's a "farmer's market" on Wednesdays, however it's mostly crafts and convenience foods... if homeless people around the stage and grassy seating area make you feel a bit uncomfortable, just don't go to that side... police are almost always present..."

Equipment/play structures........... ❸ ❸ ....Maintenance

WWW.PHOENIX.GOV/PRL/PARKSMAIN.HTML

PHOENIX—CENTRAL AVE (AT E WASHINGTON ST); 602.495.3797

Piestewa Peak Park

"...Phoenix's Central Park... it's unique to our city... many different levels of trails, something to suit everyone... bring your kids and your dogs, though no dogs are allowed on the main peak trail..."

Equipment/play structures........... ❺ ❺ ....Maintenance

WWW.PHOENIX.GOV/PRL/PARKSMAIN.HTML

PHOENIX—2701 E SQUAW PEAK LN (AT N 24TH PL & E LINCOLN); 602.262.7901

Roadrunner Park

"...baseball, basketball, lagoon, playground, pool, ramadas and picnic area, restrooms, soccer, softball, tennis, volleyball... there's a pond with ducks and geese... also has a farmer's market on Saturdays..."

Equipment/play structures........... ❹ ❹ ....Maintenance

WWW.PHOENIX.GOV/PRL/PARKSMAIN.HTML

PHOENIX—3502 E CACTUS RD (AT N 35TH ST); 602.262.6696

Sereno Park

"...facilities include baseball/softball diamond, horse arena, picnic area, playground, and restrooms..."

Equipment/play structures........... ❹ ❹ ....Maintenance

WWW.PHOENIX.GOV/PRL/PARKSMAIN.HTML

PHOENIX—N 56TH ST (AT SWEETWATER AVE); 602.262.6696

Steele Indian School Park

"...the cleanest and best park in the city!!!... includes a 2.5 acre lake, two playgrounds, one for kids age 2-5 and the other for older kids. very cool!... this is a newer park in Phoenix... a beautiful park with hills for the kids to climb, a nicely laid-out playground with age-appropriate equipment, and a lot of items surrounding native American culture..."

Equipment/play structures........... ❹ ❺ ....Maintenance

WWW.PHOENIX.GOV/PRL/PARKSMAIN.HTML

PHOENIX—3RD ST (AT INDIAN SCHOOL RD); 602.495.0739

Sueno Park

"...basketball, exercise course, picnic area, playground, restrooms, soccer, youth softball, volleyball (sand), Ramada..."

Equipment/play structures........... ❸ ❷ ....Maintenance

WWW.PHOENIX.GOV/PRL/PARKSMAIN.HTML

PHOENIX—N 43RD AVE (AT W ENCANTO BLVD); 602.262.4539

Surrey Park

"...nice little neighborhood park... good playground equipment, across from school... picnic area and ramada..."

Equipment/play structures........... ❹ ❸ ....Maintenance

WWW.PHOENIX.GOV/PRL/PARKSMAIN.HTML

PHOENIX—W JOAN DE ARC AVE (AT N 39TH AVE); 602.262.6575

Washington Park

WWW.PHOENIX.GOV/PRL/PARKSMAIN.HTML

PHOENIX—23RD AVE AND MARYLAND AVE (AT W MARYLAND AVE); 602.262.6971

Werner's Field

"...nice clean park... lots of playground equipment and benches for parents... no restrooms..."

Equipment/play structures .... ❸ ❸ .... Maintenance

WWW.PHOENIX.GOV/PRL/PARKSMAIN.HTML

PHOENIX—7TH AVE AND GROVERS AVE (AT W GROVERS AVE); 602.262.6575

Northwest Valley

Anthem Community Park

"...great place to take your children—lots of slides, sand and they also have a little water park inside the play park... they have a train that you can ride (for a small fee if you're not a resident of Anthem)—my son loves it!..."

Equipment/play structures........... ❹ ❺ ....Maintenance

WWW.PHOENIX.GOV/PARKS

ANTHEM—3500 W ANTHEM WY (AT N GAVILION PEAK PKWY); 888.233.5932

Bicentennial Park

WWW.SURPRISEAZ.COM

SURPRISE—15705 N NASH ST (OFF SANTA FE DR); 623.266.4500

Community Park

"...great city park with a lake, playground, basketball courts, tennis courts, volleyball sand courts, pool on one side and county library on the other side, a fenced dog park coming soon as well as a special needs park in the future... across Bullard is the Surprise Recreation Campus featuring the spring training facilities of the Texas Rangers and Kansas City Royals, and soccer fields..."

Equipment/play structures........... ❺ ❺ ....Maintenance

WWW.SURPRISEAZ.COM

SURPRISE—15930 N BULLARD AVE (AT W GREENWAY RD); 623.266.4500; FREE PARKING

Rio Vista Community Park

"...beautiful new park!... has a lake you can fish in, large ramadas, volleyball courts, playground and tot lot, a great splash park, as well as a walking/jogging path... clean for the most part... there's a skate park for the older kids..."

Equipment/play structures........... ❷ ❸ ....Maintenance

WWW.PEORIAAZ.COM

PEORIA—8866 W THUNDERBIRD RD (OFF LOOP 101); 623.773.7137

Sunrise Pool and Family Center

WWW.PEORIAAZ.COM

PEORIA—21321 N 86TH DR (AT W LONE CACTUS DR); 623.773.7513; CHECK SCHEDULE ONLINE

Surprise Aquatic Center

WWW.SURPRISEAZ.COM

SURPRISE—15831 N BULLARD AVE (OFF W GREENWAY RD); 623.266.4644

Northeast Valley

"lila picks"

★ Cactus Park

★ McCormick-Stillman Railroad Park

parks & playgrounds

Cactus Park

"...this place is huge... in addition to a great playground and big open field, they also have a pool, sand volleyball court, and gazebos you can rent for parties... we come here so my husband can work out while we play... clean and very well maintained... check out the pool too—it's cheap and the perfect way to cool off after a long playground visit..."

Equipment/play structures .... ❹ ❹ .... Maintenance

WWW.SCOTTSDALEAZ.GOV/PARKS/CACTUS

SCOTTSDALE—7202 E CACTUS RD (AT SCOTTSDALE RD); 480.312.7961; SUNRISE TO10:30; FREE PARKING

Chesnutt Park

"...nice park, with lots of space to run around or play games... five acres with picnic areas, two ramadas, two lighted tennis courts, two basketball courts, a playground, a spray pad, large open grass areas and restroom facilities..."

Equipment/play structures .... ❸ ❸ .... Maintenance

WWW.SCOTTSDALEAZ.GOV

SCOTTSDALE—4565 N GRANITE REEF (AT E MINNEZONA AVE); 480.312.7275; DAILY SUNRISE-10:30

Comanche Park

WWW.SCOTTSDALEAZ.GOV

SCOTTSDALE—7639 PASEO DEL NORTE (1/2 MI N OF MCCORMICK PKWY); DAILY SUNRISE-10:30

Grayhawk Neighborhood Park

WWW.SCOTTSDALEAZ.GOV

SCOTTSDALE—20726 N 76TH ST (AT GRAYHAWK DR); 480.312.7275; DAILY SUNRISE-10:30

Horizon Park

WWW.SCOTTSDALEAZ.GOV

SCOTTSDALE—15444 N 100TH ST (AT 100TH ST AND THOMPSON PARK); 480.312.2650; DAILY SUNRISE-10:30

Ironwood Park

WWW.SCOTTSDALEAZ.GOV

SCOTTSDALE—18650 N 94TH ST (OFF 94TH ST AND UNION HILLS); 480.312.7275; DAILY SUNRISE-10:30

McCormick-Stillman Railroad Park

"...my children's favorite park...they love to ride on the trains and the carousel...the playground is very nice because they have different size equipment for different ages...they have a spray area as well... lots of grass for picnics and birthday parties...great place to meet other moms..."

Equipment/play structures........... ❺ ❺ .... Maintenance

WWW.THERAILROADPARK.COM

SCOTTSDALE—7301 E INDIAN BEND RD (AT SCOTTSDALE RD); 480.312.2312; CHECK ONLINE; FREE PARKING

Mescal Park

WWW.SCOTTSDALEAZ.GOV

SCOTTSDALE—11015 N 68TH PLACE (AT E MESCAL ST); 480.312.7275; DAILY SUNRISE-10:30

Mountain View Park

WWW.SCOTTSDALEAZ.GOV

SCOTTSDALE—8625 E MOUNTAIN VIEW (OFF HAYDEN); 480.312.2584; DAILY SUNRISE-10:30; PARKING LOT

Northsight Park

WWW.SCOTTSDALEAZ.GOV

SCOTTSDALE —8400 E THUNDERBIRD RD (OFF 84TH ST); 480.312.7275; DAILY SUNRISE-10:30; PARKING LOT

Osborn Park

WWW.SCOTTSDALEAZ.GOV

SCOTTSDALE—7775 E OSBORN RD (OFF MILLER); 480.312.2771; PARKING LOT

Pima Park

WWW.SCOTTSDALEAZ.GOV

SCOTTSDALE—8600 E THOMAS RD (OFF N 86TH ST); 480.312.7275; DAILY SUNRISE-10:30; PARKING LOT

Rio Montana Park

WWW.SCOTTSDALEAZ.GOV

SCOTTSDALE—11180 N 132ND ST (SW OF VIA LINDA AND 130TH ST); 480.312.7275; DAILY SUNRISE-10:30; PARKING LOT

Southeast Valley

"lila picks"

★ Desert Breeze Park and Railroad

★ Freestone Park

parks & playgrounds

Arrowhead Meadows Pool

WWW.CHANDLERAZ.ORG

CHANDLER—1475 E ERIE ST (OFF N ALMA SCHOOL RD); 480.732.1064; CHECK SCHEDULE ONLINE

Chuparosa Park and Spray Pad

"...nice community park, one of the largest in the area... spray pad has one ground spray, run-through rings, and a candy cane shaped shower... it also has a big playground, restrooms and covered picnic areas... not a lot of shade though so be sure to bring hats or an umbrella ..."

Equipment/play structures .... ❸ ❺ .... Maintenance

WWW.CHANDLEAZ.GOV

CHANDLER—2400 S DOBSON RD (AT W GERMANN RD); 480.782.2704

Desert Breeze Park and Railroad Park

★★★★★

"...wonderful, clean, safe (though outdated) playground equipment... great for ages 2-10... the splash park is wonderful... carousel, snack bar... fun train that goes around the park only operates on weekends... top notch, very poular park..."

Equipment/play structures .... ❹ ❹ .... Maintenance

WWW.GF.STATE.AZ.US

CHANDLER—660 N DESERT BREEZE BLVD (OFF RAY RD AND MCCLINTOCK DR); 480.782.2727; DAILY 6-10:30; PARKING LOT

Espee Park & Spray Pad

"...spray pad operates seasonally—call for schedule..."

Equipment/play structures .... ❸ ❺ .... Maintenance

WWW.CHANDLERAZ.GOV

CHANDLER—450 E KNOX RD (AT N ARIZONA AVE); 480.782.2750

Folley Pool

"...has kiddie slide, sprays, wading pool... bring a cooler for drinks and snacks because there is no concession stand..."

Equipment/play structures .... ❸ ❸ .... Maintenance

WWW.CHANDLERAZ.ORG

CHANDLER—600 E FAIRVIEW (OFF S BOGLE AVE); 480.732.1063; CHECK SCHEDULE ONLINE

Freestone Park

“...a huge park complete with a train, ponds, play equipment, ball fields and restrooms... great for older toddlers... only have one section for the younger ones... hills are great for rolling down... a carnival area runs on weekends... my kids love to walk around the lake to feed the ducks... my kid begs to go there daily...”

Equipment/play structures............❹ ❹..............................Maintenance

WWW.CI.GILBERT.AZ.US

GILBERT—1045 E JUNIPER RD (AT FREESTONE PARK)

Tempe Beach Park

“...adjacent to Tempe Town Lake... home of Splash Playground, a fine spot to cool off with the kids... this is a great place to bring a young child to introduce them to water... there is more or less water flowing everywhere... only drawbacks are limited parking and crowds... a lifeguard told me that the least busy time to visit is on Sunday mornings... very fun and beautiful, with lots of fun water activities...”

Equipment/play structures............❹ ❹..............................Maintenance

WWW.TEMPE.GOV/LAKE/RECREATION/TBP.HTM

TEMPE—54 W RIO SALADO PKWY (AT W 2ND ST); 480.858.2199

Tempe Town Lake

“...fun place to take kids during the hot summer months for them to play with water—slides, fountains, hoses, etc...”

Equipment/play structures............❸ ❺..............................Maintenance

WWW.TEMPE.GOV/LAKE

TEMPE—80 W RIO SALADO PKWY (AT E CURRY RD); 480.350.8625

Tumbleweed Park

“...let your imagination flow to see what Tumbleweed Park can be in its final form... right now, tennis courts, picnic ramadas with barbecues, restrooms and large grassy areas are all there is to see, but the potential is limited only by the City's annual appropriations for recreation... eventually, a playground filled with equipment promises to cater to kids... in the meantime, there's room to spread out a blanket, dance in the grass or maneuver a soccer ball from invisible goal to invisible goal... dogs are welcome but owners are required to control and pick up after their pets...”

Equipment/play structures............❸ ❸..............................Maintenance

WWW.CI.CHANDLER.AZ.US

CHANDLER—2250 S MCQUEEN RD (AT E RYAN RD)

restaurants

Central Phoenix

"lila picks"

- ★5 & Diner
- ★Bill Johnson's Big Apple
- ★Chevy's Fresh Mex
- ★Old Spaghetti Factory
- ★Sonic Drive-In

5 & Diner

"...50's style diner... fun place to bring kids of all ages... extremely kid-friendly... awesome atmosphere and good food... they make a mean milkshake and root beer float... reasonable prices... waitstaff is very accommodating with kids..."

Children's menu	✓	$$	Prices
Changing station	✓	❹	Customer service
Highchairs/boosters	✓	❸	Stroller access

WWW.5ANDDINER.COM

PHOENIX—12802 N TATUM BLVD (AT PARADISE VALLEY MALL); 602.996.0033

PHOENIX—20216 N 27TH AVE (AT W BEARDSLEY AVE); 623.869.9311

PHOENIX—5220 N 16TH ST (AT DESERT STORM PARK); 602.264.5220

Applebee's Neighborhood Grill

"...geared to family dining—they expect you to be loud and leave a mess... Macaroni & Cheese, Hot Dogs, and tasty grilled cheese... activity book and special kids cup are a bonus... service can be slow, but they will cover you with things to snack on... stay clear on Friday and Saturday nights... comfort food in a casual atmosphere... even though it's part of a very large chain you get the feeling it's a neighborhood-type place..."

Children's menu	✓	$$	Prices
Changing station	✓	❹	Customer service
Highchairs/boosters	✓	❸	Stroller access

WWW.APPLEBEES.COM

PHOENIX—2 E CAMELBACK RD (AT N CENTRAL AVE); 602.266.3330; PARKING LOT

PHOENIX—2190 E BASELINE RD (AT S 24TH ST); 602.323.5680

PHOENIX—2547 N 44TH ST (AT ARCADIA CROSSING SHOPPING CTR); 602.952.0033

PHOENIX—2720 W BELL RD (AT BELL CANYON PAVILLIONS); 602.789.9449

PHOENIX—4609 E CHANDLER BLVD (AT S 46TH ST); 480.705.4980

Benihana

"...stir-fry meals are always prepared in front of you—it keeps everyone entertained, parents and kids alike... chefs often perform especially for the little ones... tables sit about 10 people, so it encourages talking with other diners... tend to be pretty loud so it's pretty family friendly... delicious for adults and fun for kids..."

Children's menu .... ✗ $$$ .... Prices
Changing station .... ✓ ❹ .... Customer service
Highchairs/boosters .... ✓ ❸ .... Stroller access

WWW.BENIHANA.COM

PHOENIX—4921 E RAY RD (AT S 48TH ST); 480.940.1111; CALL FOR RESERVATION

Bill Johnson's Big Apple

"...yee-haw, pardner... what kid doesn't love the cowboy atmosphere and food... sawdust on the floor. and other old west decor... a rootin' tootin' good time... terrific food and service, at great prices... I've been coming here for 20 years (my father used to take me) and I still enjoy it... a family favorite..."

Children's menu .... ✓ $$ .... Prices
Changing station .... ✓ ❹ .... Customer service
Highchairs/boosters .... ✓ ❹ .... Stroller access

WWW.BILLJOHNSONS.COM

PHOENIX—16810 N 19TH AVE (AT W BELL RD); 602.863.7921

PHOENIX—3101 W INDIAN SCHOOL RD (AT N 31ST AVE); 602.277.6291

PHOENIX—3757 E VAN BUREN ST (AT N 38TH ST); 602.275.2107

Cheesecake Factory, The

"...although their cheesecake is good, we come here for the kid-friendly atmosphere and selection of good food... eclectic menu has something for everyone... they will bring your tot a plate of yogurt, cheese, bananas and bread free of charge... we love how flexible they are—they'll make whatever my kids want... lots of mommies here... always fun and always crazy... no real kids menu, but the pizza is great to share... waits can be really long..."

Children's menu .... ✗ $$$ .... Prices
Changing station .... ✓ ❹ .... Customer service
Highchairs/boosters .... ✓ ❸ .... Stroller access

WWW.THECHEESECAKEFACTORY.COM

PHOENIX—2402 E CAMELBACK RD (AT 24TH ST); 602.778.6501; M-TH 11-11, F-SA 11-12:30, SU 10-11; MALL PARKING

Chevys Fresh Mex

"...a nice combo of good food for adults and a nice kid's menu... always a sure bet with tots in tow... tasty Mexican food with a simple kids menu (especially the quesedillas)... the tortilla making machine is sure to grab your toddler's attention until the food arrives... an occasional balloon making man... party-like atmosphere with colorful decorations... huge Margaritas for mom and dad... service generally excellent and fast, but you may have to wait for a table at peak hours... long tables can accommodate the multifamily get-together..."

Children's menu .... ✓ $$ .... Prices
Changing station .... ✓ ❹ .... Customer service
Highchairs/boosters .... ✓ ❹ .... Stroller access

WWW.CHEVYS.COM

PHOENIX—2650 E CAMELBACK RD (NEXT TO BILTMORE FASHION PARK); 602.955.6677

Chili's Grill & Bar

"...family-friendly, mild Mexican fare... delicious ribs, soups, salads... kids' menu and crayons as you sit down... on the noisy side, so you don't mind if your kids talk in their usual loud voices... service is excellent... fun night out with the family... a wide variety of menu selections for kids and their parents—all at a reasonable price... best chicken fingers on any kids' menu..."

Children's menu .... ✓ $$ .... Prices
Changing station .... ✓ ❹ .... Customer service
Highchairs/boosters .... ✓ ❹ .... Stroller access

WWW.CHILIS.COM

PHOENIX—12660 N TATUM BLVD (AT PARADISE VALLEY MALL); 602.494.1330; SU-TH 11-11, F-SA 11-12

PHOENIX—2057 E CAMELBACK ST (AT N 24TH ST); 602.955.1195; SU-TH 11-11, F-SA 11-12

PHOENIX—3039 W AGUA FRIA FWY (AT N 31ST AVE); 623.587.9100; SU-TH 11-11, F-SA 11-12

PHOENIX—4848 E CHANDLER BLVD (AT S 48TH ST); 480.753.9383; SU-TH 11-11, F-SA 11-12

PHOENIX—513 E BELL RD (AT N 7TH ST); 602.863.1093; SU-TH 11-11, F-SA 11-12

Fazoli's

"...quick, easy and satisfying Italian food... spacious and comfortable... free breadsticks to keep little minds in check before the meatballs and pasta arrive... a nice step up from the easy fast-food trap... service is quick and the food is good..."

Children's menu .... ✓ $$ .... Prices
Changing station .... ✓ ❹ .... Customer service
Highchairs/boosters .... ✓ ❸ .... Stroller access

WWW.FAZOLIS.COM

PHOENIX—2526 N 75TH AVE (AT DESERT SKY MALL); 623.247.8449; SU-TH 10:30-10, F-SA 10:30-11

PHOENIX—2910 W THUNDERBIRD (AT N BLACK CANYON FWY); 602.866.3130; SU-TH 10:30-10, F-SA 10:30-11; FREE PARKING

PHOENIX—4046 E THOMAS RD (AT N 40TH ST); 602.522.3970; SU-TH 10:30-10, F-SA 10:30-11; FREE PARKING

PHOENIX—617 W BELL RD (AT N 7TH AVE); 602.548.3484; SU-TH 10:30-10, F-SA 10:30-11

Hard Rock Cafe

"...fun and tasty if you can get in... the lines can be horrendous so be sure to check in with them first... a good spot if you have tots in tow—food tastes good and the staff is clearly used to messy eaters... hectic and loud... fun for adults as well as kids..."

Children's menu .... ✓ $$$ .... Prices
Changing station .... ✓ ❹ .... Customer service
Highchairs/boosters .... ✓ ❸ .... Stroller access

WWW.HARDROCK.COM

PHOENIX—3 S 2ND ST (AT WASHINGTON ST); 602.261.7625; SU-TH 11-11, F-SA 11-12

Islands Fine Burgers & Drinks

"...always an easy place to go with the kids... your kid can cry, scream or eat and throw food on the floor and they don't mind... burgers, tacos and lots of soda... bright, colorful decor keeps my baby's attention... the meals are large enough to share... family style, fun

place where a little noise won't bother anyone... booths are perfect for breastfeeding... not a very large selection of healthy foods, but what they have is tasty... ”

Children's menu .... ✓
Changing station.......................... ✓
Highchairs/boosters .... ✓
$$ .... Prices
❹ .... Customer service
❹ .... Stroller access

WWW.ISLANDSRESTAURANTS.COM

PHOENIX—12811 N TATUM BLVD (AT PARADISE VALLEY MALL); 602.494.4434

Jillian's

“...there is a lot of room for the kids to wiggle around... it is also loud so if have children that like to talk loud or cry a lot this is the place for them... they also have bowling that youngsters can participate in and a game room... there is a lot to do here and the food is pretty good... ”

Children's menu .... ✗
Changing station.......................... ✗
Highchairs/boosters .... ✗
$$ .... Prices
❹ .... Customer service
❹ .... Stroller access

WWW.JILLIANS.COM

PHOENIX—21001 N TATUM BLVD (AT LOOP 101); 480.538.8956; M-F 11-1, SA-SU 10-1

Luby's Cafeteria

“...I am in love with Luby's, and I consider myself to be a food snob... menu is kid-friendly and food is served super-fast, as in—you don't have to wait for your food at allL because it's served cafeteria style—which is great for hungry, fussy kids... Luby's is a great value... food is tasty and prices are reasonable... they've got highchairs on wheels, so you can push your baby/toddler along the cafeteria line, right along with you (so cute!) plus crayons, bibs, place mats for the kids... nice wide aisles... ”

Children's menu .... ✓
Changing station.......................... ✓
Highchairs/boosters .... ✓
$ .... Prices
❸ .... Customer service
❺ .... Stroller access

WWW.LUBYS.COM

PHOENIX—4550 E CACTUS RD (AT PARADISE VALLEY MALL); 602.494.9722

Market Street Coffee Co

“...nice couches to relax with your children... good coffee and treats... great place to take your children for story time...they have little toys to keep your young ones busy while you enjoy a coffee... ”

Children's menu .... ✗
Changing station.......................... ✗
Highchairs/boosters .... ✗
$$$ .... Prices
❸ .... Customer service
❸ .... Stroller access

PHOENIX—539 E GLENDALE AVE (AT N 7TH ST); 602.266.6511; STREET PARKING

Mary Coyle Ice Cream

“...very cute old-fashioned ice cream parlor... this family-owned business has been around for years!.. the homemade ice cream is great... wonderful ice cream... my kids love it... they even have a drive thru so you don't have to get out of the car... ”

Children's menu .... ✗
Changing station.......................... ✗
Highchairs/boosters .... ✓
$$ .... Prices
❹ .... Customer service
❹ .... Stroller access

WWW.MARYCOYLE.NET

PHOENIX—5521 N 7TH AVE (AT W MISSOURI AVE); 602.265.6266; DAILY 11-7

McCormick & Schmicks

"...steak and seafood are the mainstay but the menu is broad... terrific happy-hour menu... a little more formal than your regular 'tot-friendly' restaurant, but the staff is great and goes out of their way to make sure you're comfortable... try to get one of the banquet rooms—it makes breastfeeding much easier... good food for adults and more than enough for the little ones too..."

Children's menu ✓ | $$$ Prices
Changing station ✓ | ❹ Customer service
Highchairs/boosters ✓ | ❹ Stroller access

WWW.MCCORMICKANDSCHMICKS.COM

PHOENIX—2575 E CAMELBACK RD (AT N 26TH ST); 602.468.1200

My Big Fat Greek Restaurant

"...yummy, reliable pizza... nice decor, and friendly staff..."

Children's menu ✗ | $$ Prices
Changing station ✗ | ❹ Customer service
Highchairs/boosters ✗ | ❹ Stroller access

WWW.MYBIGFATGREEKRESTAURANT.NET

PHOENIX—10625 N TATUM BLVD (AT E SHEA BLVD); 480.607.1212; SU-TH 11-11, F-SA 11-12; PARKING LOT

PHOENIX—2303 N 44TH ST (AT ARCADIA CROSSSING SHOPPING CTR); 602.840.3513

Old Spaghetti Factory, The

★★★★★

"...good for a fast, cheap meal if the place isn't too packed... apple sauce for kids... fun for the whole family and easy to eat for under $25 (family of four)... if you've got a hankering for spaghetti and meatballs, look no further... relatively inexpensive and you get big portions for your money... a place with a relaxed feel... it is usually so busy that no one will notice if your toddler is crying... the staff makes it easy to hang out and have a good time..."

Children's menu ✓ | $$ Prices
Changing station ✓ | ❹ Customer service
Highchairs/boosters ✓ | ❹ Stroller access

WWW.OLDSPAGHETTIFACTORY.COM

PHOENIX—1418 N CENTRAL AVE (AT E WILLETA ST); 602.257.0380; M-F 11:30-9:30, F 5-10, SA 11:30-10, SU 11:30-9:30; PARKING IN FRONT OF BLDG

Olive Garden

"...finally a place that is both kid and adult friendly... tasty Italian chain with lot's of convenient locations... the staff consistently attends to the details of dining with babies and toddlers—minimizing wait time, highchairs offered spontaneously, bread sticks brought immediately... food is served as quickly as possible... happy to create special orders... our waitress even acted as our family photographer..."

Children's menu ✓ | $$ Prices
Changing station ✓ | ❹ Customer service
Highchairs/boosters ✓ | ❹ Stroller access

WWW.OLIVEGARDEN.COM

PHOENIX—10223 N METRO PKY E (AT N 27TH AVE); 602.943.4573; SU-TH 11-10, F-SA 11-11

PHOENIX—2626 N 75TH AVE (AT W THOMAS RD); 623.849.6533; SU-TH 11-10, F-SA 11-11

Oregano's Pizza Bistro

"...wonderful pizza... love that I don't have to worry about the kids making a mess...huge portions that you can share with your kids..."

Children's menu .... ✓ $$$ .... Prices
Changing station.......................... × ❸ .... Customer service
Highchairs/boosters .... ✓ ❸ .... Stroller access
WWW.OREGANOS.COM

PHOENIX—1008 E CAMELBACK RD (AT N 7TH ST); 602.241.0707

Pasta Pomodoro

"...California-Italian cooked up fast in an almost open kitchen... the friendly waitstaff is well prepared and trained for kid customers... crayons and coloring pages are ready and waiting, orders are taken quickly and the food is brought as soon as it is prepared... a great place for getting out with the kids and not feeling guilty about them making noise or a mess... if you want some good tasting pasta, decent service, and a break form the inside of the house, this is a good last minute pick as it is consistent and fairly inexpensive..."

Children's menu .... ✓ $$ .... Prices
Changing station.......................... ✓ ❹ .... Customer service
Highchairs/boosters .... ✓ ❹ .... Stroller access
WWW.PASTAPOMODORO.COM

PHOENIX—4669 E CACTUS RD (AT PARADISE VALLEY MALL); 602.923.6001

Pei Wei Asian Diner

"...you order at the counter and it is delivered to your table... a couple steps up from regular fast food—much nicer decor and much better food... there isn't a lot of space in the dining room, so if you can do without a stroller, you'll be better off... the restaurant is noisy, so the kids can chat as loud as they want without disturbing the table next to them... my kids love the child-friendly chop sticks..."

Children's menu .... ✓ $$ .... Prices
Changing station.......................... ✓ ❹ .... Customer service
Highchairs/boosters .... ✓ ❸ .... Stroller access
WWW.PEIWEI.COM

PHOENIX—4340 E INDIAN SCHOOL RD (AT N 44TH ST); 602.956.2300

Peter Piper Pizza

Children's menu .... ✓ ✓ .... Changing station
Highchairs/boosters .... ✓
WWW.PETERPIPERPIZZA.COM

PHOENIX—10003 N METRO PKY E (AT METRO CTR); 602.943.2807; SU-TH 11-10, F 11-11, SA 10-11

PHOENIX—245 E BELL RD (AT N 3RD ST); 602.863.0977; SU-F 11-10, SA 10-10

PHOENIX—3403 N 7TH AVE (AT W OSBORN RD); 602.266.0040

PHOENIX—3430 W BELL RD (AT N 35TH AVE); 602.942.0750; SU-TH 11-10, F 11-11, SA 10-11

PHOENIX—3945 E THOMAS RD (AT E THOMAS RD); 602.273.7600; M-SA 10-11, SU 10-10

PHOENIX—4024 N 67TH AVE (AT W INDIAN SCHOOL RD); 623.846.8000; SU-TH 11-10, F-SA 10-11

PHOENIX—4310 W THOMAS RD (AT N 43RD AVE); 602.269.0004; M-SA 10-11, SU 10-10

PHOENIX—4940 E RAY RD (AT FOOTHILLS PARK PLACE SHOPPING CTR); 480.893.0995; SU-TH 11-10, F-SA10-11

PHOENIX—5050 W INDIAN SCHOOL RD (AT N 51ST AVE); 623.247.5100; SU-TH 11-10, F-SA 11-11

PHOENIX—6040 S CENTRAL AVE (AT W SOUTHERN AVE); 602.243.7183

Pizzeria Bianco

"...good pizza, different... doesn't make you feel sick...considered the best pizza in the country... absolutely delicious, but very popular... you may have to wait awhile to get in..."

Children's menu .... ✓ $$$ .... Prices
Changing station .... ✗ ❸ .... Customer service
Highchairs/boosters .... ✓ ❸ .... Stroller access

PHOENIX—623 E ADAMS ST (AT 7TH ST); 602.258.8300; T-SA 5-10

Romano's Macaroni Grill

"...family oriented and tasty... noisy so nobody cares if your kids make noise... the staff goes out of their way to make families feel welcome... they even provide slings by the table for infant carriers... the noise level is pretty constant so it's not too loud, but loud enough so that crying babies don't disturb the other patrons... good kids' menu with somewhat healthy items... crayons for kids to color on the paper tablecloths..."

Children's menu .... ✓ $$$ .... Prices
Changing station .... ✓ ❹ .... Customer service
Highchairs/boosters .... ✓ ❹ .... Stroller access

WWW.MACARONIGRILL.COM

PHOENIX—21001 N TATUM BLVD (AT E DEER VALLEY DR); 480.538.8755; M-F 11-10, SA-SU 11-11

PHOENIX—2949 W AGUA FRIA FWY (AT W BEARDSLEY RD); 623.580.8681; M-F 11-10, SA-SU 11-11

PHOENIX—5035 E RAY RD (AT FOOTHILLS PARK PLACE SHOPPING CTR); 480.705.5661; M-F 11-10, SA-SU 11-11

Ruby Tuesday

"...nice variety of healthy choices on the kids' menu—turkey, spaghetti, chicken tenders... you can definitely find something healthy here... prices are on the high side, but at least everyone can find something they like... service is fast and efficient... my daughter makes a mess and they never let me clean it up... your typical chain, but it works—you'll be happy to see ample aisle space, storage for your stroller, and attentive staff..."

Children's menu .... ✓ $$ .... Prices
Changing station .... ✓ ❹ .... Customer service
Highchairs/boosters .... ✓ ❸ .... Stroller access

WWW.RUBYTUESDAY.COM

PHOENIX—4568 E CACTUS RD (AT PARADISE VALLEY MALL); 602.494.3033; SU-TH 11-11, F-SA 11-12; PARKING IN FRONT OF BLDG

PHOENIX—9617 METRO PKY (AT METRO CENTER); 602.997.0620; SU-TH 11-11, F-SA 11-12; PARKING IN FRONT OF BLDG

Rustler's Rooste

"...when you have extra money, it's great!.. difficult to navigate a stroller through the entrance... view is fantastic, family friendly environment... the atmosphere is great..."

Children's menu .... ✓ $$$$ .... Prices
Changing station .... ✓ ❹ .... Customer service
Highchairs/boosters .... ✓ ❸ .... Stroller access

WWW.RUSTLERSROOSTE.COM

PHOENIX—7777 S POINTE PKY W (AT W BASELINE RD); 602.431.6474; DAILY 5-10

Sonic Drive-In ★★★★★

"...the food is surprisingly good and the entertainment value is priceless... amazing cream pie shakes and breakfast all day... 50's-style

car hop service always feels like an event... quick and convenient... corn dog and wacky-pack kids meals... not exactly healthy, but a fun, occasional outing... ”*

Children's menu .... ✓
Changing station .... ×
Highchairs/boosters .... ✓
$$$ .... Prices
❸ .... Customer service
❸ .... Stroller access

WWW.SONICDRIVEIN.COM

PHOENIX—1537 W CAMELBACK RD (AT N 15TH AVE); 602.230.0828; SU-TH 6:30-11, F-SA 6:30-12AM

PHOENIX—3310 W BETHANY HOME RD (AT N 35TH AVE); 602.336.1361; SU-TH 6:30-11, F-SA 6:30-12AM

PHOENIX—3330 E THOMAS RD (AT N 32ND ST); 602.224.0830; SU-TH 6:30-11, F-SA 6:30-12AM

PHOENIX—4244 N 43RD AVE (AT W INDIAN SCHOOL RD); 623.691.9567; SU-TH 6:30-11, F-SA 6:30-12AM

PHOENIX—5002 E MCDOWELL RD (AT N 48TH ST); 602.231.0665; SU-TH 6:30-11, F-SA 6:30-12AM

PHOENIX—5021 W MCDOWELL RD (AT N 51ST AVE); 602.353.1371; SU-TH 6:30-11, F-SA 6:30-12AM

PHOENIX—6724 W THOMAS RD (AT N 67TH AVE); 623.848.8322; SU-TH 6:30-11, F-SA 6:30-12AM

PHOENIX—7440 JESSE OWENS PKWY (AT CENTRAL AVE); 602.268.6904; SU-TH 6:30-11, F-SA 6:30-12AM

PHOENIX—748 E MCDOWELL RD (AT N 7TH ST); 602.258.9320; SU-TH 6:30-11, F-SA 6:30-12AM

PHOENIX—8815 N 7TH ST (AT ALICE AVE); 602.371.3700; SU-TH 6:30-11, F-SA 6:30-12AM

Souplantation/Sweet Tomatoes

“...you can't beat the price and selection of healthy foods... all you can eat—serve yourself soup and salad bar... lots of healthy choices plus pizza and pasta... great for picky eaters... free for 2 and under and only $3 for kids under 5... booths for comfy seating and discreet breastfeeding... helps to have another adult along since it is self serve... they always bring fresh cookies to the table and offer to refill drinks... ”

Children's menu .... ✓
Changing station .... ✓
Highchairs/boosters .... ✓
$$ .... Prices
❹ .... Customer service
❹ .... Stroller access

WWW.SOUPLANTATION.COM

PHOENIX—10046 N 26TH DR (NEAR W PEORIA AVE); 602.749.9016; SU-TH 11-9, F-SA 11-10

PHOENIX—52 E CAMELBACK RD (AT CENTRAL AVE); 623.274.5414; SU-TH 11-9, F-SA 11-10

PHOENIX—9029 E INDIAN BEND RD (AT N 68TH ST); 480.991.6010; SU-TH 11-9, F-SA 11-10

Yummy China Inn

“...the best Chinese food I have tasted... I love going here to eat... highchairs and boosters make it kid-friendly... ”

Children's menu .... ×
Changing station .... ×
Highchairs/boosters .... ✓
$$ .... Prices
❹ .... Customer service
❸ .... Stroller access

PHOENIX—13843 N TATUM BLVD (AT E THUNDERBIRD RD); 602.996.6969; M-SA 11-9:30, SU 12-9

Northwest Valley

"lila picks"

- ★5 & Diner
- ★Bill Johnson's Big Apple
- ★Chevy's Fresh Mex
- ★Sonic Drive-In

5 & Diner

"...50's style diner... fun place to bring kids of all ages... extremely kid-friendly... awesome atmosphere and good food... they make a mean milkshake and root beer float... reasonable prices... waitstaff is very accommodating with kids..."

Children's menu ✓ $$ Prices
Changing station ✓ ❹ Customer service
Highchairs/boosters ✓ ❸ Stroller access

WWW.5ANDDINER.COM

PEORIA—7541 W BELL RD (AT W ARROWHEAD TWN CT); 623.979.3073

Applebee's Neighborhood Grill

"...geared to family dining—they expect you to be loud and leave a mess... Macaroni & Cheese, Hot Dogs, and tasty grilled cheese... activity book and special kids cup are a bonus... service can be slow, but they will cover you with things to snack on... stay clear on Friday and Saturday nights... comfort food in a casual atmosphere... even though it's part of a very large chain you get the feeling it's a neighborhood-type place..."

Children's menu ✓ $$ Prices
Changing station ✓ ❹ Customer service
Highchairs/boosters ✓ ❸ Stroller access

WWW.APPLEBEES.COM

GLENDALE—5880 W PEORIA AVE (AT N 59TH AVE); 623.878.3500; FREE PARKING

PEORIA—8001 W BELL RD (AT NORTH VALLEY POWER CTR); 623.878.1410; M-TH 11-12, F-SA 11-1, SU 11-11; PARKING LOT

SURPRISE—13756 W BELL RD (OFF GRAND AVE); 623.544.0368

Bill Johnson's Big Apple

"...yee-haw, pardner... what kid doesn't love the cowboy atmosphere and food... sawdust on the floor. and other Old West decor... a rootin' tootin' good time... terrific food and service, at great prices... I've been coming here for 20 years (my father used to take me) and I still enjoy it... a family favorite..."

Children's menu ✓ $$ Prices

Changing station ✓	❹ Customer service
Highchairs/boosters ✓	❹ Stroller access

WWW.BILLJOHNSONS.COM

GLENDALE—7322 W BELL RD (AT 73RD AVE); 623.776.1900

Cheesecake Factory, The

"...although their cheesecake is good, we come here for the kid-friendly atmosphere and selection of good food... eclectic menu has something for everyone... they will bring your tot a plate of yogurt, cheese, bananas and bread free of charge... we love how flexible they are—they'll make whatever my kids want... lots of mommies here... always fun and always crazy... no real kids menu, but the pizza is great to share... waits can be really long..."

Children's menu ✗	$$$ Prices
Changing station ✓	❹ Customer service
Highchairs/boosters ✓	❸ Stroller access

WWW.THECHEESECAKEFACTORY.COM

PEORIA—16134 N 83RD AVE (AT BELL RD); 623.773.2233; M-TH 11-11, F-SA 11-12:30, SU 10-10; MALL PARKING

Chevys Fresh Mex

★★★★★

"...a nice combo of good food for adults and a nice kid's menu... always a sure bet with tots in tow... tasty Mexican food with a simple kids menu (especially the quesedillas)... the tortilla making machine is sure to grab your toddler's attention until the food arrives... an occasional balloon making man... party-like atmosphere with colorful decorations... huge Margaritas for mom and dad... service generally excellent and fast, but you may have to wait for a table at peak hours... long tables can accommodate the multifamily get-together..."

Children's menu ✓	$$ Prices
Changing station ✓	❹ Customer service
Highchairs/boosters ✓	❹ Stroller access

WWW.CHEVYS.COM

GLENDALE—7700 ARROWHEAD TOWNE CTR (AT ARROWHEAD TOWNE CTR); 623.979.0055

Chili's Grill & Bar

"...family-friendly, mild Mexican fare... delicious ribs, soups, salads... kids' menu and crayons as you sit down... on the noisy side, so you don't mind if your kids talk in their usual loud voices... service is excellent... fun night out with the family... a wide variety of menu selections for kids and their parents—all at a reasonable price... best chicken fingers on any kids' menu..."

Children's menu ✓	$$ Prices
Changing station ✓	❹ Customer service
Highchairs/boosters ✓	❹ Stroller access

WWW.CHILIS.COM

PEORIA—7717 W BELL RD (AT N 77TH AVE); 623.979.5850; SU-TH 11-11, F-SA 11-12

Fazoli's

"...quick, easy and satisfying Italian food... spacious and comfortable... free breadsticks to keep little minds in check before the meatballs and pasta arrive... a nice step up from the easy fast-food trap... service is quick and the food is good..."

Children's menu ✓	$$ Prices
Changing station ✓	❹ Customer service
Highchairs/boosters ✓	❸ Stroller access

WWW.FAZOLIS.COM

GLENDALE—6738 W BELL RD (AT N 67TH AVE); 623.979.4334; SU-TH 10:30-10, F-SA 10:30-11

PEORIA—9030 W PEORIA AVE (AT N 91ST AVE); 623.486.0105; SU-TH 10:30-10, F-SA 10:30-11

SURPRISE—13746 W BELL RD (AT LITCHFIELD RD); 623.544.5818; SU-TH 10:30-10, F-SA 10:30-11

Olive Garden

"...finally a place that is both kid and adult friendly... tasty Italian chain with lot's of convenient locations... the staff consistently attends to the details of dining with babies and toddlers—minimizing wait time, highchairs offered spontaneously, bread sticks brought immediately... food is served as quickly as possible... happy to create special orders... our waitress even acted as our family photographer..."

Children's menu .... ✓ $$ .... Prices
Changing station .... ✓ ❹ .... Customer service
Highchairs/boosters .... ✓ ❹ .... Stroller access

WWW.OLIVEGARDEN.COM

PEORIA—7889 W BELL RD (AT N 79TH AVE); 623.412.4955; SU-TH 11-10, F-SA 11-11

SURPRISE—13379 W GRAND AVE (AT W BELL RD); 623.975.6774; SU-TH 11-10, F-SA 11-11

Pei Wei Asian Diner

"...you order at the counter and it is delivered to your table... a couple steps up from regular fast food—much nicer decor and much better food... there isn't a lot of space in the dining room, so if you can do without a stroller, you'll be better off... the restaurant is noisy, so the kids can chat as loud as they want without disturbing the table next to them... ..."

Children's menu .... ✓ $$ .... Prices
Changing station .... ✓ ❹ .... Customer service
Highchairs/boosters .... ✓ ❸ .... Stroller access

WWW.PEIWEI.COM

GLENDALE—20022 N 67TH AVE (AT W WAHALLA DR); 623.825.9949

Peter Piper Pizza

Children's menu .... ✓ ✓ .... Changing station
Highchairs/boosters .... ✓

WWW.PETERPIPERPIZZA.COM

GLENDALE—4315 W GLENDALE AVE (AT N 43RD AVE); 623.937.9253

GLENDALE—4324 W OLIVE AVE (AT N 43RD AVE); 623.842.1500

PEORIA—10006 N 91ST AVE (AT W CINNABAR AVE); 623.878.0608

PEORIA—6821 W PEORIA AVE (AT N 67TH AVE); 623.776.8320

Red Robin

"...very kid-oriented—loud, balloons, bright lights, colorful decor and a cheerful staff make Red Robin a favorite among parents and children... the food is mainly burgers (beef or chicken)... loud music covers even the most boisterous of screaming... lots of kids—all the time... sometimes the wait can be long, but the arcade games and balloons help pass the time..."

Children's menu .... ✓ $$ .... Prices
Changing station .... ✓ ❹ .... Customer service
Highchairs/boosters .... ✓ ❹ .... Stroller access

WWW.REDROBIN.COM

PEORIA—16233 N 83RD AVE (AT N VALLEY POWER CTR); 623.334.4600

Sonic Drive-In

"...the food is surprisingly good and the entertainment value is priceless... amazing cream pie shakes and breakfast all day... 50's-style car hop service always feels like an event... quick and convenient... corn dog and wacky-pack kids meals... not exactly healthy, but a fun, occasional outing..."

Children's menu .... ✓ $$$ .... Prices
Changing station .... × ❸ .... Customer service
Highchairs/boosters .... ✓ ❸ .... Stroller access

WWW.SONICDRIVEIN.COM

PEORIA—10969 N 83RD AVE (AT EDWARDS ST); 623.412.1500; SU-TH 6:30-11, F-SA 6:30-12AM

Souplantation/Sweet Tomatoes

"...you can't beat the price and selection of healthy foods... all you can eat—serve yourself soup and salad bar... lots of healthy choices plus pizza and pasta... great for picky eaters... free for 2 and under and only $3 for kids under 5... booths for comfy seating and discreet breastfeeding... helps to have another adult along since it is self serve... they always bring fresh cookies to the table and offer to refill drinks..."

Children's menu .... ✓ $$ .... Prices
Changing station .... ✓ ❹ .... Customer service
Highchairs/boosters .... ✓ ❹ .... Stroller access

WWW.SOUPLANTATION.COM

PEORIA—7565 W BELL RD (AT 75TH AVE); 623.487.0307; SU-TH 11-9, F-SA 11-10

Northeast Valley

"lila picks"

★Sonic Drive-In

Applebee's Neighborhood Grill

"...geared to family dining—they expect you to be loud and leave a mess... Macaroni & Cheese, Hot Dogs, and tasty grilled cheese... activity book and special kids cup are a bonus... service can be slow, but they will cover you with things to snack on... stay clear on Friday and Saturday nights... comfort food in a casual atmosphere... even though it's part of a very large chain you get the feeling it's a neighborhood-type place..."

Children's menu	✓	$$	Prices
Changing station	✓	❹	Customer service
Highchairs/boosters	✓	❸	Stroller access

WWW.APPLEBEES.COM

SCOTTSDALE—10460 N 90TH ST (AT E SHEA BLD); 480.391.3535

Arizona Bread Co

"...very good food... child-friendly... lots for the kids to eat... also good for breakfast...yummy sandwiches and salads and soups..."

Children's menu	×	$	Prices
Changing station	×	❹	Customer service
Highchairs/boosters	✓	❹	Stroller access

WWW.ARIZONABREADCOMPANY.COM

SCOTTSDALE—7000 E SHEA BLVD (AT SCOTTSDALE RD); 480.948.8338; M-F 6:30-3, SA-SU 7-3

Benihana

"...stir-fry meals are always prepared in front of you—it keeps everyone entertained, parents and kids alike... chefs often perform especially for the little ones... tables sit about 10 people, so it encourages talking with other diners... tend to be pretty loud so it's pretty family friendly... delicious for adults and fun for kids..."

Children's menu	×	$$$	Prices
Changing station	✓	❹	Customer service
Highchairs/boosters	✓	❸	Stroller access

WWW.BENIHANA.COM

SCOTTSDALE—16403 N SCOTTSDALE RD (AT E FRANK LLOYD WRIGHT BLVD); 480.444.0068

Carrabba's Italian Grill

"...classic Italian dishes... noisy enough to drown out a fussy baby... lovely and patient waitstaff... slings for car carriers... one or two looks from the non-family diners, but the staff were totally welcoming... the bread is a must and helps hungry kids while waiting for food..."

Children's menu .... ✓ $$$ .... Prices
Changing station.......................... ✓ ❹......................... Customer service
Highchairs/boosters .... ✓ ❸.............................Stroller access

WWW.CARRABBAS.COM

SCOTTSDALE—17027 N SCOTTSDALE RD (AT E FRANK LLOYD WRIGHT BLVD); 480.948.8881

Cheesecake Factory, The

"...although their cheesecake is good, we come here for the kid-friendly atmosphere and selection of good food... eclectic menu has something for everyone... they will bring your tot a plate of yogurt, cheese, bananas and bread free of charge... we love how flexible they are—they'll make whatever my kids want... lots of mommies here... always fun and always crazy... no real kids menu, but the pizza is great to share... waits can be really long..."

Children's menu .... ✗ $$$ .... Prices
Changing station.......................... ✓ ❹......................... Customer service
Highchairs/boosters .... ✓ ❸.............................Stroller access

WWW.THECHEESECAKEFACTORY.COM

SCOTTSDALE—15230 N SCOTTSDALE RD (AT GREENWAY HAYDEN LOOP); 480.607.0083; M-TH 11-11, F-SA 11-12:30, SU 10-11; MALL PARKING

Chili's Grill & Bar

"...family-friendly, mild Mexican fare... delicious ribs, soups, salads... kids' menu and crayons as you sit down... on the noisy side, so you don't mind if your kids talk in their usual loud voices... service is excellent... fun night out with the family... a wide variety of menu selections for kids and their parents—all at a reasonable price... best chicken fingers on any kids' menu..."

Children's menu .... ✓ $$ .... Prices
Changing station.......................... ✓ ❹......................... Customer service
Highchairs/boosters .... ✓ ❹.............................Stroller access

WWW.CHILIS.COM

SCOTTSDALE—8612 E SHEA BLVD (AT N 85TH PL); 480.948.7373; SU-TH 11-11, F-SA 11-12

Maggiano's Little Italy

"...Southern Italian cuisine served in huge, family-style portions... so much food, we didn't even need a kid's meal... yummy for both adults and kids... fun atmosphere and friendly staff... not the easiest place with a baby, but servers are helpful... they will help you store your stroller... where else can I eat with my kids and listen to Sinatra playing... rather noisy which is great if baby gets fussy... kids love all the activity..."

Children's menu .... ✓ $$$ .... Prices
Changing station.......................... ✓ ❹......................... Customer service
Highchairs/boosters .... ✓ ❸.............................Stroller access

WWW.MAGGIANOS.COM

SCOTTSDALE—16405 N SCOTTSDALE RD (AT BELL RD); 972.781.0776; SU-TH 11-10, F-SA 11-11

Olive Garden

"...finally a place that is both kid and adult friendly... tasty Italian chain with lot's of convenient locations... the staff consistently attends to the details of dining with babies and toddlers—minimizing wait time, highchairs offered spontaneously, bread sticks brought immediately... food is served as quickly as possible... happy to create special orders... our waitress even acted as our family photographer..."

Children's menu .... ✓ $$ .... Prices
Changing station.......................... ✓ ❹......................... Customer service

Highchairs/boosters .... ✓ ❹ .... Stroller access

WWW.OLIVEGARDEN.COM

SCOTTSDALE—3380 N SCOTTSDALE RD (AT E OSBORN RD); 480.874.0212; SU-TH 11-10, F-SA 11-11

SCOTTSDALE—4868 E CACTUS RD (AT TATUM BLVD); 602.494.4327; SU-TH 11-10, F-SA 11-11

Original Pancake House ★★★★½

"...consistently the best breakfast around... great flapjacks and appropriately-sized kids meals... food comes quickly... the most amazing apple pancakes ever... service is always friendly, but sometimes it can take a while to actually get the food... the highlight for my daughter is the free balloon when we leave... always a lot of families here with small children on the weekends, so you don't have to worry about being the only one..."

Children's menu .... ✓ $$ .... Prices
Changing station .... ✓ ❹ .... Customer service
Highchairs/boosters .... ✓ ❸ .... Stroller access

WWW.ORIGINALPANCAKEHOUSE.COM

SCOTTSDALE—6840 E CAMELBACK RD (AT N GOLDWATER BLVD); 480.946.4902

Pei Wei Asian Diner ★★★★☆

"...you order at the counter and it is delivered to your table... a couple steps up from regular fast food—much nicer decor and much better food... there isn't a lot of space in the dining room, so if you can do without a stroller, you'll be better off... the restaurant is noisy, so the kids can chat as loud as they want without disturbing the table next to them... ..."

Children's menu .... ✓ $$ .... Prices
Changing station .... ✓ ❹ .... Customer service
Highchairs/boosters .... ✓ ❸ .... Stroller access

WWW.PEIWEI.COM

FOUNTAIN HILLS—14835 E SHEA BLVD (AT E EAGLE MOUNTAIN PKY); 480.837.0926; DAILY 11-9

SCOTTSDALE—20851 N SCOTTSDALE RD (AT E GRAYHAWK DR); 480.365.6002

SCOTTSDALE—32607 N SCOTTSDALE RD (AT E ALOE VERA DR); 480.488.8630

SCOTTSDALE—8787 N SCOTTSDALE RD (AT E SUNNYVALE RD); 480.365.6000

Peter Piper Pizza

Children's menu .... ✓ ✓ .... Changing station
Highchairs/boosters .... ✓

WWW.PETERPIPERPIZZA.COM

SCOTTSDALE—7607 E MCDOWELL RD (AT N MILLER RD); 480.947.9901; SU-TH 11-10, F-SA 10-11

Red Robin ★★★½☆

"...very kid-oriented—loud, balloons, bright lights, colorful decor and a cheerful staff make Red Robin a favorite among parents and children... the food is mainly burgers (beef or chicken)... loud music covers even the most boisterous of screaming... lots of kids—all the time... sometimes the wait can be long, but the arcade games and balloons help pass the time..."

Children's menu .... ✓ $$ .... Prices
Changing station .... ✓ ❹ .... Customer service
Highchairs/boosters .... ✓ ❹ .... Stroller access

WWW.REDROBIN.COM

SCOTTSDALE—8970 E SHEA BLVD (AT N 90TH ST); 480.661.7114

Romano's Macaroni Grill

"...family oriented and tasty... noisy so nobody cares if your kids make noise... the staff goes out of their way to make families feel welcome... they even provide slings by the table for infant carriers... the noise level is pretty constant so it's not too loud, but loud enough so that crying babies don't disturb the other patrons... good kids' menu with somewhat healthy items... crayons for kids to color on the paper tablecloths..."

Children's menu	✓	$$$	Prices
Changing station	✓	❹	Customer service
Highchairs/boosters	✓	❹	Stroller access

WWW.MACARONIGRILL.COM

SCOTTSDALE—7245 E GOLD DUST AVE (AT N SCOTTSDALE RD); 480.596.6676; M-F 11-10, SA-SU 11-11

Sonic Drive-In

"...the food is surprisingly good and the entertainment value is priceless... amazing cream pie shakes and breakfast all day... 50's-style car hop service always feels like an event... quick and convenient... corn dog and wacky-pack kids meals... not exactly healthy, but a fun, occasional outing..."

Children's menu	✓	$$$	Prices
Changing station	×	❸	Customer service
Highchairs/boosters	✓	❸	Stroller access

WWW.SONICDRIVEIN.COM

SCOTTSDALE—2870 N HAYDEN RD (AT THOMAS RD); 480.941.6096; SU-TH 6:30-11, F-SA 6:30-12AM

Sugar Bowl Ice Cream Parlor

"...wonderful ice cream... the kids will love it!..."

Children's menu	×	$$$	Prices
Changing station	×	❸	Customer service
Highchairs/boosters	×	❸	Stroller access

SCOTTSDALE—4005 N SCOTTSDALE RD (AT E 1ST AVE); 480.946.0051; M-TH 11-11, F-SA 11-2, SU 11-10

Southeast Valley

"lila picks"

- ★5 & Diner
- ★Bill Johnson's Big Apple
- ★Chevy's
- ★Gordon Biersch
- ★Organ Stop Pizza

5 & Diner ★★★★★

"...50's style diner... fun place to bring kids of all ages... extremely kid-friendly... awesome atmosphere and good food... they make a mean milkshake and root beer float... reasonable prices... waitstaff is very accommodating with kids..."

Children's menu ✓ $$ Prices
Changing station ✓ ❹ Customer service
Highchairs/boosters ✓ ❸ Stroller access

WWW.5ANDDINER.COM

CHANDLER—960 N 54TH ST (AT W RAY RD); 480.753.1114

MESA—2252 E BASELINE RD (AT S 24TH ST); 480.892.1952

MESA—6353 E SOUTHERN AVE (AT SUPERSTITION SPRINGS MALL); 480.641.1958

TEMPE—5025 S ARIZONA MILLS CIR (AT S PRIEST DR); 480.752.1958

Applebee's Neighborhood Grill

"...geared to family dining—they expect you to be loud and leave a mess... macaroni & cheese, hot dogs, and tasty grilled cheese... activity book and special kids cup are a bonus... service can be slow, but they will cover you with things to snack on... stay clear on Friday and Saturday nights... comfort food in a casual atmosphere... even though it's part of a very large chain you get the feeling it's a neighborhood-type place..."

Children's menu ✓ $$ Prices
Changing station ✓ ❹ Customer service
Highchairs/boosters ✓ ❸ Stroller access

WWW.APPLEBEES.COM

CHANDLER—1245 W CHANDLER BLVD (AT N ALMA SCHOOL RD); 480.917.3535; M-TH 11-12, F-SA 11-1, SU 11-11; PARKING LOT

GILBERT—830 W WARNER RD (AT S COOPER RD); 480.892.5250; SU-T 11-11, W-SA 11-12; PARKING LOT

MESA—1143 N HIGLEY RD (AT E BROWN RD); 480.981.4667

MESA—2032 E BASELINE RD (AT S GILBERT RD); 480.545.4299; M-TH 11-12, SA 11-1, SU 11-11; PARKING LOT

MESA—2053 S ALMA SCHOOL RD (AT W BASELINE RD); 480.831.7557; M-TH 11-12, F-SA 11-1, SU 11-11; PARKING LOT

MESA—6259 E SOUTHERN AVE (AT SUPERSTITION SPRINGS CTR); 480.830.3099; M-TH 11-12, F-SA 11-1, SU 11-11; PARKING LOT

TEMPE—1655 W ELLIOT RD (AT PRIEST DR); 480.893.2878

TEMPE—909 E BROADWAY RD (AT S RURAL RD); 480.736.1100; FREE PARKING

Benihana

"...stir-fry meals are always prepared in front of you—it keeps everyone entertained, parents and kids alike... chefs often perform especially for the little ones... tables sit about 10 people, so it encourages talking with other diners... tend to be pretty loud so it's pretty family friendly... delicious for adults and fun for kids..."

Children's menu .... ✗ $$$ .... Prices
Changing station.......................... ✓ ❹......................... Customer service
Highchairs/boosters .... ✓ ❸............................Stroller access

WWW.BENIHANA.COM

TEMPE—411 S MILL AVE (AT E 5TH ST); 480.990.9256

Bill Johnson's Big Apple

"...yee-haw, pardner... what kid doesn't love the cowboy atmosphere and food... sawdust on the floor. and other old west decor... a rootin' tootin' good time... terrific food and service, at great prices... I've been coming here for 20 years (my father used to take me) and I still enjoy it... a family favorite..."

Children's menu .... ✓ $$ .... Prices
Changing station.......................... ✓ ❹......................... Customer service
Highchairs/boosters .... ✓ ❹............................Stroller access

WWW.BILLJOHNSONS.COM

MESA—950 E MAIN ST (AT S TEMPLE ST); 480.969.6504

Cheesecake Factory, The

"...although their cheesecake is good, we come here for the kid-friendly atmosphere and selection of good food... eclectic menu has something for everyone... they will bring your tot a plate of yogurt, cheese, bananas and bread free of charge... we love how flexible they are—they'll make whatever my kids want... lots of mommies here... always fun and always crazy... no real kids menu, but the pizza is great to share... waits can be really long..."

Children's menu .... ✗ $$$ .... Prices
Changing station.......................... ✓ ❹......................... Customer service
Highchairs/boosters .... ✓ ❸............................Stroller access

WWW.THECHEESECAKEFACTORY.COM

CHANDLER—3111 W CHANDLER BLVD (AT PRICE RD); 480.792.1300; M-TH 11-11, F-SA 11-12:30, SU 10-10; MALL PARKING

Chevys Fresh Mex

"...a nice combo of good food for adults and a nice kid's menu... always a sure bet with tots in tow... tasty Mexican food with a simple kids menu (especially the quesedillas)... the tortilla making machine is sure to grab your toddler's attention until the food arrives... an occasional balloon making man... party-like atmosphere with colorful decorations... huge Margaritas for mom and dad... service generally excellent and fast, but you may have to wait for a table at peak hours... long tables can accommodate the multifamily get-together..."

Children's menu .... ✓ $$ .... Prices
Changing station.......................... ✓ ❹......................... Customer service
Highchairs/boosters .... ✓ ❹............................Stroller access

WWW.CHEVYS.COM

MESA—1335 S ALMA SCHOOL RD (AT FIESTA MALL); 480.833.1300

Chili's Grill & Bar

"...family-friendly, mild Mexican fare... delicious ribs, soups, salads... kids' menu and crayons as you sit down... on the noisy side, so you don't mind if your kids talk in their usual loud voices... service is excellent... fun night out with the family... a wide variety of menu selections for kids and their parents—all at a reasonable price... best chicken fingers on any kids' menu..."

Children's menu .... ✓ $$.. Prices
Changing station .... ✓ ❹ ....Customer service
Highchairs/boosters .... ✓ ❹ .... Stroller access

WWW.CHILIS.COM

CHANDLER—2025 N ALMA SCHOOL RD (AT W WARNER RD); 480.899.5050; SU-TH 11-11, F-SA 11-12

CHANDLER—3015 W CHANDLER BLVD (AT N PRICE RD); 480.786.1289; SU-TH 11-11, F-SA 11-12

GILBERT—3917 S GILBERT RD (AT WILLIAMS FIELD RD); 480.812.4636; SU-TH 11-11, F-SA 11-12

MESA—1435 S POWER RD (AT E HAMPTON AVE); 480.807.6003; SU-TH 11-11, F-SA 11-12

MESA—1637 S STAPLEY DR (AT SUPERSTITION FWY); 480.633.2900; SU-TH 11-11, F-SA 11-12

MESA—6648 E MCKELLIPS RD (AT N POWER RD); 480.325.7582; SU-TH 11-11, F-SA 11-12

TEMPE—1190 W ELLIOT RD (AT S PRIEST DR); 480.838.8441; SU-TH 11-11, F-SA 11-12

TEMPE—801 S MILL AVE (E UNIVERSITY DR); 480.731.9482; SU-TH 11-11, F-SA 11-12

Damon's Grill

"...'kid's night' features cartoons on the big screen tv's... chocolate-chip cookies come with the kids' meals... tends to be filled with an older crowd... food is decent enough..."

Children's menu .... ✓ $$$...................................... Prices
Changing station .... ✓ ❸ ....Customer service
Highchairs/boosters .... ✓ ❷ .... Stroller access

WWW.DAMONS.COM

GILBERT—940 S GILBERT RD (AT CIVIC CTR DR); 480.813.7427; SU-TH 11-10, F-SA 11-11

Fazoli's

"...quick, easy and satisfying Italian food... spacious and comfortable... free breadsticks to keep little minds in check before the meatballs and pasta arrive... a nice step up from the easy fast-food trap... service is quick and the food is good..."

Children's menu .... ✓ $$.. Prices
Changing station .... ✓ ❹ ....Customer service
Highchairs/boosters .... ✓ ❸ .... Stroller access

WWW.FAZOLIS.COM

CHANDLER—2170 N ARIZONA AVE (AT W WARNER RD); 480.855.5947; SU-TH 10:30-10, F-SA 10:30-11

CHANDLER—4989 W RAY RD (AT N RURAL RD); 480.705.5862; SU-TH 10:30-10, F-SA 10:30-11

GILBERT—2135 E BASELINE (AT S GILBERT RD); 480.503.3729; SU-TH 10:30-10, F-SA 10:30-11

MESA—1353 W MAIN ST (AT S ALMA SCHOOL RD); 480.610.1891; SU-TH 10:30-10, F-SA 10:30-11; FREE PARKING

MESA—6742 E MAIN ST (AT N POWER RD); 480.981.7418; SU-TH 10:30-10, F-SA 10:30-11

Gordon Biersch

"...a fantastic brewery that serves delicious food... awesome beer that is brewed onsite... fun atmosphere that works well for kids... high-end bar food... staff seems to adore babies... server was very doting and attentive to my family's needs... best to go early before the after work scene gets going... the big vats and pipes provide for a fun walk-around with my tot..."

Children's menu .... ✓ $$$ .... Prices
Changing station .... ✓ ❹ .... Customer service
Highchairs/boosters .... ✓ ❹ .... Stroller access

WWW.GORDONBIERSCH.COM

TEMPE—420 S MILL AVE (AT 5TH ST); 480.736.0033

IKEA

"...Swedish meatballs and funny berry drinks—all very yummy and cheap... a clean, comfortable place to eat... the restaurant sells baby food and has bottle/jar warmers... worth visiting even if you aren't shopping—the food is cheap, but good... totally kid-friendly... lines can sometimes be long—especially during peak shopping hours..."

Children's menu .... ✓ $$ .... Prices
Changing station .... ✓ ❹ .... Customer service
Highchairs/boosters .... ✓ ❹ .... Stroller access

WWW.IKEA.COM

TEMPE—2110 W IKEA WY (AT WARNER AND PRIEST); 480.496.5658; M-SA 10-9, SU 10-7; PARKING LOT

Joe's Crab Shack

"...for the young and the young at heart... newspaper lined tables, crabs done every which way... the staff sings and dances and so do my kids... dining inside and out... this is a kick back place where we always have a good time and a good crab... plenty for the kids to choose from even if they're not into crab... lots of fun items on the walls and ceilings—keeps kids entertained until the food comes... perfect for appetizers and beer when you need a break..."

Children's menu .... ✓ $$$ .... Prices
Changing station .... ✓ ❹ .... Customer service
Highchairs/boosters .... ✓ ❸ .... Stroller access

WWW.JOESCRABSHACK.COM

TEMPE—1604 E SOUTHERN AVE (AT S MCCLINTOCK DR); 480.730.0303

TEMPE—1606 W BASELINE RD (AT ARIZONA MILLS S); 480.345.0972

Olive Garden

"...finally a place that is both kid and adult friendly... tasty Italian chain with lot's of convenient locations... the staff consistently attends to the details of dining with babies and toddlers—minimizing wait time, highchairs offered spontaneously, bread sticks brought immediately... food is served as quickly as possible... happy to create special orders... our waitress even acted as our family photographer..."

Children's menu .... ✓ $$ .... Prices
Changing station .... ✓ ❹ .... Customer service
Highchairs/boosters .... ✓ ❹ .... Stroller access

WWW.OLIVEGARDEN.COM

CHANDLER—3430 W CHANDLER BLVD (OFF N PRICE WY); 480.857.0126; SU-TH 11-10, F-SA 11-11

MESA—6201 E SOUTHERN AVE (AT E SUPERSTITION SPRINGS BLVD); 480.807.0207; SU-TH 11-10, F-SA 11-11

TEMPE—1010 W ELLIOTT RD (AT S HARDY DR); 480.777.0032; SU-TH 11-10, F-SA 11-11

Organ Stop Pizza ★★★★★

"...what a whacky place—my kids love to go there because of the organ music... the food is good, but what makes it great is the environment... the staff 'gets' kids and is very accommodating... good for children of all ages... very laid back and great for parties..."

Children's menu .... ✗ | $$ .... Prices
Changing station .... ✗ | ❹ .... Customer service
Highchairs/boosters .... ✓ | ❹ .... Stroller access

WWW.ORGANSTOPPIZZA.COM

MESA—1149 E SOUTHERN AVE (AT S STAPLEY DR); 480.813.5700

Pasta Pomodoro ★★★★☆

"...California-Italian cooked up fast in an almost open kitchen... the friendly waitstaff is well prepared and trained for kid customers... crayons and coloring pages are ready and waiting, orders are taken quickly and the food is brought as soon as it is prepared... a great place for getting out with the kids and not feeling guilty about them making noise or a mess... if you want some good tasting pasta, decent service, and a break form the inside of the house, this is a good last minute pick as it is consistent and fairly inexpensive..."

Children's menu .... ✓ | $$ .... Prices
Changing station .... ✓ | ❹ .... Customer service
Highchairs/boosters .... ✓ | ❹ .... Stroller access

WWW.PASTAPOMODORO.COM

CHANDLER—3395 W CHANDLER BLVD (AT CHANDLER FASHION MALL); 480.855.3736; M-TH 11-9, F-SA 11:30-10, SU 11:30-9

Pei Wei Asian Diner ★★★★☆

"...you order at the counter and it is delivered to your table... a couple steps up from regular fast food—much nicer decor and much better food... there isn't a lot of space in the dining room, so if you can do without a stroller, you'll be better off... the restaurant is noisy, so the kids can chat as loud as they want without disturbing the table next to them... ..."

Children's menu .... ✓ | $$ .... Prices
Changing station .... ✓ | ❹ .... Customer service
Highchairs/boosters .... ✓ | ❸ .... Stroller access

WWW.PEIWEI.COM

CHANDLER—7131 W RAY RD (AT N PRIEST DR); 480.940.3800

GILBERT—1084 S GILBERT RD (AT W JASPER DR); 480.926.9749

MESA—3426 E BASELINE RD (AT E BASELINE RD); 480.539.4454

Peter Piper Pizza

Children's menu .... ✓ | ✓ .... Changing station
Highchairs/boosters .... ✓

WWW.PETERPIPERPIZZA.COM

CHANDLER—3029 N ALMA SCHOOL RD (AT W ELLIOT RD); 480.838.6880

TEMPE—1803 E BASELINE RD (AT S MCCLINTOCK DR); 480.345.9700; SU-TH 11-10, F-SA 11-11

Rainforest Cafe ★★★½☆

"...like eating in the jungle... the decor keeps the kids entertained and the food is decent... kids either love it or are terrified at first and need to ease into the wild animal thing... I get at least 20 extra minutes of hang time with my friends because my daughter is so enchanted by the setting... waiters tend to be very accommodating... they always give me (with my three kiddos) an extra-large table... watch the toy section chock full of 'but I want it' items..."

Children's menu .... ✓ | $$$ .... Prices

Changing station ✓ | ❹ Customer service
Highchairs/boosters ✓ | ❹ Stroller access

WWW.RAINFORESTCAFE.COM

TEMPE—5000 S ARIZONA MILLS CIR (AT ARIZONA MILLS MALL); 480.752.9100; M-SA 11-9:30, SU 11-8

Red Robin ★★★½☆

"...very kid-oriented—loud, balloons, bright lights, colorful decor and a cheerful staff make Red Robin a favorite among parents and children... the food is mainly burgers (beef or chicken)... loud music covers even the most boisterous of screaming... lots of kids—all the time... sometimes the wait can be long, but the arcade games and balloons help pass the time..."

Children's menu ✓ | $$ Prices
Changing station ✓ | ❹ Customer service
Highchairs/boosters ✓ | ❹ Stroller access

WWW.REDROBIN.COM

CHANDLER—3420 W CHANDLER BLVD (AT CHANDLER FASHION CTR); 480.814.7766

MESA—1636 S STAPLEY DR (AT RT 181); 480.892.7626

TEMPE—1375 W ELLIOT RD (AT SPORTS AUTHORITY PLAZA); 480.940.9900

Restaurant Mexico ★★★★☆

"...cheap, fast, tasty Mexican food... very accommodating to kids, and they bring the food quickly... they will make 1 scrambled egg for dinner or 1/ 2 an avocado, or other special requests from my son..."

Children's menu ✗ | $ Prices
Changing station ✗ | ❺ Customer service
Highchairs/boosters ✓ | ❺ Stroller access

TEMPE—120 E UNIVERSITY DR (AT S MYRTLE AVE); 480.967.3280

Romano's Macaroni Grill ★★★★☆

"...family oriented and tasty... noisy so nobody cares if your kids make noise... the staff goes out of their way to make families feel welcome... they even provide slings by the table for infant carriers... the noise level is pretty constant so it's not too loud, but loud enough so that crying babies don't disturb the other patrons... good kids' menu with somewhat healthy items... crayons for kids to color on the paper tablecloths..."

Children's menu ✓ | $$$ Prices
Changing station ✓ | ❹ Customer service
Highchairs/boosters ✓ | ❹ Stroller access

WWW.MACARONIGRILL.COM

MESA—1705 S STAPLEY DR (AT E BASELINE DR); 480.632.2699; M-F 11-10, SA-SU 11-11

Ruby Tuesday ★★★½☆

"...nice variety of healthy choices on the kids' menu—turkey, spaghetti, chicken tenders... you can definitely find something healthy here... prices are on the high side, but at least everyone can find something they like... service is fast and efficient... my daughter makes a mess and they never let me clean it up... your typical chain, but it works—you'll be happy to see ample aisle space, storage for your stroller, and attentive staff..."

Children's menu ✓ | $$ Prices
Changing station ✓ | ❹ Customer service
Highchairs/boosters ✓ | ❸ Stroller access

WWW.RUBYTUESDAY.COM

MESA—6555 E SOUTHERN AVE (AT SUPERSTITION SPRINGS CTR); 480.641.8188; SU-TH 11-11, F-SA 11-12; PARKING IN FRONT OF BLDG

TEMPE—4 E UNIVERSITY DR (AT MILL AVE); 480.303.9660; SU-TH 11-11, F-SA 11-12; PARKING IN FRONT OF BLDG

Serrano's Mexican Food

"...my kids love the chips and salsa and bean dip... I really like the bean dip too... prices are very reasonable... atmosphere is great for kids..."

Children's menu .... ✓ | $ .... Prices
Changing station .... ✗ | ❹ .... Customer service
Highchairs/boosters .... ✓ | ❸ .... Stroller access

MESA—1955 W GUADALUPE RD (AT S DUBSON RD); 480.756.2992

Sonic Drive-In

"...the food is surprisingly good and the entertainment value is priceless... amazing cream pie shakes and breakfast all day... 50's-style car hop service always feels like an event... quick and convenient... corn dog and wacky-pack kids meals... not exactly healthy, but a fun, occasional outing..."

Children's menu .... ✓ | $$$ .... Prices
Changing station .... ✗ | ❸ .... Customer service
Highchairs/boosters .... ✓ | ❸ .... Stroller access

WWW.SONICDRIVEIN.COM

MESA—235 W UNIVERSITY (AT COUNTRY CLUB DR); 602.649.7931; SU-TH 6:30-11, F-SA 6:30-12AM

MESA—3033 E MCKELLIPS RD (AT LINDSAY RD); 480.854.9101; SU-TH 6:30-11, F-SA 6:30-12AM

MESA—618 W SOUTHERN AVE (AT COUNTRY CLUB DR); 480.649.5651; SU-TH 6:30-11, F-SA 6:30-12AM

MESA—647 E MCKELLIPS RD (AT MESA DR); 602.964.8380; SU-TH 6:30-11, F-SA 6:30-12AM

TEMPE—1122 E BROADWAY RD (AT RURAL RD); 480.902.1800; SU-TH 6:30-11, F-SA 6:30-12AM

Souplantation/Sweet Tomatoes

"...you can't beat the price and selection of healthy foods... all you can eat—serve yourself soup and salad bar... lots of healthy choices plus pizza and pasta... great for picky eaters... free for 2 and under and only $3 for kids under 5... booths for comfy seating and discreet breastfeeding... helps to have another adult along since it is self serve... they always bring fresh cookies to the table and offer to refill drinks..."

Children's menu .... ✓ | $$ .... Prices
Changing station .... ✓ | ❹ .... Customer service
Highchairs/boosters .... ✓ | ❹ .... Stroller access

WWW.SOUPLANTATION.COM

AHWATUKEE—4723 E RAY RD (AT AHWATUKEE FOOTHILLS TOWNE CTR); 480.705.8774; SU-TH 11-9, F-SA 11-10

TEMPE—1410 E SOUTHERN AVE (AT S MCCLINTOCK DR); 480.831.1600; SU-TH 11-9, F-SA 11-10

West Valley

"lila picks"

★Bill Johnson's Big Apple

restaurants

Applebee's Neighborhood Grill

"...geared to family dining—they expect you to be loud and leave a mess... macaroni & cheese, hot dogs, and tasty grilled cheese... activity book and special kids cup are a bonus... service can be slow, but they will cover you with things to snack on... stay clear on Friday and Saturday nights... comfort food in a casual atmosphere... even though it's part of a very large chain you get the feeling it's a neighborhood-type place..."

Children's menu .... ✓ $$ .... Prices
Changing station .... ✓ ❹ .... Customer service
Highchairs/boosters .... ✓ ❸ .... Stroller access

WWW.APPLEBEES.COM

GOODYEAR—13832 W MCDOWELL RD (AT N LITCHFIELD RD); 623.536.8440

Bill Johnson's Big Apple

"...yee-haw, pardner... what kid doesn't love the cowboy atmosphere and food... sawdust on the floor. and other Old West decor... a rootin' tootin' good time... terrific food and service, at great prices... I've been coming here for 20 years (my father used to take me) and I still enjoy it... a family favorite..."

Children's menu .... ✓ $$ .... Prices
Changing station .... ✓ ❹ .... Customer service
Highchairs/boosters .... ✓ ❹ .... Stroller access

WWW.BILLJOHNSONS.COM

AVONDALE—1330 N DYSART RD (AT VAN BUREN ST); 623.882.8288

Chili's Grill & Bar

"...family-friendly, mild Mexican fare... delicious ribs, soups, salads... kids' menu and crayons as you sit down... on the noisy side, so you don't mind if your kids talk in their usual loud voices... service is excellent... fun night out with the family... a wide variety of menu selections for kids and their parents—all at a reasonable price... best chicken fingers on any kids' menu..."

Children's menu .... ✓ $$ .... Prices
Changing station .... ✓ ❹ .... Customer service
Highchairs/boosters .... ✓ ❹ .... Stroller access

WWW.CHILIS.COM

GOODYEAR—1371 N LITCHFIELD RD (AT W MCDOWELL RD); 623.535.4222; SU-TH 11-11, F-SA 11-12

Fazoli's

"...quick, easy and satisfying Italian food... spacious and comfortable... free breadsticks to keep little minds in check before the meatballs and pasta arrive... a nice step up from the easy fast-food trap... service is quick and the food is good..."

Children's menu .... ✓ | $$ .... Prices
Changing station .... ✓ | ❹ .... Customer service
Highchairs/boosters .... ✓ | ❸ .... Stroller access

WWW.FAZOLIS.COM

GOODYEAR—1340 N LITCHFIELD RD (AT W MCDOWELL RD); 623.536.9404; SU-TH 10:30-10, F-SA 10:30-11

Red Robin

"...very kid-oriented—loud, balloons, bright lights, colorful decor and a cheerful staff make Red Robin a favorite among parents and children... the food is mainly burgers (beef or chicken)... loud music covers even the most boisterous of screaming... lots of kids—all the time... sometimes the wait can be long, but the arcade games and balloons help pass the time..."

Children's menu .... ✓ | $$ .... Prices
Changing station .... ✓ | ❹ .... Customer service
Highchairs/boosters .... ✓ | ❹ .... Stroller access

WWW.REDROBIN.COM

AVONDALE—10240 W MCDOWELL RD (AT N 103RD AVE); 623.907.3460

doulas & lactation consultants

Editor's Note: Doulas and lactation consultants provide a wide range of services and are very difficult to classify, let alone rate. In fact the terms 'doula' and 'lactation consultant' have very specific industry definitions that are far more complex than we are able to cover in this brief guide. For this reason we have decided to list only those businesses and individuals who received overwhelmingly positive reviews, without listing the reviewers' comments.

Greater Phoenix Area

Association of Labor Assistants & Childbirth Educators (ALACE)

Labor doula .... ✓ ✗ .... Postpartum doula
Pre & post natal massage .... ✗ ✗ .... Lactation consultant

WWW.ALACE.ORG

PHOENIX—617.441.2500 52924

Baby Mother & More

Labor doula .... ✗ ✗ .... Postpartum doula
Pre & post natal massage .... ✗ ✓ .... Lactation consultant

WWW.MILKSMILE.COM

MESA—1235 S GILBERT RD (AT SOUTHERN); 480.890.1870; M-SA 10-6, SU 12-4; PARKING LOT

Banner Baywood Medical Center (Lactation Center)

Labor doula .... ✗ ✗ .... Postpartum doula
Pre & post natal massage .... ✗ ✓ .... Lactation consultant

WWW.BANNERHEALTH.COM

MESA—644 E BAYWOOD AVE (AT S CHESTNUT); 602.981.4482; CALL FOR SCHEDULE

Banner Desert Medical Center (Lactation Center)

Labor doula .... ✗ ✗ .... Postpartum doula
Pre & post natal massage .... ✗ ✓ .... Lactation consultant

WWW.BANNERHEALTH.COM

MESA—1400 S DOBSON RD (AT W SOUTHERN AVE); 480.512.3035

Banner Good Samaritan Medical Center (Lactation Services)

Labor doula .... ✗ ✗ .... Postpartum doula
Pre & post natal massage .... ✗ ✓ .... Lactation consultant

PHOENIX—1111 E MCDOWELL RD (AT N 11TH ST); 602.239.3502; CALL FOR SCHEDULE

Banner Thunderbird Medical Center

Labor doula .... ✗ ✗ .... Postpartum doula
Pre & post natal massage .... ✗ ✓ .... Lactation consultant

WWW.BANNERHEALTH.COM

GLENDALE—5555 W THUNDERBIRD RD (AT N 55TH AVE); 602.865.5920; CALL FOR SCHEDULE

BestFed

Labor doula .... ✗ ✗ .... Postpartum doula
Pre & post natal massage .... ✗ ✓ .... Lactation consultant

WWW.EBESTFED.COM

MESA—2025 S ALMA SCHOOL RD (AT W BASELINE RD); 480.820.4424; M-SA 9-7, SU 12-5

Chandler Regional Hospital (Lactation Services)

Labor doula .... ✗ | ✗ .... Postpartum doula
Pre & post natal massage .... ✗ | ✓ .... Lactation consultant

WWW.CHANDLERHOSPITAL.COM

CHANDLER—475 S DOBSON RD (AT W PECOS RD); 480.821.3163

Doulas of North America (DONA)

Labor doula .... ✓ | ✓ .... Postpartum doula
Pre & post natal massage .... ✗ | ✗ .... Lactation consultant

WWW.DONA.ORG

PHOENIX—888.788.3662

John C Lincoln Hospital (Lactation Services)

Labor doula .... ✗ | ✗ .... Postpartum doula
Pre & post natal massage .... ✗ | ✓ .... Lactation consultant

PHOENIX—250 E DUNLAP AVE (AT N 2ND WAY); 602.870.6060; CALL FOR SCHEDULE

La Leche League

Labor doula .... ✗ | ✗ .... Postpartum doula
Pre & post natal massage .... ✗ | ✓ .... Lactation consultant

WWW.LALECHELEAGUE.ORG

PHOENIX—VARIOUS LOCATIONS; 847.519.7730; CHECK SCHEDULE ONLINE

Paradise Valley Hospital (Lactation Services)

Labor doula .... ✗ | ✗ .... Postpartum doula
Pre & post natal massage .... ✗ | ✓ .... Lactation consultant

WWW.PARADISEVALLEYHOSPITAL.COM

PHOENIX—3929 E BELL RD (AT N 40TH ST); 602.923.5748

Phoenix Children's Hospital (Lactation Services)

Labor doula .... ✗ | ✗ .... Postpartum doula
Pre & post natal massage .... ✗ | ✓ .... Lactation consultant

PHOENIX—1919 E THOMAS RD (AT N 20TH ST); 602.546.1937; CALL FOR SCHEDULE

Scottsdale Healthcare (Lactation Services)

Labor doula .... ✗ | ✗ .... Postpartum doula
Pre & post natal massage .... ✗ | ✗ .... Lactation consultant

WWW.SHC.ORG

SCOTTSDALE—7400 E OSBORN (AT BY SCOTTSDALE STADIUM); 480.323.3563; CALL FOR SCHEDULE

SCOTTSDALE—7400 E THOMPSON PEAK PKWY; 480.882.4636; CALL FOR SCHEDULE

SCOTTSDALE—9003 E SHEA (AT N 90TH ST); 480.882.4636

exercise

Central Phoenix

"lila picks"

★Baby Boot Camp

★Stroller Strides

Baby Boot Camp

"...a great, low-cost, outdoor mom and baby workout... I've met some really fun moms and babies at these classes... not only fun, but more importantly I got results... the first class is free so there's no excuse not to give it a try... instructors are well-trained physical therapists that really know their stuff... class sizes are limited... it's like a personal trainer and motivational system all in one... I do their exercises even when I'm on my own with my baby..."

Prenatal	✗	$$$	Prices
Mommy & me	✓	❸	Decor
Child care available	✗	❸	Customer service

WWW.BABYBOOTCAMP.COM

PHOENIX—VARIOUS LOCATIONS (AT N 3RD ST); 602.526.8992; CHECK SCHEDULE ONLINE

Bally Total Fitness

"...whirlpool, child play center, personal trainers—this place really has it all... their day care makes it possible to have a great time working out and not worry about leaving your child behind... some locations have pools and spas too... lots of group classes so it's a nice way to meet new (postnatal) moms..."

Prenatal	✗	$$$$	Prices
Mommy & me	✗	❺	Decor
Child care available	✓	❺	Customer service

WWW.BALLY.COM

PHOENIX—15401 N 29TH AVE (AT W GREENWAY RD); 602.993.3366; CHECK SCHEDULE ONLINE; PARKING LOT

PHOENIX—3921 E INDIAN SCHOOL RD (AT N 40TH ST); 602.956.4116; CHECK SCHEDULE ONLINE; PARKING LOT

Biltmore Family Fitness

Prenatal	✗	✓	Mommy & me
Child care available	✗		

WWW.BILTMOREFAMILYFITNESS.COM

PHOENIX—4836 N 16TH ST (AT E PIERSON ST); 602.266.3494

Desert Song Yoga

"...love the pre-natal yoga class!.. they have one on a Saturday—thanks for recognizing that pregnant women may be working outside the home... everyone is great, and the location is like a little oasis in the center of Phoenix.... wonderful massages, too!..."

Prenatal ✓
Mommy & me ✓
Child care available ✗
$$$ Prices
❺ Decor
❺ Customer service
WWW.ADESERTSONG.COM

PHOENIX—4811 N 7TH ST (AT E CAMELBACK RD); 602.265.8222; CHECK SCHEDULE ONLINE; FREE

Jazzercise At ASA

"...the most fun I have ever had exercising... the dancing is a blast and the classes combine cardio with weights and stretching for a complete workout... not only a good workout, but it's actually fun too... nothing specifically postnatal about it—just a good sweaty workout..."

Prenatal ✗
Mommy & me ✗
Child care available ✗
$$$ Prices
❹ Decor
❺ Customer service

PHOENIX—5125 E THOMAS RD (AT N 40TH ST); 480.759.1199; CALL FOR SCHEDULE

Phoenix Jazzercise Center

"...love it!.. low impact and light..."

Prenatal ✗
Mommy & me ✗
Child care available ✓
$$$ Prices
❷ Decor
❸ Customer service
WWW.JAZZERCISE.COM

PHOENIX—12228 N CAVE CREEK RD (AT E THUNDERBIRD RD); 602.992.1552; DAILY 5:30AM-8PM; YES

Stroller Fit

"...a great workout for parents and the kids are entertained the whole time... a great way to ease back into exercise after your baby's birth... the instructor is knowledgeable about fitness and keeping babies happy... motivating, supportive, and fun for kids and moms... sometimes they even set up a play group for after class... not just a good workout, but also a great chance to meet other moms and kids..."

Prenatal ✗
Mommy & me ✓
Child care available ✗
$$$ Prices
❸ Decor
❸ Customer service
WWW.STROLLERFIT.COM

PHOENIX—VARIOUS LOCATIONS; 602.312.5389

Stroller Strides

"...fantastic fun and very effective for losing those post-baby pounds... this is the greatest way to stay in shape as a mom—you have your baby in the stroller with you the whole time... the instructors are very professional, knowledgeable and motivating... beautiful, outdoor locations... classes consist of power walking combined with body toning exercises using exercise tubing and strollers... a great way to bond with my baby and other moms..."

Prenatal ✗
Mommy & me ✓
Child care available ✗
$$$ Prices
❹ Decor
❹ Customer service
WWW.STROLLERSTRIDES.NET

PHOENIX—VARIOUS LOCATIONS; 800.917.4561; CHECK SCHEDULE ONLINE

YMCA

"...the variety of fitness programs offered is astounding... class types and quality vary from facility to facility, but it's a must for new moms to check out... most facilities offer some kind of kids' activities or childcare so you can time your workouts around the classes... aerobics,

yoga, pool—our Y even offers Pilates now... my favorite classes are the mom & baby yoga... the best bang for your buck... they have it all—great programs that meet the needs of a diverse range of families... ❞

Prenatal .... ✓ $$$ .... Prices
Mommy & me .... ✓ ❸ .... Decor
Child care available .... ✓ ❸ ....Customer service

WWW.VALLEYYMCA.ORG

PHOENIX—1030 E LIBERTY LN (AT S DESERT FOOTHILLS PKWY); 480.460.3959; CHECK SCHEDULE ONLINE

Yoga Pura

❝*...the best yoga studio around... love Jane & Eric... amazing place... also have massages and kids yoga!...* ❞

Prenatal .... ✗ $ .... Prices
Mommy & me .... ✗ ❺ .... Decor
Child care available .... ✗ ❺ ....Customer service

WWW.YOGAPURA.COM/

PHOENIX—15440 N 7TH ST (AT E CORAL GABLES DR); 602.843.7872; CHECK SCHEDULE ONLINE

Northeast Valley

"lila picks"

★Stroller Strides

At One Yoga

"...I love the mommy and me yoga class here... my baby started at 6 weeks... it was very soothing to her believe it or not... once she heard the music start after the first few classes she instantly was calm..."

Prenatal .... ✗ | $$ .... Prices
Mommy & me .... ✓ | ❺ .... Decor
Child care available .... ✗ | ❺ .... Customer service

WWW.ATONEYOGA.COM

SCOTTSDALE—10050 N SCOTTSDALE RD (AT E MOUNTAIN VIEW RD); 480.556.6044; CHECK SCHEDULE ONLINE

Gainey Village Health Club & Spa

"...outstanding facility with great child care, group exercise programs, equipment and cafe... you get what you pay for and this place is the best!..."

Prenatal .... ✗ | $$$$ .... Prices
Mommy & me .... ✗ | ❺ .... Decor
Child care available .... ✓ | ❺ .... Customer service

WWW.DMBCLUBS.COM

SCOTTSDALE—7477 E DOUBLETREE RANCH RD (AT N SCOTTSDALE RD); 480.609.6979; CHECK SCHEDULE ONLINE

Mountainside Fitness

"...great group fitness instructors... clean and beautiful... child care is good, too..."

Prenatal .... ✗ | $$$ .... Prices
Mommy & me .... ✗ | ❺ .... Decor
Child care available .... ✓ | ❺ .... Customer service

WWW.MOUNTAINSIDEFITNESS.COM

SCOTTSDALE—9375 E BELL RD (AT N 94TH ST); 480.502.2096; M-TH 4:30AM-11PM F 4:30AM-9PM SA-SU 6-9PM; PARKING LOT

Stroller Strides

"...fantastic fun and very effective for losing those post-baby pounds... this is the greatest way to stay in shape as a mom—you have your baby in the stroller with you the whole time... the instructors are very professional, knowledgeable and motivating... beautiful, outdoor locations... classes consist of power walking combined with body toning exercises using exercise tubing and strollers... a great way to bond with my baby and other moms..."

Prenatal .... ✗ | $$ .... Prices

Mommy & me .... ✓ ❹ .... Decor
Child care available .... × ❺ ....Customer service

WWW.STROLLERSTRIDES.NET

SCOTTSDALE—VARIOUS LOCATIONS (AT N 47TH PL); 800.917.4561; CHECK SCHEDULE ONLINE

SURPRISE—VARIOUS LOCATIONS; 602.319.7853; CHECK SCHEDULE ONLINE

Southeast Valley

"lila picks"

★Stroller Strides

Allstar Jazzercise Center ★★★★☆

"...I enjoyed it very much... jazzercise combines elements of jazz dance, resistance training, Pilates, yoga, kickboxing, and more to create truly effective programs for people of every age and fitness level..."

Prenatal ✗ | $$ Prices
Mommy & me ✗ | ❹ Decor
Child care available ✗ | ❹ Customer service

TEMPE—931 E ELLIOT RD (AT S RURAL RD); 480.503.0002

Bikram Yoga Tempe ★★★★☆

"...Bikram yoga is wonderful... more flexibility, weight loss, strength, muscle tone, anti-aging, discipline, improved circulation, relaxation, vitality, balance, deeper breathing, improved posture, strengthened immune system, normalize hormone levels... I love the staff..."

Prenatal ✗ | $$$ Prices
Mommy & me ✗ | ❸ Decor
Child care available ✗ | ❹ Customer service

WWW.BIKRAMYOGATEMPE.COM

TEMPE—1825 E GUADALUPE RD (AT S MCCLINTOCK DR); 480.777.0939; M-SU; YES

Bodyworks Studio Center For The Arts ★★★½☆

"...great mommy and me class... Wendy blends the verbal, experiential and non-verbal approaches in her practice by using movement, dream exploration, art, creative dance, yoga and voice... holistic health..."

Prenatal ✓ | $$ Prices
Mommy & me ✓ | ❹ Decor
Child care available ✗ | ❹ Customer service

WWW.BODYWORKS-STUDIO.COM

TEMPE—1801 S JEN TILLY LN (AT E BROADWAY RD); 480.894.2090; CHECK SCHEDULE ONLINE

Dahn Holistic Fitness ★★★★★

"...a combination of physical exercise, stretching, visualization, and meditation... tai chi, holistic healing, and kids camp... really enjoy this studio..."

Prenatal ✓ | $$$ Prices
Mommy & me ✓ | ❺ Decor
Child care available ✗ | ❺ Customer service

WWW.DAHNWORLD.COM

MESA—1404 W SOUTHERN AVE (AT FIESTA MALL); 480.464.9068; M-F 8-8 SA 10 ; PARKING LOT

Inner Vision Yoga ★★★★½

"...a nice yoga center for the serious yoga student... a great place to learn and meet like-minded people... wonderful prenatal yoga class... also have kids yoga at a reasonable rate... very experienced instructors that make you feel comfortable..."

Prenatal .... ✓ | $$$ .... Prices
Mommy & me .... ✓ | ❺ .... Decor
Child care available .... ✗ | ❺ .... Customer service

WWW.INNERVISIONYOGA.COM

CHANDLER—1949 W RAY RD (AT N DOBSON RD); 480.632.7899; CHECK SCHEDULE ONLINE; PARKING LOT

Lifetime Fitness ★★★★½

"...top-notch, beautiful, and huge facilities... plenty of equipment, both cardio and weights—never a wait for equipment... the childcare center is incredible—my kids think they're going to an indoor playground... many family and child activities... some locations offer a full service Aveda salon and spa... state-of-the-art and extremely family friendly..."

Prenatal .... ✗ | $ .... Prices
Mommy & me .... ✗ | ❺ .... Decor
Child care available .... ✓ | ❸ .... Customer service

WWW.LIFETIMEFITNESS.COM

GILBERT—381 E WARNER RD (AT CIVIC CTR DR); 480.892.5020; CHECK SCHEDULE ONLINE; PARKING LOT

TEMPE—1616 W RUBY DR (AT S PRIEST DR); 480.735.5200; CHECK SCHEDULE ONLINE; PARKING LOT

Mountainside Fitness ★★★★★

"...a great gym!.. the equipment is very nice, and you can make your membership include different things—including child care!..."

Prenatal .... ✓ | $ .... Prices
Mommy & me .... ✗ | ❺ .... Decor
Child care available .... ✓ | ❸ .... Customer service

WWW.MOUNTAINSIDEFITNESS.COM

CHANDLER—1920 S ALMA SCHOOL RD (AT W GERMANN RD); 480.732.9777; M-TH 4:30AM-9PM F 4:30AM-9PM SA-SU 6-9PM; PARKING LOT

Premier Pilates ★★★★★

"...Colleen is very knowledgeable... great people, and great energy... a thorough workout..."

Prenatal .... ✓ | $$ .... Prices
Mommy & me .... ✓ | ❺ .... Decor
Child care available .... ✗ | ❺ .... Customer service

WWW.PREMIER-PILATES.COM

GILBERT—425 W GUADALUPE RD (AT N NEELY ST); 480.777.1061; M-F 6-8, SA 7-12; AVAILABLE FREE

Red Mountain Multigenerational Center ★★★★★

"...a fantastic place with children's activities, exercise classes, walking track, gym equipment, and childcare while mom/dad works out... no swimming pool, but it's great anyways..."

Prenatal .... ✗ | $$ .... Prices
Mommy & me .... ✗ | ❹ .... Decor
Child care available .... ✗ | ❺ .... Customer service

WWW.REDMOUNTAINCENTER.COM

MESA—7550 E ADOBE RD (AT BETWEEN N 80TH AND N SUNVALLEY BLVD); 480.644.4810; M-F 5:30-10 SA 8-1

Stroller Strides

“...fantastic fun and very effective for losing those post-baby pounds... this is the greatest way to stay in shape as a mom—you have your baby in the stroller with you the whole time... the instructors are very professional, knowledgeable and motivating... beautiful, outdoor locations... classes consist of power walking combined with body toning exercises using exercise tubing and strollers... a great way to bond with my baby and other moms...”

Prenatal	×	$$$	Prices
Mommy & me	✓	❸	Decor
Child care available	×	❸	Customer service

WWW.STROLLERSTRIDES.NET

AHWATUKEE—VARIOUS LOCATIONS; 480.540.3380; CHECK SCHEDULE ONLINE

YMCA

“...the variety of fitness programs offered is astounding... class types and quality vary from facility to facility, but it's a must for new moms to check out... most facilities offer some kind of kids' activities or childcare so you can time your workouts around the classes... aerobics, yoga, pool—our Y even offers Pilates now... my favorite classes are the mom & baby yoga... the best bang for your buck... they have it all—great programs that meet the needs of a diverse range of families...”

Prenatal	✓	$$$	Prices
Mommy & me	✓	❸	Decor
Child care available	✓	❹	Customer service

WWW.VALLEYYMCA.ORG

MESA—207 N MESA DR (AT E 2ND ST); 480.969.8166; CHECK SCHEDULE ONLINE

TEMPE—7070 S RURAL RD (AT E BELL DE MAR DR); 480.730.4523; CHECK SCHEDULE ONLINE; FREE PARKING

Yoga Planet

“...great for beginners, too... love the instructors, classes, and atmosphere... very personable and experienced staff...”

Prenatal	✓	$$$	Prices
Mommy & me	×	❺	Decor
Child care available	×	❺	Customer service

WWW.PLANETYOGA.COM/

TEMPE—21 E 6TH ST (AT S MILL AVE); 480.303.9642; CHECK SCHEDULE ONLINE

parent education & support

Greater Phoenix Area

"lila picks"

★Best Fed

★Bethany Womens Healthcare Center

★Chandler Regional Hospital

★Scottsdale Healthcare

Arrowhead Community Hospital And Medical Center

Childbirth classes .... ✗ ✓ .... Breastfeeding support
Parent group/club .... ✗ ✗ .... Child care info

WWW.ARROWHEADHOSPITAL.COM

GLENDALE —18701 N 67TH AVE (AT W UNION HILLS DR); 623.561.4535

Baby Signs (Jenny Hodges, Helping Hands)

Childbirth classes .... ✗ ✗ .... Breastfeeding support
Parent group/club .... ✓ ✗ .... Child care info

WWW.BABYSIGNS.COM

CHANDLER—1812 W ROSAL DR (AT W NOPAL DR); 480.917.4811; CHECK SCHEDULE ONLINE

Banner Baywood Medical Center

Childbirth classes .... ✗ ✓ .... Breastfeeding support
Parent group/club .... ✗ ✗ .... Child care info

WWW.BANNERHEALTH.COM

MESA—644 E BAYWOOD AVE (AT S CHESTNUT); 602.230.2273; CALL FOR SCHEDULE

Banner Desert Medical Center

Childbirth classes .... ✗ ✓ .... Breastfeeding support
Parent group/club .... ✗ ✗ .... Child care info

WWW.BANNERHEALTH.COM

MESA—1400 S DOBSON RD (AT W SOUTHERN AVE); 602.230.2273; CALL FOR SCHEDULE

Banner Good Samaritan Medical Center

Childbirth classes .... ✗ ✓ .... Breastfeeding support
Parent group/club .... ✗ ✗ .... Child care info

PHOENIX—1111 E MCDOWELL RD (AT N 11TH ST); 602.230.2273; CALL FOR SCHEDULE

Banner Mesa Medical Center

Childbirth classes .... ✗ ✓ .... Breastfeeding support
Parent group/club .... ✗ ✗ ....Child care info

WWW.BANNERHEALTH.COM

MESA—1010 N COUNTRY CLUB DR (AT W 10TH ST); 602.230.2273

Banner Thunderbird Medical Center

Childbirth classes .... ✗ ✓ .... Breastfeeding support
Parent group/club .... ✗ ✗ ....Child care info

WWW.BANNERHEALTH.COM

GLENDALE—5555 W THUNDERBIRD RD (AT N 55TH AVE); 602.230.2273; CALL FOR SCHEDULE

BestFed ★★★★★

"...you will learn everything you ever wanted to know about breastfeeding from this place... they made it so much easier than I thought it was going to be... no matter what came up, I always felt like I had somewhere to turn to... wonderful staff who are truly devoted to babies and their mothers..."

Childbirth classes .... ✗ $$$ .... Prices
Parent group/club .... ✗ ❸ .... Class selection
Breastfeeding support .... ✓ ❸ .... Staff knowledge
Child care info .... ✗ ❸ .... Customer service

WWW.EBESTFED.COM

MESA—2025 S ALMA SCHOOL RD (AT W BASELINE RD); 480.820.4424; M-SA 9-7, SU 12-5

Bethany Womens Healthcare Center ★★★★★

"...the classes we took here were well taught and helped us imagine what the real child birth would be like... we felt prepared and ready when the big day came... practical advice, not just a bunch of statistics... just the real nitty-gritty (delivered with humor and tact, of course)... wonderful people who really care about you and your baby, before and after the delivery..."

Childbirth classes .... ✓ $ .... Prices
Parent group/club .... ✗ ❺ .... Class selection
Breastfeeding support .... ✗ ❺ .... Staff knowledge
Child care info .... ✗ ❹ .... Customer service

WWW.BETHANYWOMEN.COM

PHOENIX—3660 W BETHANY HOME RD (AT N 35TH AVE); 602.973.3200

Chandler Regional Hospital ★★★★★

"...I had a wonderful experience delivering here and enjoyed their birthing class... the breastfeeding class was especially helpful... tons of information and I am sure that their breastfeeding class contributed to our success because I felt prepared... CPR and new mom classes, too... don't miss the big sib classes..."

Childbirth classes .... ✓ $$ .... Prices
Parent group/club .... ✗ ❹ .... Class selection
Breastfeeding support .... ✓ ❹ .... Staff knowledge
Child care info .... ✗ ❹ .... Customer service

WWW.CHANDLERHOSPITAL.COM

CHANDLER—475 S DOBSON RD (AT W PECOS RD); 480.821.3935; CALL FOR SCHEDULE

Desert Samaritan Care Center

Childbirth classes .... ✗ ✓ .... Breastfeeding support

Parent group/club ✓ ✓ Child care info

WWW.BANNERHEALTH.COM

MESA—2145 W SOUTHERN AVE (AT S DOBSON RD); 602.230.2273

East Valley Family Resource Center

Childbirth classes ✗ ✓ Breastfeeding support
Parent group/club ✓ ✓ Child care info

WWW.CHILDCRISIS.ORG/FRC/INDEX.HTML

MESA—170 W UNIVERSITY DR (AT N COUNTRY CLUB DR); 480.834.9424

John C Lincoln Hospital

Childbirth classes ✗ ✓ Breastfeeding support
Parent group/club ✗ ✗ Child care info

PHOENIX—250 E DUNLAP AVE (AT N 2ND WAY); 602.870.6300; CALL FOR SCHEDULE

Lamaze International ★★★★☆

"...thousands of women each year are educated about the birth process by Lamaze educators... their web site offers a list of local instructors... they follow a basic curriculum, but invariably class quality will depend on the individual instructor... in many ways they've set the standard for birth education classes..."

Childbirth classes ✓ $$$ Prices
Parent group/club ✗ ❸ Class selection
Breastfeeding support ✗ ❸ Staff knowledge
Child care info ✗ ❸ Customer service

WWW.LAMAZE.ORG

PHOENIX—VARIOUS LOCATIONS; 800.368.4404; CHECK SCHEDULE AND LOCATIONS ONLINE

Mocha Moms ★★★★½

"...a wonderfully supportive group of women—the kind of place where both mother and child will make lifelong friends... a comfortable forum for bouncing ideas off of other moms with same-age children... easy to get involved and not too demanding... the annual membership dues seem a small price to pay for the many activities, play groups, field trips, Moms Nights Out and book club meetings... local chapters in cities nationwide..."

Childbirth classes ✗ $ Prices
Parent group/club ✓ ❸ Class selection
Breastfeeding support ✗ ❸ Staff knowledge
Child care info ✗ ❹ Customer service

WWW.MOCHAMOMS.ORG

PHOENIX—VARIOUS LOCATIONS

MOMS Club ★★★★☆

"...an international nonprofit with lots of local chapters and literally tens of thousands of members... designed to introduce you to new mothers with same-age kids wherever you live... they organize all sorts of activities and provide support for new mothers with babies... very inexpensive for all the activities you get... book clubs, moms night out, play group connections... generally a very diverse group of women..."

Childbirth classes ✗ $$$ Prices
Parent group/club ✓ ❸ Class selection
Breastfeeding support ✗ ❸ Staff knowledge
Child care info ✗ ❸ Customer service

WWW.MOMSCLUB.ORG

CENTRAL PHOENIX—VARIOUS LOCATIONS

Mothers and More

"...a very neat support system for moms who are deciding to stay at home... a great way to get together with other moms in your area for organized activities... book clubs, play groups, even a 'mom's only' night out... local chapters offer more or less activities depending on the involvement of local moms..."

Childbirth classes .... ×
Parent group/club .... ✓
Breastfeeding support .... ×
Child care info .... ×

$$$ .... Prices
❸ .... Class selection
❸ .... Staff knowledge
❸ .... Customer service

WWW.MOTHERSANDMORE.COM

PHOENIX—VARIOUS LOCATIONS; CHECK SCHEDULES & LOCATIONS ONLINE

Paradise Valley Hospital

Childbirth classes .... ×
Parent group/club .... ✓
✓ .... Breastfeeding support
× .... Child care info

WWW.PARADISEVALLEYHOSPITAL.COM

PHOENIX—3929 E BELL RD (AT N 40TH ST); 877.784.5005; CALL FOR SCHEDULE

Phoenix Children's Hospital

Childbirth classes .... ×
Parent group/club .... ×
✓ .... Breastfeeding support
× .... Child care info

PHOENIX—1919 E THOMAS RD (AT N 20TH ST); 602.546.1000; CALL FOR SCHEDULE

Scottsdale Healthcare

"...great classes all around and I especially enjoyed the infant CPR and birth basics... terrific instructors... I felt prepared for the delivery after the birth basics class... the best place in the Valley to have a baby!.. very informative..."

Childbirth classes .... ✓
Parent group/club .... ×
Breastfeeding support .... ✓
Child care info .... ×

$$$ .... Prices
❸ .... Class selection
❸ .... Staff knowledge
❸ .... Customer service

WWW.SHC.ORG

SCOTTSDALE—7400 E OSBORN (AT BY SCOTTSDALE STADIUM); 480.882.4636; CALL FOR SCHEDULE

SCOTTSDALE—7400 E THOMPSON PEAK PKWY (AT E THOMPSON PEAK PKWY); 480.882.4636; CALL FOR SCHEDULE

SCOTTSDALE—9003 E SHEA (AT N 90TH ST); 480.882.4636; CALL FOR SCHEDULE

St Joseph's Hospital Medical Center

Childbirth classes .... ×
Parent group/club .... ×
✓ .... Breastfeeding support
× .... Child care info

WWW.ICHOSESTJOES.COM

PHOENIX—222 W THOMAS RD (AT N CENTRAL AVE); 602.406.3420; CALL FOR SCHEDULE

pediatricians

Editor's Note: Pediatricians provide a tremendous breadth of services and are very difficult to classify and rate in a brief guide. For this reason we list only those practices for which we received overwhelmingly positive reviews. We hope this list of pediatricians will help you in your search.

Greater Phoenix Area

Ahwatukee Pediatrics

WWW.AHWATUKEEPEDS.COM

PHOENIX—4545 E CHANDLER BLVD (AT S 46TH ST); 480.496.6444; M-F 9-5 SA 8:30-4

All About Kids Pediatrics

TEMPE—4450 S RURAL RD (AT S LAKESHORE DR); 480.820.3188; M-TH 8-5 F 8-3

Arrowhead Pediatrics

WWW.ARROWHEADHOSPITAL.COM

GLENDALE—18700 N 64TH DR (AT W UNION HILLS DR); 623.561.5437; M-TH 8:30-5:30 F 8:30-5

SUN CITY WEST—14300 W GRANITE VALLEY DR (AT MEEKER BLVD); 623.556.5437; M-F 8:30-5:30; PARKING IN FRONT OF BLDG

East Valley Childrens Center

WWW.EVCC.NET

TEMPE—3200 S GEORGE DR (AT E GENEVA DR); 480.839.9097; M-F 8-5

East Valley Pediatrics

MESA—6553 E BAYWOOD AVE (AT VALLEY LUTHERAN HOSPITAL); 480.615.2010; M-F 8-5

Gentile, Mark MD

CHANDLER—908 W CHANDLER BLVD (AT N PLEASANT DR); 480.857.0222; M-F 8-4:30

Gilbert Pediatrics

MESA—4540 E BASELINE RD (AT S GREENFIELD RD); 480.892.3880; M-F 8:30-5

Happy Kids Pediatrics

MESA—135 S POWER RD (AT E MAIN); 480.214.0051; M-F 9-5

Kids First Pediatrics

TEMPE—4653 S LAKESHORE DR (AT E MINSTON DR); 480.838.9797; M-TH 8-5, F 8-3

Kids Kare Pediatrics

PHOENIX—515 W BUCKEYE RD (AT W BUCKEYE RD); 602.254.0390; M-F 8-5

McAuley Pediatrics P C

PHOENIX—500 W THOMAS RD (AT W THOMAS RD); 602.776.9511; M-F 9-5 SA 9-12

Mesa Pediatrics

WWW.MESAPEDS.COM

PHOENIX—5110 E WARNER RD (AT 6 KI DR); 480.785.8700; M-F 8-5

Pediatric Associates

PHOENIX—7600 N 15TH ST (AT N 15TH ST); 602.861.1611; M-F 8-6

Pediatrix

PHOENIX—2316 W BETHANY HOME RD (AT W BETHANY HOME RD); 602.242.7190; M-F 8-6

Phoenix Pediatrics

PHOENIX—6702 N 19TH AVE (AT PARADISE VALLEY HOSPITAL); 602.971.5121; M-F 8-4:30

Rainbow Pediatrics

PHOENIX—301 W MCDOWELL RD (AT N 3RD AVE); 602.257.8070; M-F 9-5

Saguaro Pediatrics

PHOENIX—4530 E RAY RD (AT S 44TH ST); 480.783.8960; M-F 8-5; PARKING LOT

Scottsdale Children's Group

WWW.SCOTTSDALECHILDRENSGROUP.COM

SCOTTSDALE—7555 E OSBORN RD (AT N MILLER RD); 480.609.8100; M-F 8-5

Sierra Pediatrics

GILBERT—1546 N PKWY DR (AT N VAL VISTA DR); 480.644.1466; M-F 8:30-4:30

breast pump sales & rentals

Greater Phoenix Area

"lila picks"

- ★Babies R Us
- ★Baby Mother & More
- ★BestFed
- ★Mothers' Milk Boutique

Babies R Us

"...Medela pumps, Boppy pillows and lots of other breastfeeding supplies... staff knowledge varies from store to store, but everyone was friendly and helpful... clean and well-stocked... not a huge selection, but what they've got is great and very competitively priced..."

Customer Service .... ❹ $$$ .... Prices

WWW.BABIESRUS.COM

GLENDALE—7540 W BELL RD (AT ARROWHEAD TOWNE CTR); 623.878.3810; M-SA 9:30-9:30, SU11-7; PARKING IN FRONT OF BLDG

PHOENIX—4835 E RAY RD (AT 14TH ST); 480.705.0400; M-SA 9:30-9:30, SU 11-7; PARKING LOT

SCOTTSDALE—7000 E MAYO BLVD (AT SCOTTSDALE RD); 480.585.7362; M-SA 9:30-9:30, SU 11-7; PARKING LOT

Baby Mother & More

"...they carry everything a nursing mom needs to be successful... reasonable prices... great selection of nursing bras... a lactation specialist will help you find the right breast pump for you..."

Customer Service .... ❺ $$$ .... Prices

WWW.MILKSMILE.COM

MESA—1235 S GILBERT RD (AT SOUTHERN); 480.890.1870; M-SA 10-6, SU 12-4; PARKING LOT

BestFed

"...specializes in nursing supplies and clothing... knowledgeable staff who are easy to approach... the lactation consultants are very helpful and offers breastfeeding classes... hospital-grade breast pumps available... they do their best to remember your name... Web site and newsletters are loaded with information on breastfeeding..."

Customer Service .... ❹ $$$ .... Prices

WWW.EBESTFED.COM

MESA—2025 S ALMA SCHOOL RD (AT W BASELINE RD); 480.820.4424; M-SA 9-7, SU 12-5

PHOENIX—4920 W THUNDERBIRD RD (AT N 49TH AVE); 602.843.4111; M-SA 9-7, SU 12-5; PARKING LOT

Breastfeeding Pump N Go

"...I got a great pump here, at a reasonable price... Doris is wonderful—she holds a free moms' support group twice a week..."

Customer Service .... ❹ $$ .... Prices

WWW.PUMP-N-GO.COM

MESA—2464 E MENLO ST (AT N 24TH ST); 480.833.2262

Good Samaritan Gift Shop

WWW.BANNERHEALTH.COM/PATIENTS+AND+VISITORS/FACILITIES/ARIZONA/GOOD+SAMARITAN/DEFAULT.ASP

PHOENIX—1111 E MCDOWELL RD (AT GOOD SAMARITAN HOSPITAL); 602.239.5677; M-F 7:30-8

Mothers' Milk Boutique

"...locally-owned and operated store carrying unique maternity and nursing products... amazing lactation counseling... great place for alternatives... interesting selection of diaper bags... authorized Medela retailer... staff are helpful, kind and not pushy... you may pay a little more here, but you'll receive outstanding service..."

Customer Service .... ❺ $$$ .... Prices

WWW.MOTHERSMILKBOUTIQUE.COM

SCOTTSDALE—10816 N SCOTTSDALE RD (AT E SHEA BLVD); 480.922.4615; M-F 10-6, SA 10-5 ; PARKING LOT

Paradise Valley Hospital (Lactation Services)

WWW.PARADISEVALLEYHOSPITAL.COM

PHOENIX—3929 E BELL RD (AT N 40TH ST); 602.923.5748

Scottsdale Healthcare Shea

"...loved renting my breast pump from here... they show you how to use it and charge fair prices... informative and attentive nurses... if they don't have something they can help you find it..."

Customer Service .... ❺ $$ .... Prices

WWW.SHC.ORG

SCOTTSDALE—9003 E SHEA BLVD (AT N PIMA RD); 480.860.3655; M-F 8-8, SA 9-6, SU 10-5

USA Baby

WWW.USABABY.COM

PHOENIX—10630 N 32ND ST (AT E SHEA BLVD); 602.788.8200; M F 10-8, T-TH SA 10-6, SU 12-5; MALL PARKING

TEMPE—3143 S MCCLINTOCK DR (AT E SOUTHERN AVE); 480.897.2229; T TH SA 10-6, M W F 10-8, SU 12-5; MALL PARKING

Online

amazon.com

"...I'm always amazed by the amount of stuff Amazon sells—including a pretty good selection of pumps... Medela, Avent, Isis, Ameda... prices range from great to average... pretty easy shopping experience... free shipping on bigger orders..."

babycenter.com

"...they carry all the major brands... prices are competitive, but keep in mind you'll need to pay for shipping too... the comments from parents are incredibly helpful... excellent customer service... easy shopping experience..."

birthexperience.com

"...Medela and Avent products... great deal with the Canadian currency conversion... get free shipping with big orders... easy site to navigate..."

breast-pumps.com

breastmilk.com

ebay.com

"...you can get Medela pumps brand new in packaging with the warranty for $100 less than retail... able to buy immediately instead of having to bid and wait... wide variety... be sure to check for shipping price... great place to find deals, but research the seller before you bid..."

express-yourself.net

healthchecksystems.com

lactationconnection.com

"...Ameda and Whisper Wear products... nice selection and competitive prices... quick delivery of any nursing or lactation product you can imagine... the selection of mom and baby related items is fantastic..."

medela.com

"...well worth the money... fast, courteous and responsive... great site for a full listing of Medela products and links to purchase online... quality of customer service by phone varies... licensed lactation specialist answers e-mail via email at no charge and with quick turnaround..."

mybreastpump.com

"...a great online one-stop-shop for all things breast feeding... you can purchase hospital grade pumps from them... fast service for all your breastfeeding needs..."

diaper delivery services

Greater Phoenix Area

Baby Love Diaper Service ★★★★☆

"...worth it for babies with allergies or really sensitive skin... we had our little one two weeks early, and Chuck was great about getting diapers on our doorstep the very next day... he also has a breastfeeding supply store, and delivered my breast pump with the diapers one week..."

Customer Service ....❸ $$$.. Prices

Service Area .. greater 'Mesa, AZ' area

WWW.MILKSMILE.COM

MESA—320 E 10TH DR (AT S WILBUR); 480.890.9004

Bare Care Diaper Service ★★★★½

"...I received a gift certificate for this service and they were wonderful... very reliable and flexible... excellent service, family owned and operated, friendly service..."

Customer Service ....❸ $$$.. Prices

Service Area ....call for info

SURPRISE—15287 W LAUREL LN (AT W GARNETTE DR); 623.556.2820

haircuts

Greater Phoenix Area

"lila picks"

★Cool Cuts 4 Kids

★Snip-its Haircuts For Kids

Big & Tiny Cuts

"...the girls who cut hair here are the greatest... the staff treats my girl like a little princess... wonderful and fun..."

Customer Service .... 5 $$.. Prices

EL MIRAGE—12550 W THUNDERBIRD RD (AT N 126TH AVE); 623.933.2214

Camargos Kid Cuts

MESA—1706 E BROADWAY RD (AT S GILBERT RD); 480.834.3636; CALL FOR APPT

Cool Cuts 4 Kids

"...they're quick and keep kids engaged... fun cars to sit in and videos galore... it's almost like going on a play date rather than a haircut... the colorful waiting area is well-equipped to keep youngsters busy... kids can sit in cars, watch movies, or play video games while getting their hair cut... an ideal place for that first haircut because of all of the distractions... call ahead for an appointment—walk-ins usually have a long wait time..."

Customer Service .... 4 $$.. Prices

WWW.COOLCUTS4KIDS.COM

GILBERT—756 S GILBERT RD (AT SONORA TOWN); 480.545.0272; M-F 10-7, SA 9-7, SU 11-5

GLENDALE—7260 W BELL RD (AT N 75TH AVE); 623.776.7229; M-F 10-8, SA 9-7, SU 11-5

MESA—2120 S POWER RD (AT FACTORY STORES OF AMERICA); 480.654.6574; M-F 10-8, SA 9-7, SU 11-5

PHOENIX—420 E BELL RD (AT N 3RD ST); 602.504.2413; M-F 10-7, SA 9-7, SU 11-5

PHOENIX—4515 E CACTUS RD (AT N TATUM BLVD); 602.493.9090; M-F 9-7, SA 9-7, SU 11-5

SCOTTSDALE—15640 N PIMA RD (AT E FRANK LLYOD WRIGHT BLVD); 480.951.3234; M-F 10-7, SA 9-7, SU 11-5

TEMPE—1020 W ELLIOT RD (AT S HARDY DR); 480.831.6102; M-F 10-8, SA 9-7, SU 11-5

Cost Cutters Family Hair Care

"...these guys are great for a quick, cheap hair cut for kids... although they are a chain, they treat the kids really well... only $9.95 for a cut for all kids 10 and under... the best part is that they get a toy after their haircut —it's different each month and is pretty much the highlight of our visit..."

Customer Service .... 3 $$.. Prices

WWW.COSTCUTTERS.COM

GILBERT—3701 E BASELINE RD (OFF N VAL VISTA DR); 480.926.2651; DAILY 9-7; FREE PARKING

Headlines

PEORIA—16610 N 75TH AVE (AT W BELL RD); 623.939.0552; CALL FOR APPT

Kid's Kuts

“...very attentive and excellent with children... a great place to go for the big event—they make it special and my kids were beaming...”

Customer Service .... ❺ $$ .... Prices

SCOTTSDALE—7115 E MERCER LN (AT N SCOTTSDALE RD); 480.483.8447; CALL FOR APPT

Madrid's

“...a great barber shop—especially if you have tight, curly hair... they do everything for adults and kids...great for African American hair...”

Customer Service .... ❺ $$ .... Prices

WWW.MADRIDSBARBERSHOP.COM

PHOENIX—648 W PIERSON ST (AT N 7TH AVE); 602.264.9686; T-F 8:30-6, SA 8-6

Mini Cuts

“...a great place for kids haircuts... cars to sit in, videos to watch and toys for siblings to play with while they wait... a very fun atmosphere... it doesn't feel like going to a hair salon -, but almost like going to an amusement park...”

Customer Service .... ❸ $$ .... Prices

WWW.MINICUTS.COM

CHANDLER—3855 W RAY RD (AT N MCCLINTOCK DR); 480.812.3600; M-F 10-7, SA 9-7, SU 11-5

Minnows Kids Cuts

WWW.CANYONFALLS.COM

SCOTTSDALE—14891 N NORTHSIGHT BLVD (AT E RAINTREE DR); 480.998.0333; M-F 8-8, SA 8-6, SU 9-5

Snip-its Haircuts For Kids

“...the entertainment is unbeatable... kids' haircuts without all the stress... the only place we ever go... quick, painless and relatively cheap... they really know kids and how to keep them entertained while snipping away... they do a fabulous job... long waits (can be an hour or more) and they don't take appointments unless you join a VIP club... bubbles, videos, games and lollipops kept my daughter busy throughout the cut... patient stylists who know all the tricks to put your little one at ease... pricey, but worth it for a stylist used to squirming kids...”

Customer Service .... ❸ $$$ .... Prices

WWW.SNIPITS.COM

CHANDLER—3415 W FRYE RD (AT CHANDLER VILLAGE CTR); 480.963.0800; M-F 10-8, SA 9-8, SU 11-6; MALL PARKING

nanny & babysitter referrals

Greater Phoenix Area

"lila picks"

★A Plus Nannies Inc

A Plus Nannies Inc

"...A Plus Nannies has been a life saver!.. knowledgeable and experienced staff... high quality nannies... everything is done by the book... very professional and very friendly... I felt very comfortable talking with them, and at the end of our conversation I knew I would never find a better nanny company... noticed they were a member of the BBB and the Alliance of Professional Nanny Agencies—evidence of their commitment to customer service, as well as high business ethics..."

Baby nurses	✗	$$	Prices
Nannies	✓	❺	Candidate selection
Au pairs	✗	❺	Staff knowledge
Babysitters	✗	❺	Customer service

WWW.APLUSNANNIESINC.COM

MESA—1859 N MORRIS (AT W JASMINE ST); 480.699.7558

All About Nannies

"...the owner Dianna is great and really wants to work with you as a family... very personable, thorough, and dedicated... they make the process pretty easy..."

Baby nurses	✓	$$$	Prices
Nannies	✓	❸	Candidate selection
Au pairs	✗	❸	Staff knowledge
Babysitters	✗	❸	Customer service

WWW.ALLABOUTNANNIES.ORG

SCOTTSDALE—8912 E PINNACLE PEAK RD (AT N PIMA RD); 480.948.3901

Child Care Resource & Referral

"...free service—provides resource listings for child care by age group... able to pull listings near home, work, or your route to work... you'll still need to do a lot of your own searching using the listings they provide, but it's a great place to start..."

Baby nurses	✗	$$	Prices
Nannies	✗	❹	Candidate selection
Au pairs	✗	❹	Staff knowledge
Babysitters	✗	❹	Customer service

WWW.AZCHILDCARE.ORG

TEMPE—3910 S RURAL RD (AT US HWY 60); 602.244.2678; M-F 8-5

Nanny Exchange Inc

"...provide a wide variety of caretaking employees, ranging from babysitters, to nannies, to personal chefs!.. they really have everything you need, for a reasonable fee... especially good if you are new in town and don't know where to begin looking for help..."

Baby nurses	×	$$$$	Prices
Nannies	✓	❸	Candidate selection
Au pairs	×	❸	Staff knowledge
Babysitters	✓	❶	Customer service

WWW.NANNYEXCHANGE.COM

TEMPE—4625 S WENDLER DR (AT RT 10); 602.458.9700

Nanny On The Net, A

"...a national agency that places experienced (at least three years) nannies... easy to use and efficient... detailed background checks... all prospects are trained in CPR... legal, financial, and practical help for first-time 'employer' families... about $75 for the application fee and then additional placement fees when you succeed in finding a nanny..."

Baby nurses	✓	$$$	Prices
Nannies	✓	❸	Candidate selection
Au pairs	×	❸	Staff knowledge
Babysitters	×	❸	Customer service

WWW.ANANNYONTHENET.COM

PHOENIX—888.436.0222; M-F 9-5

Parents Time Out

"...very informative and easy to work with... a reasonable way to find a nanny... a great babysitting resource, although a bit pricey..."

Baby nurses	✓	$$$	Prices
Nannies	✓	❸	Candidate selection
Au pairs	×	❹	Staff knowledge
Babysitters	×	❹	Customer service

WWW.PTOFAMILY.COM

PHOENIX—951 E S FORK DR (AT E S FORK DR); 480.460.1200

Peace of Mind Referral Service

Baby nurses	×	✓	Nannies
Au pairs	×	×	Babysitters

GILBERT—1014 E BETSY LN (AT S NIELSON ST); 480.732.1234

Village Connection

"...tend to be a bit on the pricier side—however, they are very thorough in terms of doing background checks and pre-screening... a nice plus is that they have a 90 day placement guarantee... they also refer therapists and tutors..."

Baby nurses	×	$$$	Prices
Nannies	✓	❸	Candidate selection
Au pairs	×	❸	Staff knowledge
Babysitters	×	❸	Customer service

WWW.VILLAGECONNECTION.COM

MESA —2650 E SOUTHERN AVE (OFF S LINDSAY RD); 480.969.3493

Online

"lila picks"

★craigslist.org

4nannies.com

Baby nurses .... ✗ | ✓ .... Nannies
Au pairs .... ✗ | ✗ .... Babysitters
Service Area .... nationwide
WWW.4NANNIES.COM

aupaircare.com

Baby nurses .... ✗ | ✗ .... Nannies
Au pairs .... ✓ | ✗ .... Babysitters
Service Area .... International
WWW.AUPAIRCARE.COM

aupairinamerica.com

Baby nurses .... ✗ | ✗ .... Nannies
Au pairs .... ✓ | ✗ .... Babysitters
Service Area .... International
WWW.AUPAIRINAMERICA.COM

babysitters.com

Baby nurses .... ✗ | ✗ .... Nannies
Au pairs .... ✗ | ✓ .... Babysitters
Service Area .... nationwide
WWW.BABYSITTERS.COM

craigslist.org ★★★★★

"...you can find just about anything on craigslist... good starting point, especially if you don't want to spend a lot of money and are willing to do your own screening... we received at least 50 responses to our 'nanny wanted' ad... helped me find very qualified baby-sitters... includes all major cities in the US..."

Baby nurses .... ✓ | ✓ .... Nannies
Au pairs .... ✗ | ✓ .... Babysitters
WWW.CRAIGSLIST.ORG

enannysource.com

Baby nurses .... ✗ | ✓ .... Nannies
Au pairs .... ✗ | ✗ .... Babysitters
Service Area .... nationwide
WWW.ENANNYSOURCE.COM

findcarenow.com

Baby nurses .... ✗ | ✗ .... Nannies
Au pairs .... ✗ | ✓ .... Babysitters
Service Area .... nationwide

WWW.FINDCARENOW.COM

get-a-sitter.com

Baby nurses ✗ | ✗ Nannies
Au pairs ✗ | ✓ Babysitters
Service Area nationwide
WWW.GET-A-SITTER.COM

householdstaffing.com

Baby nurses ✓ | ✓ Nannies
Au pairs ✗ | ✗ Babysitters
WWW.HOUSEHOLDSTAFFING.COM

interexchange.org

Baby nurses ✗ | ✗ Nannies
Au pairs ✓ | ✗ Babysitters
Service Area International
WWW.INTEREXCHANGE.ORG

nannies4hire.com

Baby nurses ✗ | ✓ Nannies
Au pairs ✗ | ✗ Babysitters
WWW.NANNIES4HIRE.COM

nannylocators.com ★★★½☆

"...many listings of local nannies available... I have found that the listings are not always up to date... $100 subscriber fee to respond and contact nannies that have posted... different regions have varying amounts of listings available..."

Baby nurses ✗ | ✓ Nannies
Au pairs ✗ | ✗ Babysitters
Service Area Nationwide
WWW.NANNYLOCATORS.COM

sittercity.com ★★★★☆

"...wonderful online resource... an online baby-sitter database filled with mostly college and graduate students looking for babysitting and nanny jobs... candidates are not pre-screened so you must check references... fee to access the database is $35 plus $5 per month... tends to be more useful for babysitters than regular daytime nannies..."

Baby nurses ✗ | ✗ Nannies
Au pairs ✗ | ✓ Babysitters
Service Area nationwide
WWW.SITTERCITY.COM

student-sitters.com

Baby nurses ✗ | ✗ Nannies
Au pairs ✗ | ✓ Babysitters
WWW.STUDENT-SITTERS.COM

photographers

Greater Phoenix Area

"lila picks"

★Kiddie Kandids

Contempo Portraits

MESA—1235 S GILBERT RD (AT E SOUTHERN AVE); 480.926.2216

Donna Hackney Photography ★★★☆☆

"...specializes in motherhood and child photography... very personalized and elegant... very natural looking photographs..."

Customer service........................❸ $$$..Prices

WWW.DONNAHACKNEY.COM

PHOENIX—602.432.4235

JCPenney Portrait Studio ★★★½☆

"...don't expect works of art, but they are great for a quick wallet photo... photographers and staff range from great to not so good... a quick portrait with standard props and backdrops... definitely join the portrait club and use coupons... waits are especially long around the holidays, so consider taking your Christmas pictures early... the e-picture option is a time saver... wait time for prints can be up to a month... look for coupons and you'll never have to pay full price..."

Customer service........................❹ $$..Prices

WWW.JCPENNEYPORTRAITS.COM

MESA—6525 E SOUTHERN AVE (AT SUPERSTITION SPRINGS CTR); 480.396.3311

Kathryn Smith Photography ★★★★☆

"...she is a talented photographer, and does wonderful work.... she tries very hard to work with you as much as possible... state-of-the-art photo equipment... very pretty, artistic pictures..."

Customer service........................❹ $$$..Prices

WWW.KATSMITHPHOTO.COM

CHANDLER—480.241.5544

Kiddie Kandids ★★★★★

"...good quality photos for all occasions... they made a big effort to get a smile out of my grumpy son... you don't need to make a reservation, just pop in and have the pictures taken... no sitting fee... photographers take the extra time necessary to get a great shot and they have the cutest props... lots of items to buy with your pictures on them—cups, bags, mouse pads... buy the CD of pictures rather than buying the prints... pictures are available right after the sitting..."

Customer service........................❹ $$$..Prices

WWW.KIDDIEKANDIDS.COM

AHWATUKEE—4835 E RAY RD (AT BABIES R US); 480.763.4228; M-SA 9:30-8, SU 11-6

CHANDLER—3111 W CHANDLER BLVD (AT CHANDLER FASHION CTR); 480.899.4066

GLENDALE—ARROWHEAD CENTER (AT BELL RD); 623.979.4000; M-SA 10-9, SU 11-6

MESA—6555 E SOUTHERN AVE (AT SUPERSTITION SPRINGS CTR); 480.654.8926

PHOENIX—4550-128 E CACTUS RD (AT PARADISE VALLEY); 602.494.4494

PHOENIX—9617 METRO PKWY WEST (AT METRO CENTER); 602.395.1884; M-SA 10-9, SU 11-6

TEMPE—5000 ARIZONA MILLS PKWY (AT RT 10); 480.897.6100

Kneka Smith Photography

"...excellent at drawing out a child's personality... beautiful photos of pregnant women... very professional... makes a true connection with children and it shows in her fabulous pictures... her great personality makes everyone feel comfortable... the web site is very user friendly and you can view your proofs and share them with friends and family and order all right online..."

Customer service .... ❺ $$ .... Prices

WWW.KNEKA.COM

PHOENIX—602.636.0211

Lisa Maynard Designs

"...she did the photographs at my children's school and they were not your typical school photos... these photos were creative and beautiful... she also makes lovely jewelry that you can put your photo inside of and show off!..."

Customer service .... ❺ $$$ .... Prices

PHOENIX—480.968.2417

Photography by Leanna

Customer service .... ❸ $$$ .... Prices

WWW.PHOTOSBYLEANNA.COM

PHOENIX—2312 E INDIAN SCHOOL RD (AT N 24TH ST); 602.224.7939; CALL FOR APPT; NA

Picture People

"...this well-known photography chain offers good package deals that get even better with coupons... generally friendly staff despite the often 'uncooperative' little customers... they don't produce super fancy, artistic shots, but you get your pictures in under an hour... reasonable quality for a fast portrait... kind of hit-or-miss quality and customer service..."

Customer service .... ❹ $$$ .... Prices

WWW.PICTUREPEOPLE.COM

CHANDLER—3111 W CHANDLER BLVD (AT CHANDLER FASHION CTR); 480.722.9004

GLENDALE—7700 W ARROWHEAD TOWNE CTR (AT BELL RD); 623.334.2350

MESA—6555 E SOUTHERN AVE (AT SUPERSTITION SPRINGS CTR); 480.396.6392

PHOENIX—4550-92 E CACTUS RD (AT PARADISE VALLEY MALL); 602.867.9357

SCOTTSDALE—7014 E CAMELBACK RD (AT SCOTTSDALE FASHION SQUARE); 480.941.2847

Sears Portrait Study

"...the price is right, but the service and quality are variable... make an appointment to cut down on the wait time... bring your coupons for even better prices... perfect for getting a nice wallet size portrait without spending a fortune... I wish the wait time for prints wasn't so long (2 weeks)... the quality and service-orientation of the photographers really vary a lot—some are great, some aren't..."

Customer service........................❸ $$..Prices

WWW.SEARSPORTRAIT.COM

CHANDLER—3177 W CHANDLER BLVD (AT CHANDLER FASHION CTR); 480.726.6599

GLENDALE—7780 W ARROWHEAD TOWN CTR (AT W ARROWHEAD TOWN CTR); 623.776.2283

MESA—1425 W SOUTHERN AVE (AT FIESTA MALL); 480.969.3140

MESA—6515 E SOUTHERN AVE (AT SUPERSTITION SPRINGS CTR); 480.981.7999

PHOENIX—10001 N METRO PKWY W (AT N METRO PARKWAY); 602.674.5523

PHOENIX—4531 E THOMAS RD (AT ARCADIA CROSSING SHOPPING CTR); 602.954.0821; M-F 10-8, SA 9-8, SU 10-6

PHOENIX—4604 E CACTUS RD (AT PARADISE VALLEY MALL); 602.953.7231; M-F 10-8, SA 9-8, SU 10-6

PHOENIX—7611 W THOMAS RD (AT DESERT SKY MALL); 623.873.6805

Target Portrait Studio

"...no sitting fee, reasonable prices (especially with the frequent buyers club), a shopping trip for me and the digital preview system for immediate gratification... pretty hit or miss with the photographer—some are patient and others are not... lots of backgrounds to choose from... even with an appointment we often have to wait... we've gotten some great pictures, enough to share with the entire extended family..."

Customer service........................❹ $$..Prices

WWW.TARGET.COM

GILBERT—1515 E WARNER RD (AT S VAL VISTA DR); 480.892.2283

Online

clubphoto.com

WWW.CLUBPHOTO.COM

dotphoto.com

WWW.DOTPHOTO.COM

flickr.com

WWW.FLICKR.COM

kodakgallery.com

"...the popular ofoto.com is now under it's wings... very easy to use desktop software to upload your pictures on their site... prints, books, mugs and other photo gifts are reasonably priced and are always shipped promptly... I like that there is no limit to how many pictures and albums you can have on their site..."

WWW.KODAKGALLERY.COM

photoworks.com

WWW.PHOTOWORKS.COM

shutterfly.com

"...I've spent hundreds of dollars with them—it's so easy and the quality of the pictures is great... they use really nice quality photo paper... what a lifesaver—since I store all of my pictures with them I didn't lose any when my computer crashed... most special occasions are taken care of with a personal photo calendar, book or other item with the cutest pictures of our kids... reasonable prices..."

WWW.SHUTTERFLY.COM

snapfish.com

"...great photo quality and never a problem with storage limits... we love their photo books and flip books—easy to make and fun to give... good service and a good price... we have family that lives all over the country and yet everyone still gets to see and order pictures of our new baby..."

WWW.SNAPFISH.COM

indexes

alphabetical

by city/neighborhood

alphabetical

participate in our survey at

by city/neighborhood

Goodyear

Litchfield Park

Mesa

Paradise Valley

Peoria

Phoenix

participate in our survey at

Queen Creek

Scottsdale

Sun City

Sun City West

Surprise

Tempe

Notes

YOUR RECOMMENDATIONS MAKE THE LILAGUIDE BETTER!
PLEASE SHARE YOUR NOTES WITH US AT WWW.LILAGUIDE.COM

YOUR RECOMMENDATIONS MAKE THE LILAGUIDE BETTER!
PLEASE SHARE YOUR NOTES WITH US AT WWW.LILAGUIDE.COM

Notes

YOUR RECOMMENDATIONS MAKE THE LILAGUIDE BETTER!
PLEASE SHARE YOUR NOTES WITH US AT WWW.LILAGUIDE.COM

YOUR RECOMMENDATIONS MAKE THE LILAGUIDE BETTER!
PLEASE SHARE YOUR NOTES WITH US AT WWW.LILAGUIDE.COM

Notes

YOUR RECOMMENDATIONS MAKE THE LILAGUIDE BETTER!
PLEASE SHARE YOUR NOTES WITH US AT WWW.LILAGUIDE.COM

Notes

YOUR RECOMMENDATIONS MAKE THE LILAGUIDE BETTER!
PLEASE SHARE YOUR NOTES WITH US AT WWW.LILAGUIDE.COM

Notes

YOUR RECOMMENDATIONS MAKE THE LILAGUIDE BETTER!
PLEASE SHARE YOUR NOTES WITH US AT WWW.LILAGUIDE.COM

Notes

YOUR RECOMMENDATIONS MAKE THE LILAGUIDE BETTER!
PLEASE SHARE YOUR NOTES WITH US AT WWW.LILAGUIDE.COM

Notes

YOUR RECOMMENDATIONS MAKE THE LILAGUIDE BETTER!
PLEASE SHARE YOUR NOTES WITH US AT WWW.LILAGUIDE.COM

Notes

YOUR RECOMMENDATIONS MAKE THE LILAGUIDE BETTER!
PLEASE SHARE YOUR NOTES WITH US AT WWW.LILAGUIDE.COM

Notes

YOUR RECOMMENDATIONS MAKE THE LILAGUIDE BETTER!
PLEASE SHARE YOUR NOTES WITH US AT WWW.LILAGUIDE.COM

Notes

YOUR RECOMMENDATIONS MAKE THE LILAGUIDE BETTER!
PLEASE SHARE YOUR NOTES WITH US AT WWW.LILAGUIDE.COM

Notes

Notes

YOUR RECOMMENDATIONS MAKE THE LILAGUIDE BETTER!
PLEASE SHARE YOUR NOTES WITH US AT WWW.LILAGUIDE.COM